Criminology

An Introduction Using *ExplorIt*®

Fourth Edition

Steven F. Messner
University at Albany, SUNY

Rodney Stark
University of Washington

MC MicroCase® CORPORATION

14110 NE 21st Street
Bellevue, WA 98007

CRIMINOLOGY: An Introduction Using ExplorIt, 4/e is published by MicroCase Corporation.

Editor	David J. Smetters
Production Manager	Jodi B. Gleason
Software, Lead Developer	David H. Simmons
Data Archivists	Meredith Reitman
	Chris Bader
Copy Editor	Margaret Moore
Cover Design	Michael Brugman Design
Cover Photo	Photodisc, Inc.

Printed in the United States of America
2 3 4 5 6 7 8 9 10—02 01 00

CONTENTS

About the Authors

Steven F. Messner is Professor of Sociology at the University of Albany, State University of New York. He received his Ph.D. from Princeton University and has taught at Columbia University and Nankai University in the People's Republic of China. His research has focused primarily on the relationship between features of social organization and violent crime rates. Messner is co-author with Richard Rosenfeld of *Crime and the American Dream*, co-author with Allen E. Liska of *Perspectives on Crime and Deviance*, co-editor with Marvin D. Krohn and Allen E. Liska of *Theoretical Integration in the Study of Deviance and Crime*, and author of numerous articles and book chapters on the topic of criminal violence.

Rodney Stark began his career as a newspaper reporter and then received his Ph.D. from the University of California, Berkeley. While in Berkeley, he spent eight years as a Research Sociologist at the Survey Research Center and then joined the staff of the Center for the Study of Law and Society where, for two years, he directed and conducted field research on student protest and on the police. He subsequently became Professor of Sociology and Comparative Religion at the University of Washington in Seattle. Stark is the author or co-author of 21 books and more than 100 scholarly articles.

ACKNOWLEDGMENTS

As the new co-author for the fourth edition, I have had the distinct pleasure of working with the professional staff at MicroCase for the first time. I am thoroughly impressed with their expertise and very grateful for their willingness to offer me assistance. In particular, Julie Aguilar, Chris Bader, Jodi Gleason, Meredith Reitman, and Dana Schlatter have come to my rescue on multiple occasions. David Smetters has been a superb editor, offering invaluable advice and guidance throughout the project. Thanks to all in Bellevue, Washington. Finally, I would like to acknowledge Rodney Stark's pioneering work developing a computer-based criminology workbook. The previous editions of this workbook were innovative, imaginative, and remarkably effective in the classroom. I am thus delighted to have had the opportunity to serve as co-author for the current edition.

PREFACE

Welcome to the real world of criminological research. There is nothing make-believe about what you will be doing with these exercises. You will be addressing some of the basic issues of concern to criminologists today, and you will be using many of the same research techniques they use. All the data are real. In fact, they are the kinds of data currently used by professional researchers. As you work through the chapters, you will find out a lot about criminology for yourself. In other words, you will learn criminology by doing what criminologists actually do.

The software is easy to use. You will be pleasantly surprised to discover that you can master it without any special effort—just start with the first chapter and follow along. But, despite being easy, this software is not a toy. It is a powerful package that allows you to perform sophisticated data analysis.

What's New in the Fourth Edition

The most obvious change from previous editions is the introduction of the ExplorIt software. The new software is more flexible and easier to use than ever. Both a Windows 95 and a DOS version have been provided with the workbook. This gives you the flexibility to use ExplorIt on almost any Windows- or DOS-compatible computer.

The introductory sections of the chapters have also been expanded to provide more substantive content and to position the discussions more firmly in the contemporary criminological literature. In addition, several chapters have been restructured to illustrate and emphasize the importance of theory testing in criminological research (see Part II). Appendix A has been lengthened to provide a greater number of independent projects.

Three of the data files from the previous edition—the file with information on U.S. states, the General Social Survey file, and the survey of college students—have been retained but updated to reflect more recent information. Three new data files have been added. One file is based on robbery incidents from the National Crime Victimization Survey (NCVS). The NCVS provides rich detail on the circumstances surrounding crimes, and it is the most widely cited source of data on criminal victimizations in the United States. Another new data file in the workbook is based on the final wave of the National Youth Survey (NYS). The NYS is a nationally representative survey of the U.S. population containing self-reports of criminal behavior. Many of the more important research studies in criminology over recent years have been based on NYS data. At the time of the seventh wave of the survey, respondents were young adults, approximately the same age as respondents in the college survey data file. Finally, a historical trends file has been added which includes longitudinal data on crime from the Uniform Crime Reports and the NCVS, and data on selected attitudes toward crime and criminal justice from national surveys.

GETTING STARTED

INTRODUCTION

Criminology is an empirical science. It involves the testing of claims about crime with data from the real world. The goal of this workbook is to provide you with an opportunity to participate in the criminological enterprise. You will learn how to use data to gain a better understanding of crime and public opinion about crime.

Each chapter in this workbook has two sections. The first section introduces a particular topic of criminology and demonstrates how data are used to support, augment, and test the ideas proposed. This is followed by a worksheet section. The worksheets begin with a few review questions on the material covered in the preliminary section. Then, additional data analysis exercises are provided which further explore the topics under investigation in the chapter. You will use the student version of ExplorIt to complete these worksheets.

When you finish this workbook, you'll have a better understanding of criminology because you will have done what criminologists actually do!

SYSTEM REQUIREMENTS

Two versions of Student ExplorIt have been provided with this book: a Windows version and a DOS version. The Windows version can be used only on computers running Windows 95 (or higher). The DOS version of the software will run on almost any DOS- or Windows-compatible computer, including those using Windows 3.1 (or higher). Here is more detailed information about the minimum computer requirements for each version of the student software.

> **Student ExplorIt for Windows**—This version will run on almost any computer using Windows 95 (or higher).[1] For installation purposes, a CD-ROM drive and a 3.5" floppy drive are also required.
>
> **Student ExplorIt for DOS** (or Windows 3.1)—This version requires an IBM or compatible computer with 286 or better processor, 640K RAM, DOS 3.1 or higher (or Windows 3.1 or higher), VGA-level graphics, and a mouse. A CD-ROM drive is ***not*** required.

Before installing any software on a hard drive, check with your instructor to see if a network version of Student ExplorIt has already been installed. If a network version has already been installed, skip to the section "Starting Student ExplorIt."

If the operating system on your computer is DOS or Windows 3.1, then you must use *Student ExplorIt for DOS*. If this is your case, skip to the section "Starting Student ExplorIt." Even if your computer has Windows 95 (or higher), there are some situations in which you should still use *Student ExplorIt for DOS*:

---

[1] *Student ExplorIt for Windows* requires 8 megabytes of RAM, 10 megabytes of free hard disk space (network installations require about 1 megabyte of temporary storage on hard drives of user terminals), VGA-level graphics, and a mouse.

- Your teacher has instructed you to use the DOS version (yes, the DOS version can be used on Windows computers).
- You are not allowed to install software on the hard drive of the computer (such as in a lab setting).
- Your computer does not have a CD-ROM drive.
- Your computer does not have a CD-ROM drive and a floppy drive that can be used at the same time (as with some notebook computers).

If any of these conditions apply, you should skip to the section "Starting Student ExplorIt."

NETWORK VERSIONS OF STUDENT EXPLORIT

Network versions are available for both the Windows and DOS versions of Student ExplorIt. These special versions of the software are available at no charge to instructors who adopt this book for their courses (instructors should contact MicroCase Corporation for additional information). It's worth noting that *Student ExplorIt for DOS* can be run directly from the diskette on virtually any computer network—regardless of whether a network version of Student ExplorIt has been installed.

INSTALLING STUDENT EXPLORIT FOR WINDOWS

If you will be using *Student ExplorIt for DOS* (see above discussion), you do not need to read this section. Skip to "Starting Student ExplorIt."

To install *Student ExplorIt for Windows*, you will need the diskette and CD-ROM that are packaged inside the back cover of this book. Then follow these steps:

1. Start your computer and wait until the Windows desktop is showing on your computer.
2. Insert the diskette into the A drive (or B drive) of your computer.
3. Insert the CD-ROM disc into the CD-ROM drive.
4. Click [Start] from the Windows desktop, click [Run], type **D:\SETUP** (if your CD-ROM drive is not the D drive, replace the letter D with the proper drive letter), and click [OK].
5. During the installation, you will be presented with several screens (described below). In some cases you will be required to make a selection or entry and then click [Next] to continue.

The first screen that appears is the **Welcome** screen. This provides some introductory information and suggests that you shut down any other programs that may be running. Click [Next] to continue.

You are next presented with a **Software License Agreement**. Read this screen and click [Yes] if you accept the terms of the software license.

If this is the first time you are installing Student ExplorIt, an **Install License** screen appears. (If this software has been previously installed or used, it already contains the licensing information. A screen simply confirming your name will appear instead.) Here you are asked to type in your name. It is important to type your name correctly, since it cannot be changed after this point. Your name will appear on all printouts, so make sure you spell it completely and correctly! Then click [OK] to continue.[2]

The next screen has you **Choose the Destination** for the program files. You are strongly advised to use the destination directory shown on the screen. Click [Next] to continue.

The **Install Checkbox** screen requires you to make a choice as to whether or not to copy the data files (currently located on the diskette) to your hard drive. Carefully read the choices on the screen before making your selection.

When the **Setup Complete** window appears, click [Finish]. You will find it easier to start Student ExplorIt if you place a "shortcut" icon on your Windows desktop. A folder named "MicroCase" should now be showing on the horizontal task bar at the bottom of your Windows desktop. Click on this button and a window will appear with a "shortcut" icon for Student ExplorIt.[3] Place your mouse pointer over this icon, then press down *and* hold the left mouse button as you drag the icon outside the window to an open space on your Windows desktop. Once the Student ExplorIt icon has been moved to your desktop, you can close the window that previously contained the icon by clicking the little "x" button that appears in the top right corner of the window. From this point on, you will be able to double-click the Student ExplorIt shortcut icon to start the software.

STARTING STUDENT EXPLORIT

The first section below describes how to start *Student ExplorIt for Windows*, while the second section describes how to start *Student ExplorIt for DOS*. Read the section that is appropriate for you.

Starting Student ExplorIt for Windows

Student ExplorIt for Windows must be installed on a hard drive (or a computer network) before you can start it. If the program has not been installed, review the software installation section above.

If the data files were not copied to the hard drive of the computer during the installation of *Student ExplorIt for Windows*, it will be necessary for you to insert your 3.5" data file diskette into the A or B drive of your computer. (If you are starting Student ExplorIt from a network, you *must* insert your diskette before continuing.) Don't worry, you will be prompted to insert your diskette if you forget.

If the software was installed properly, there should be a "shortcut" icon on your Windows desktop that looks something like this:

---

[2] If an installation of Student ExplorIt is already on your hard drive, you will get a warning message indicating that a copy of the program is already present on your computer. If your intention is to *replace* the previously installed version of Student ExplorIt, use the default directory offered by the installation program. If you want to create a completely separate installation of Student ExplorIt, select a new directory using the "Browse" button.

[3] If you have another installation of Student ExplorIt on your hard drive (including a version distributed with a different MicroCase book), make sure to rename the label for its "shortcut" icon on your Windows desktop before following the instructions in the next sentence (you can name it anything except "Student ExplorIt"). To rename a shortcut, click once on the shortcut label, then click it again. This causes the text for the shortcut to be highlighted, after which it can be modified.

To start *Student ExplorIt for Windows*, position your mouse pointer over the shortcut icon and double-click (that is, click it twice in rapid succession). If you did not move the shortcut icon onto your desktop during the install process, you can alternatively follow these directions to start the software:

Click [Start] from the Windows desktop.

Click [Programs].

Click MicroCase.

Click Student ExplorIt.

After a few seconds, Student ExplorIt should appear on your screen. Skip down to the "Main Menu of Student ExplorIt" section below to continue your introduction to the software.

Starting Student ExplorIt for DOS

This section explains how to start *Student ExplorIt for DOS*. You can run *Student ExplorIt for DOS* directly from the diskette on almost any DOS or Windows computer (including computers using Windows 3.1 or higher).

The instructions for starting *Student ExplorIt for DOS* differ depending on the operating system you are using. In all cases, you will first need to place the 3.5" diskette in the A or B drive. Do that now. Then follow the appropriate instructions below to start *Student ExplorIt for DOS* on your computer.

MS-DOS:

Type **A:EXPLORIT** (or **B:EXPLORIT**) and press <Enter>.

Windows 3.1:

From the Program Manager, click [File].

Click [Run].

Type **A:EXPLORIT** (or **B:EXPLORIT**) and click [OK].

Windows 95 (or higher):

Click [Start].

Click [Run].

Type **A:EXPLORIT** (or **B:EXPLORIT**) and click [OK].

The first time you start *Student ExplorIt for DOS,* you will be asked to enter your name. It is important to type your name correctly, since it will appear on all printouts. Type your name and click [OK] or press <Enter>. If your name is correct, simply click [OK] or press <Enter> in response to the next prompt. (If you wish to correct a mistake, click [Cancel] to make a correction.) To continue to the main menu of the program, press <Enter> or click the left mouse button.

Note: If you are using Windows 3.1 and the mouse fails to appear or it does not work properly, refer to Appendix B.

MAIN MENU OF STUDENT EXPLORIT

Student ExplorIt is extremely easy to use. All you do is point and click your way through the program. That is, use your mouse arrow to point at the selection you want, then click the left button on the mouse. The main menu is the starting point for everything you will do in Student ExplorIt. Let's look at how it works.

Student ExplorIt for Windows—Not all options on the menu are always available. In the Windows version of Student ExplorIt, you will know which options are available at any given time by looking at the colors of the options. For example, when you first start the software, only the OPEN FILE option is immediately available. As you can see, the colors for this option are brighter than those for the other tasks shown on the screen. Also, when you move your mouse pointer over this option, it is highlighted.

Student ExplorIt for DOS—When you are at the main menu of the DOS version of Student ExplorIt, only those tasks that have a bright yellow background are available. As you can see, no tasks are available until you select a data file with which to work.

EXPLORIT GUIDES

Throughout this workbook, there are "ExplorIt Guides" that provide you with the basic information needed to carry out each task. Here is an example:

➤ *Data File:* **STATES**
➤ *Task:* **Mapping**
➤ *Variable 1:* **2) HOMICIDE**
➤ *View:* **Map**

Each line of the ExplorIt Guide is actually an instruction. Let's follow the simple steps to carry out this task.

Step 1: Select a Data File

Before you can do almost anything in Student ExplorIt, you need to open a data file.

Student ExplorIt for Windows—To open a data file, click the OPEN FILE task. A list of data files will appear in a window (e.g., GSS, STATES, etc.). If you click on a file name *once*, a description of the highlighted file is shown in the window next to this list. In the ExplorIt Guide shown above, the ➤ symbol to the left of the Data File step indicates that you should open the STATES data file. To do so, click STATES and then click the [Open] button (or just double-click STATES). The next window that appears (labeled File Settings) provides additional information about the data file, including a file description, the number of cases in the file, and the number of variables, among other things. To continue, click the [OK] button. You are now returned to the main menu of Student ExplorIt. (You won't need to repeat this step until you want to open a different data file.) Notice that you can always see which data file is currently open by looking at the file name shown on the top line of the screen.

Student ExplorIt for DOS—In the DOS version of Student ExplorIt, the available data files are listed in the window at the left of the screen, and the description of the highlighted file is shown in the window beneath this list. To see the description of a file, click it once. To select a file, double-click its name. The "x" in the box next to the name of the file indicates which file is open. In this example, you should open the STATES data file. (You won't need to repeat this step until you want to use a different data file.)

Step 2: Select a Task

Once you have selected a data file, the next step is to select a program task. Eight analysis tasks are offered in this version of Student ExplorIt. Not all tasks are available for each data file, because some tasks are appropriate only for certain kinds of data. Mapping, for example, is a task that applies only to ecological data, and thus cannot be used with survey data files.

In the ExplorIt Guide we're following, the ➤ symbol on the second line indicates that the MAPPING task should be selected, so click the MAPPING option with your left mouse button.

Step 3: Select a Variable

After a task is selected, you will be shown a list of the variables in the open data file. Notice that the first variable is highlighted and a description of that variable is shown in the Variable Description window at the lower right. You can move this highlight through the list of variables by using the up and down cursor keys (as well as the <Page Up> and <Page Down> keys). You can also click once on a variable name to move the highlight and update the variable description. Go ahead—move the highlight to a few other variables and read their descriptions.

If the variable you want to select is not showing in the variable window, click on the scroll bars located on the right side of the variable list window to move through the list. See the following figure:

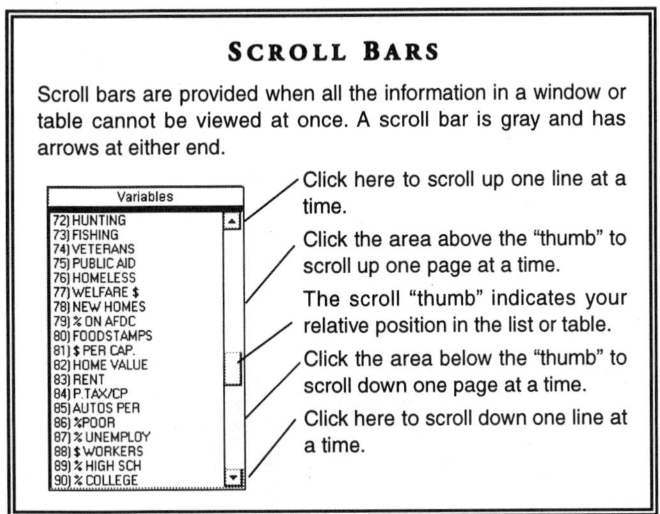

SCROLL BARS

Scroll bars are provided when all the information in a window or table cannot be viewed at once. A scroll bar is gray and has arrows at either end.

By the way, you will find an appendix section at the back of this workbook (Appendix C) that contains a list of the variable names for key data files provided in this package.

Each task requires you to select one or more variables, and the ExplorIt Guides indicate which variables should be selected. The ExplorIt Guide example here indicates that you should select 2) HOMICIDE as Variable 1. On the screen, there is a box labeled Variable 1. Inside this box, there is a vertical cursor that indicates that this box is currently an active option. When you select a variable, it will be placed in this box. Before selecting a variable, be sure that the cursor is in the appropriate box. If it is not, place the cursor inside the appropriate box by clicking the box with your mouse. This is important because in some tasks the ExplorIt Guide will require more than one variable to be selected, and you want to be sure that you put each selected variable in the right place.

To select a variable, use any one of the methods shown below. (Note: If the name of a previously selected variable is in the box, use the <Delete> or <Backspace> key to remove it—or click the [Clear All] button.)

- Type in the **number** of the variable and press <Enter>.
- Type in the **name** of the variable and press <Enter>. Or, you can type just enough of the name to distinguish it from other variables in the data—HOM would be sufficient for this example.
- Double-click the desired variable in the variable list window. This selection will then appear in the variable selection box. (If the name of a previously selected variable is in the box, the newly selected variable will replace it.)
- In *Student ExplorIt for Windows*, you have a fourth way to select a variable. First highlight the desired variable in the variable list, then click the arrow that appears to the left of the variable selection box. The variable you selected will now appear in the box. (If the name of a previously selected variable is in the box, the newly selected variable will replace it.)

Once you have selected your variable (or variables), click the [OK] button to continue to the final results screen.

Step 4: Select a View

The next screen that appears shows the final results of your analysis. In most cases, the screen that first appears matches the "view" indicated in the ExplorIt Guide. In this example, you are instructed to look at the Map view—that's what is currently showing on the screen. In some instances, however, you may need to make an additional selection to produce the desired screen.

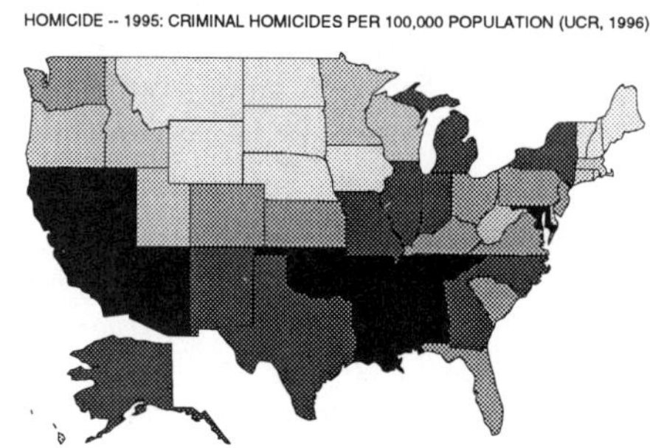

(OPTIONAL) Step 5: Select an Additional Display

Some ExplorIt Guides will indicate that an additional "Display" should be selected. In that case, simply click on the option indicated for that additional display. For example, this ExplorIt Guide may have included an additional line that requires you to select the Legend display.

Step 6: Continuing to the Next ExplorIt Guide

Some instructions in the ExplorIt Guide may be the same for at least two examples in a row. For instance, after you display the map for HOMICIDE in the example above, the following ExplorIt Guide may be given:

Data File: **STATES**
Task: **Mapping**
➤ *Variable 1:* **10) VIOCRIME**
➤ *View:* **Map**

Notice that the first two lines in the ExplorIt Guide do not have the ➤ symbol located in front of the items. That's because you already have the data file STATES open and you have already selected the MAPPING task. With the results of your first analysis showing on the screen, there is no need to return to the main menu to complete this next analysis. Instead, all you need to do is select VIOCRIME as your new variable. If you are using *Student ExplorIt for Windows*, click the [⮌] button located in the top left corner of your screen (if you are using *Student ExplorIt for DOS*, click the [Exit] button once). The variable selection screen for the MAPPING task appears again. Replace the variable with 10) VIOCRIME and click [OK].

To repeat: You need only do those items in the ExplorIt Guide that have the ➤ symbol in front of them. If you start from the top of the ExplorIt Guide, you're simply wasting your time.

If the ExplorIt Guide instructs you to select an entirely new task or data file, you will need to return to the main menu. To return to the main menu using *Student ExplorIt for Windows*, simply click the [Menu] button located at the top left corner of the screen. To return to the main menu using *Student ExplorIt for DOS*, click the [Exit] button until the main menu appears. At this point, select the new data file and/or task that is indicated in the ExplorIt Guide.

That's all there is to the basic operation of Student ExplorIt. Just follow the instructions given in the ExplorIt Guide and point and click your way through the program.

EXITING FROM STUDENT EXPLORIT

If you are continuing to the next section of this workbook, it is *not* necessary to exit from Student ExplorIt quite yet. But when you are finished using the program, it is very important that you properly exit the software—do not just walk away from the computer or remove your diskette. To exit Student ExplorIt, return to the main menu and select the [Exit] button that appears on the screen.

Important: If you inserted your diskette before starting Student ExplorIt, remember to remove it before leaving the computer.

Part I

UNDERSTANDING CRIME AND VICTIMIZATION

CHAPTER 1

THE GEOGRAPHY OF OFFICIAL CRIME RATES

Understanding crime requires understanding where it happens as well as to whom and by whom.

DENNIS W. RONCEK,
CRIMINOLOGIST SPECIALIZING IN THE MAPPING OF CRIME[1]

Tasks: Mapping
Data Files: STATES

Criminologists devote a good deal of time and effort to the measurement of crime for both practical and theoretical reasons. From a practical standpoint, knowledge about how much crime occurs, and where, is extremely useful to law enforcement officials when they make decisions about how to allocate resources. It often makes sense, for example, to have the police patrol high-risk areas more frequently and thoroughly than relatively low-risk areas. Also, from a theoretical standpoint, hypotheses about the causes of crime can be tested only if levels of criminal involvement can be measured. For example, to test the claim that a certain type of person commits more crimes than another type of person, we have to be able to measure (or at least estimate) how much crime is committed by the different types of persons.

Generally, criminologists rely on three major data sources to measure crime. *Official crime data* are based on crimes reported to or discovered by law enforcement agencies and on arrests made by these agencies. You will use this type of data source in the present chapter. *Victimization data* are based on reports from respondents in surveys who are asked about crimes committed against them or members of their household. You will explore some victimization data in the next chapter. Finally, many studies of crime are based on *self-reports*. These data are also based on survey responses, but respondents are asked to report on offenses that they themselves have committed rather than offenses committed against them. Chapter 3 uses self-report data. Each data source has strengths and weaknesses. As a result, criminologists are most confident in findings that are consistent across the different data sources.

When measuring crime, the focus of criminological inquiry is on **variables**. A variable is anything that varies or exhibits different values among the things being studied—what social scientists call the **units of analysis**. Since we are about to examine the 50 U.S. states, let's consider things that vary among them. All 50 states have homicides every year, therefore *having* homicides is *not* a variable

[1] Dennis W. Roncek, "Mapping Crime: An Inescapable But Valuable Task for Intracommunity Analysis," in *Questions and Answers in Lethal and Non-lethal Violence*, edited by Carolyn Rebecca Block and Richard L. Block (Washington, D.C.: National Institute of Justice, 1993), pp. 155–161.

among the 50 states. However, the frequency of homicides does vary among the states, and thus the *total number* of homicides for each state in a given year is a variable. States also vary with respect to a large number of other social, economic, and environmental factors. Of course, individual persons, like states, also vary on many traits or attributes—height, weight, political opinions, religious beliefs—and all of these are variables as well.

The basic task of social science is to explain *variation*. We do this by trying to discover connections among variables, that is, by finding out whether values of a given variable tend to "link up" with values of another variable. Suppose, for example, we found that people who differ in terms of their political opinions also differ in terms of their religious affiliation. If so, the next step would be to try to discover *why* these variables are connected.

So, let's begin to look at variables using data from the *Uniform Crime Reports* (or the UCR). The UCR is published annually by the Department of Justice and is also made available to the public on the Internet. It contains information on the number of crimes known to police and on arrests for various offenses. The data from the UCR are commonly referred to as "official crime statistics" because they are compiled initially by local police agencies and are then forwarded to the Federal Bureau of Investigation. These data have the advantage of having been carefully screened—the police must believe there is a good chance that a crime actually occurred for a report to be counted. These data have the disadvantage of being limited to the crimes that citizens report to the police or that the police discover. The results of victimization surveys indicate that substantial numbers of persons do not, in fact, report many types of crimes to the police, implying that the official crime statistics underestimate the true volume of crime. Nevertheless, criminologists have found over the years that the official crime statistics are extremely useful for many research purposes.

One of the offenses recorded in the UCR is **larceny-theft**. This includes all thefts in which no use of force or fraud was involved, excluding thefts of motor vehicles, which are recorded separately. Shoplifting, stripping or breaking into cars, and stealing bicycles are all examples of larceny-thefts. We can look at variation across states in the number of larcenies reported to the police in 1995 using ExplorIt's MAPPING task.

➤ *Data File:* **STATES**
➤ *Task:* **Mapping**
➤ *Variable 1:* **9) #LARCENIES**
➤ *View:* **Map**

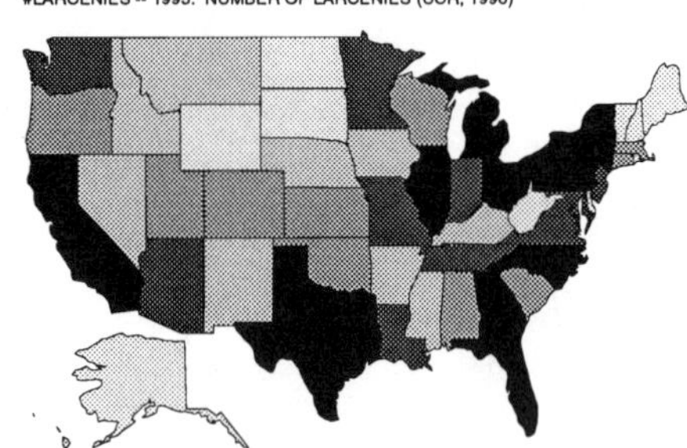

To reproduce this graphic on the computer screen using ExplorIt, review the instructions in the "Getting Started" section. For this example, you would open the STATES data file, select the MAPPING task, and select 9) #LARCENIES for Variable 1. The first view shown is the Map view. (Remember, the ➤ symbol indicates which steps you need to perform if you are doing all the examples as you follow along in the text. So in the next example below, you only need to select a new view—that is, you don't need to repeat the first three steps because they were already done in this example.)

The map on your screen depicts states in different colors varying in intensity from very dark to very light. The darker the state, the greater is the number of larceny-thefts that occurred in that state during 1995; the lighter the state, the lower is the number of larceny-thefts. Select the display option [Legend] to call up a window which identifies the range of values represented by the various colors. Click the [Legend] option again to remove the legend window from the screen.

ExplorIt provides another display option which allows you to highlight a particular case. Select the [Find Case] option, and scroll down the list of states until you find Florida. Click the box next to Florida and then click [OK] to close the window. Florida is now highlighted in a distinctive color, and the number of larcenies in Florida is displayed (612,311), along with its rank (3rd in the nation). Click the [Find Case] box again to return to the original map.

ExplorIt provides a third option for representing the mapping of larcenies graphically. Click on the display option for [Spot Fill]. In the new map on your screen, the number of larcenies in a state is represented by a circle. The color scheme for the circles remains the same as in the original mapping. However, the size of the circle is drawn to reflect the relative magnitude of the number of larcenies in each state.

Now let's take a look at the actual totals for the number of larcenies in all of the different states.

Data File: **STATES**
Task: **Mapping**
Variable 1: **9) #LARCENIES**
➤ *View:* **List: Rank**

#LARCENIES: 1995: Number of larcenies

RANK	CASE NAME	VALUE
1	California	902456
2	Texas	632468
3	Florida	612311
4	New York	425184
5	Illinois	357143
6	Ohio	297624
7	Michigan	280712
8	Georgia	264872
9	Pennsylvania	236991
10	North Carolina	234911

As indicated by the ➤ symbol, if you are continuing from the previous example, select the [List: Rank] option. The number of rows shown on your screen may be different from that shown here. Use the cursor keys and scroll bar to move through this list if necessary.

California had the greatest number of larcenies—902,456—followed by Texas with 632,468. The remaining states are listed in descending order. If you scroll to the bottom of the list, you will see that the state ranked 50th is Vermont, with 14,150 larcenies.

Looking over the entire ranking of states, you probably begin to see a pattern. The states at the top of the list tend to be the more populous states, while those at the bottom tend to be the less populous states. We can observe this pattern more directly by creating two maps—one for the number of larcenies and another for the number of people residing in the states—and comparing these maps.

Data File: **STATES**
Task: **Mapping**
Variable 1: **9) #LARCENIES**
➤ Variable 2: **20) POPULATION**
➤ Views: **Map**

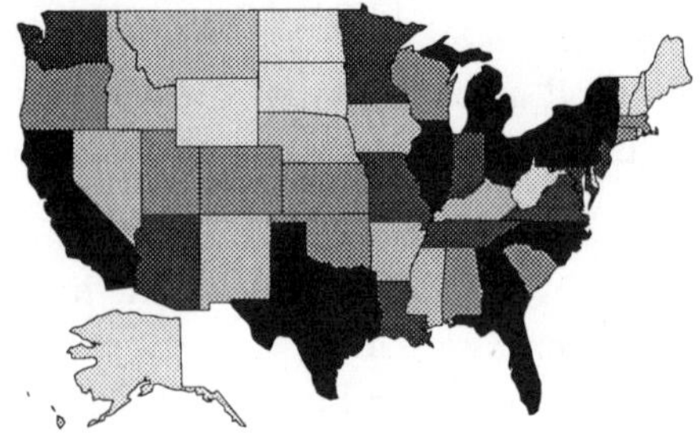

r = 0.966**

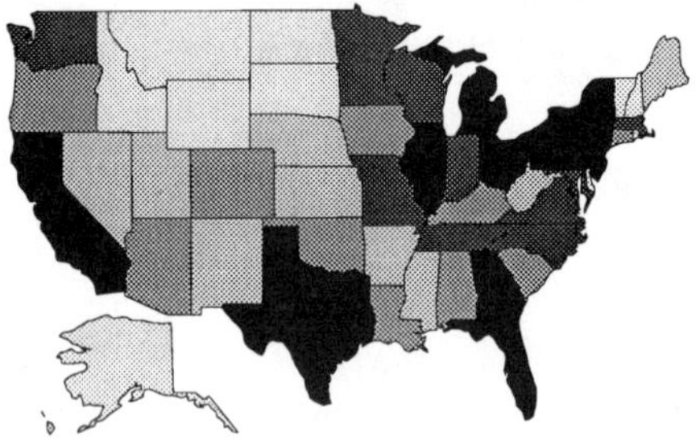

If you are continuing from the previous example, return to the variable selection screen for the MAPPING task. Select 20) POPULATION for Variable 2.

The two maps are highly similar. States with dark colors on the larceny map tend to have dark colors on the population map, and those with light colors on the larceny map tend to have light colors on the population map. This is really not very surprising. Larceny-thefts are committed by people, and where there are more people, there are more potential thieves. What we would really like to know is whether people in some states are unusually prone to commit larceny-thefts. To address this question, we need to adjust for differences in population size across states. The most common way of doing this in criminological research is to convert the raw numbers of crimes into a crime **rate**.

A rate is created by expressing the numbers for each case—in this instance, each state—in terms of a common base, such as the resident population. For example, we can compute a larceny-theft rate by dividing the number of larceny-thefts in a state by that state's population, and then multiplying by 100,000. (Multiplying by 100,000 does not affect the ranking of states; it simply enables us to avoid having to work with small numbers when examining relatively rare events). The resulting rate is the number of larceny-thefts per 100,000 population. This rate allows us to look at any variation in levels of crime across states that does not simply reflect differences in the number of people living in those states.

Now let's compare the map for the larceny rate with the map for the total numbers of larcenies.

Data File: **STATES**
Task: **Mapping**
Variable 1: **9) #LARCENIES**
➤ Variable 2: **7) LARCENY**
➤ Views: **Map**

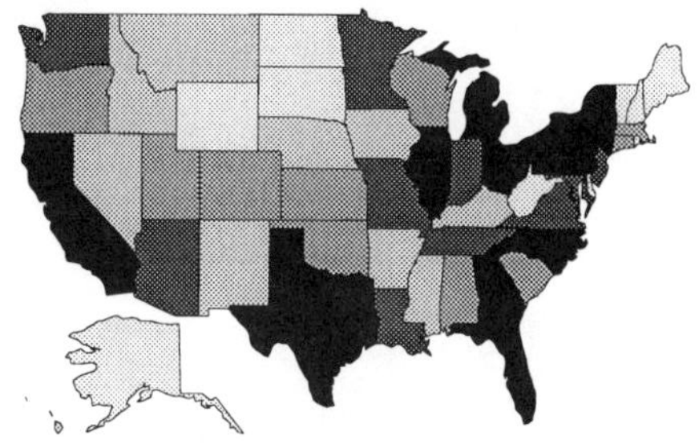

r = 0.129

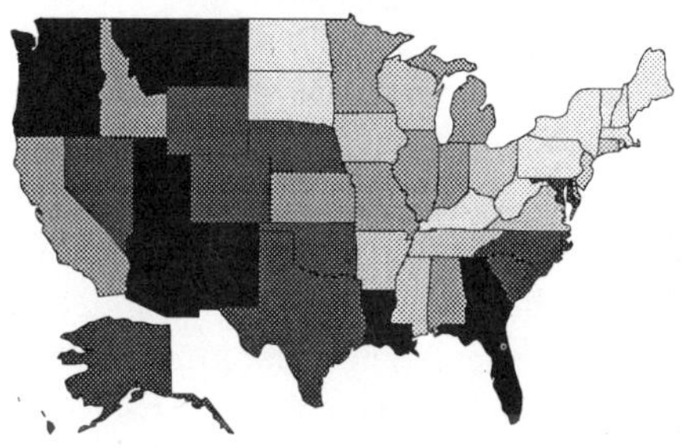

If you are continuing from the previous example, return to the variable selection screen for the MAPPING task. 9) #LARCENIES will still be selected for Variable 1. Select 7) LARCENY for Variable 2.

The two maps are quite different. States shown in dark colors on one map are often shown in light colors on the other map, and vice versa.

Let's rank both variables but focus on the list that appears at the bottom of the screen (larceny-theft rates.)

Data File: **STATES**
Task: **Mapping**
Variable 1: **9) #LARCENIES**
Variable 2: **7) LARCENY**
➤ Views: **Rank**

#LARCENIES: 1995: Number of larcenies

RANK	CASE NAME	VALUE
1	California	902456
2	Texas	632468
3	Florida	612311
4	New York	425184
5	Illinois	357143
6	Ohio	297624
7	Michigan	280712
8	Georgia	264872
9	Pennsylvania	236991
10	North Carolina	234911

LARCENY: 1995: Larcenies per 100,000 population

RANK	CASE NAME	VALUE
1	Hawaii	5046.9
2	Arizona	4925.6
3	Utah	4572.1
4	Florida	4322.4
5	Oregon	4236.7
6	Washington	4140.3
7	Montana	4105.5
8	Louisiana	3838.5
9	Georgia	3678.3
10	New Mexico	3648.5

To obtain a ranked list for both maps, you must select the [List: Rank] option for both Variable 1 and Variable 2.

Looking at the list at the bottom of the screen, you see that the highest ranking state is Hawaii, with a rate of 5046.9 larcenies per 100,000 population, followed by Arizona (4925.6) and Utah (4572.1). However, if you locate these three states in the list that appears at the top of the screen (the one representing *actual* larcenies), you'll see that Hawaii ranks 36th, Arizona ranks 12th, and Utah ranks 28th. (By the way, the easiest way to locate a state in a list is to show the cases alphabetically using the [List: Alpha] option.) These rankings illustrate quite clearly that the variation in the numbers of crimes and the variation in crime rates can differ dramatically. In practice, criminologists most often examine crime rates rather than raw numbers when studying population aggregates (e.g., cities, states, or nations).

One benefit of mapping crime rates is that it helps us detect any spatial clustering of crime. Criminologists have been particularly interested in the spatial clustering of a very serious offense—criminal homicide. As far back as the 1880s, and continuing up to more recent years, scholars have noted a tendency for homicide rates to be high in southern regions of the United States. This observation has lead to an influential and somewhat controversial explanation of homicide, an explanation referred to as the "southern culture of violence thesis." The core claim of the southern culture of violence thesis is that southerners are socialized into a distinctive culture which endorses the use of lethal violence in a wide range of circumstances, especially when someone's honor has been challenged. Southern areas are thus expected to be characterized by high rates of homicide, but not necessarily high rates of other types of crime.

The origins of the southern culture of violence have been attributed to a variety of historical, psychological, and social factors.[2] For example, the historian Sheldon Hackney proposed that a distinctive southern "world view" emerged as a result of the defeat of the South in the Civil War. This world view is allegedly characterized by feelings of grievance and persecution, which predispose Southerners to resort to violence more readily than those who are raised in non-southern regions. The geographer Raymond Gastil also identified features of southern history and tradition that, in his view, have contributed to emergence of a southern culture of violence. Specifically, Gastil cited the following factors: the institutionalization of dueling, a keen interest in military affairs, an exaggerated sense of honor, and an attraction to firearms.

---

[2] For a review of this literature, see Steven F. Messner, "Research on Cultural and Socioeconomic Factors in Criminal Violence," *Psychiatric Clinics of North America* 11 (December 1988): 511–525.

Let's consider the contemporary spatial patterning of homicide rates.

Data File: **STATES**
Task: **Mapping**
➤ *Variable 1:* **2) HOMICIDE**
➤ *View:* **Map**

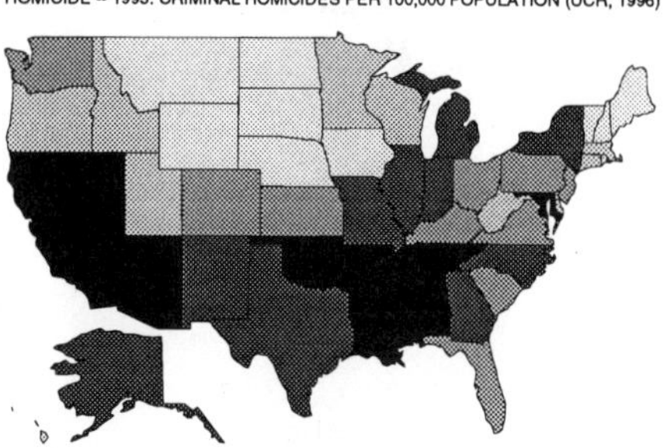

If continuing from the previous example, you can use the [Clear All] button to clear both variables previously selected.

The map reveals rather striking regional patterns. Southern states tend to be depicted in darker colors, indicating high homicide rates. Some western and mountain states (e.g., California, Nevada, and Arizona) also exhibit high homicide rates. In contrast, the upper plains states and New England states exhibit comparatively low homicide rates.

Now, let's look at the ranking of states on homicide.

Data File: **STATES**
Task: **Mapping**
Variable 1: **2) HOMICIDE**
➤ *View:* **List: Rank**

HOMICIDE: 1995: Criminal homicides per 100,000 population

RANK	CASE NAME	VALUE
1	Louisiana	17.0
2	Mississippi	12.9
3	Oklahoma	12.2
4	Maryland	11.8
5	Alabama	11.2
5	California	11.2
7	Nevada	10.7
8	Tennessee	10.6
9	Arizona	10.4
9	Arkansas	10.4

Louisiana is ranked first, with a homicide rate of 17.0 per 100,000 population. The next two states are Mississippi (12.9) and Oklahoma (12.2). Continuing down the list, it is clear that southern states do indeed tend to rank highly on homicide rates, although some states from other regions occasionally appear near the top (e.g., the rate for California is 11.2). We see that the map of homicide rates is generally consistent with the southern culture of violence thesis.

As noted earlier, identifying connections between variables (such as between homicide and region) is a critical first step in criminological inquiry. The next step is to try to explain why two variables are related. Recall that the southern culture of violence thesis postulates that the reason southern states exhibit high homicide rates is because they share a culture that is supportive of violence. However, before accepting this interpretation, we should also consider additional possibilities. Perhaps southern states differ from non-southern states in other ways that might account for high homicide rates in the South. For example, in popular media accounts, killings are often linked with illegal drugs. Let's explore the possibility that higher levels of cocaine addiction in the South might explain the observed regional pattern for homicide.

Data File: **STATES**
Task: **Mapping**
➤ *Variable 1:* **66) COKEUSER**
➤ *View:* **Map**

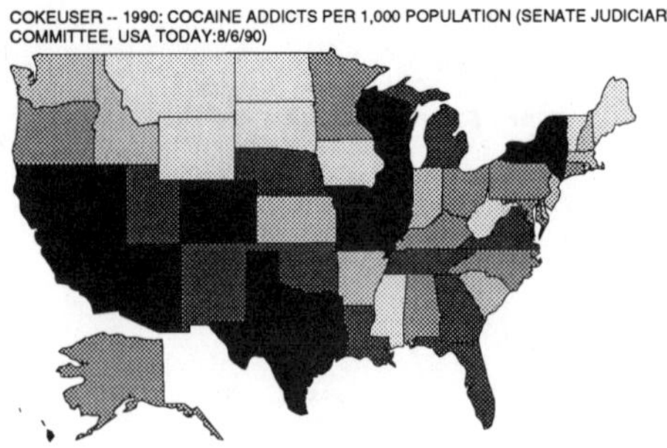

The map for cocaine addiction (cocaine addicts per 1,000 population) does not reveal much regional patterning. States with dark and light colors are scattered throughout the nation, with the exception of a clustering of light-colored states in the upper plains.

We can also see evidence of the geographic scattering in the rankings of states on cocaine addiction.

Data File: **STATES**
Task: **Mapping**
Variable 1: **66) COKEUSER**
➤ *View:* **List: Rank**

COKEUSER: 1990: Cocaine addicts per 1,000 population

RANK	CASE NAME	VALUE
1	Nevada	24.9
2	New York	24.5
3	Illinois	13.8
4	Arizona	13.7
5	California	12.2
6	Missouri	11.5
7	Wisconsin	10.8
8	Hawaii	10.5
8	Colorado	10.5
10	Texas	10.3

The ranking of the top three states covers three different regions. The top state is Nevada, a mountain state. The next state—New York—is in the Northeast. New York is followed by a mid-western state—Illinois. The fifth ranking state is California, a western state. Cocaine use thus does not seem to be a promising candidate to explain the regional patterning of homicide.

Let's compare maps for a variable reflecting fertility levels of states—the number of births per 1,000 population—and the homicide rate.

Data File: **STATES**
Task: **Mapping**
➤ *Variable 1:* **35) BIRTHS**
➤ *Variable 2:* **2) HOMICIDE**
➤ *Views:* **Map**

BIRTHS -- 1993: BIRTHS PER 1000 POPULATION (SA,1996)

r = 0.431**

HOMICIDE -- 1995: CRIMINAL HOMICIDES PER 100,000 POPULATION (UCR, 1996)

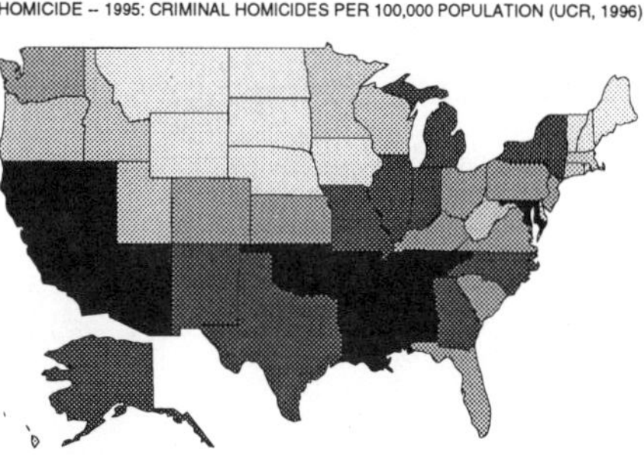

Looking first at the map for the birth rate, we see a distinct regional patterning. A cluster of dark colored states appear in the Southwest (including California). These states also tend to appear in dark colors in the map for homicide rates, suggesting that there is some association between birth rates and homicide rates. However, states in the Deep South tend to be colored in dark in the map of homicide rates but not in the map of birth rates. It is unlikely, therefore, that regional differences in fertility levels fully account for the comparatively high homicide rates in the South.

Finally, let's compare maps for the percent of the state's population living below the poverty level and homicide rates.

Data File: **STATES**
Task: **Mapping**
➤ *Variable 1:* **44) %POOR**
➤ *Variable 2:* **2) HOMICIDE**
➤ *Views:* **Map**

%POOR -- 1994: PERCENT BELOW POVERTY LEVEL (SA,1996)

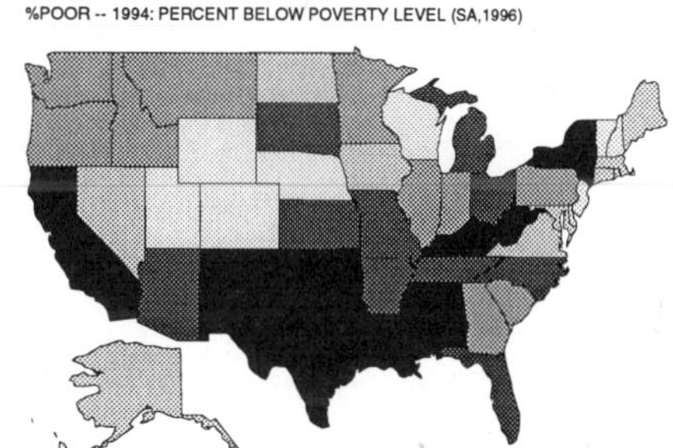

r = 0.701**

HOMICIDE -- 1995: CRIMINAL HOMICIDES PER 100,000 POPULATION (UCR, 1996)

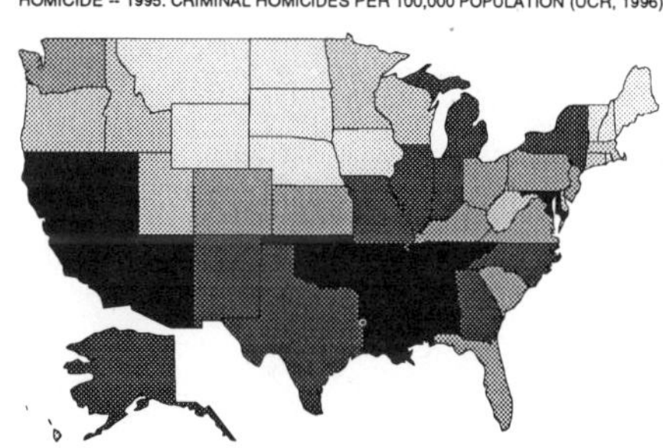

The two maps are very similar to one another. Note, in particular, that southern states are represented in relatively dark colors in both maps. What do these maps imply about the southern culture of violence thesis? They suggest that a satisfactory explanation for the relatively high homicide rates in the South must take into account similarities in poverty levels across regions, as well as any shared cultural attributes.

Now, it's your turn to examine and compare some maps in the worksheet section that follows.

WORKSHEET	CHAPTER
NAME:	1
COURSE:	
DATE:	

REVIEW QUESTIONS

Based on the first part of this chapter, answer True or False to the following items:

A noteworthy advantage of the *Uniform Crime Reports* as a data source for criminological research is that the police transmit to the FBI only crimes that they believe are likely to have occurred.	T	F
The map depicting the larceny rate per 100,000 population for U.S. states closely resembles the map depicting the total number of larcenies for states.	T	F
Southern states tend to exhibit comparatively high homicide rates.	T	F
Poverty levels are dispersed fairly evenly across the different regions of the United States.	T	F

EXPLORIT QUESTIONS

You will need to use the ExplorIt software for the remainder of the questions. Make sure you have already gone through the "Getting Started" section that is located prior to the first chapter. If you have any difficulties using the software to obtain the appropriate information, or if you want to learn about additional features of the MAPPING task, refer to Appendix B.

1. Let's look at the homicide rates for all southern states (as defined by the U.S. Census Bureau) and the rankings of these states.

➤ *Data File:* **STATES**
➤ *Task:* **Mapping**
➤ *Variable 1:* **2) HOMICIDE**
➤ *View:* **List: Alpha**

To create this map using ExplorIt, open the STATES data file, select the MAPPING task, and select 2) HOMICIDE as Variable 1, and click the display box for [List: Alpha]

a. The table that follows contains a list of states that are sometimes classified as "southern." In the first column, record the homicide rate; in the second column, record the ranking of the state.

	HOMICIDE RATE	RANK
ALABAMA	____________	____________
ARKANSAS	____________	____________
DELAWARE	____________	____________
FLORIDA	____________	____________
GEORGIA	____________	____________
KENTUCKY	____________	____________
LOUISIANA	____________	____________
MARYLAND	____________	____________
MISSISSIPPI	____________	____________
NORTH CAROLINA	____________	____________
OKLAHOMA	____________	____________
SOUTH CAROLINA	____________	____________
TENNESSEE	____________	____________
TEXAS	____________	____________
VIRGINIA	____________	____________
WEST VIRGINIA	____________	____________

b. Using the results from your work above, how many southern states rank within the top ten in the nation on homicide rates? ____________

c. How many southern states rank within the bottom ten (41–50) in homicide rates? ____________

2. Let's consider two social characteristics of states that might exhibit a geographic clustering similar to that of homicide rates: the unemployment rate and the percent of households headed by females.

Data File: **STATES**
Task: **Mapping**
➤ *Variable 1:* **48) UNEMPLMNT**
➤ *Variable 2:* **42) FEM.HEAD**
➤ *Views:* **Map**

For which variable is there a more pronounced clustering of high values in the South? (circle one) UNEMPLMNT FEM.HEAD

3. Let's look more closely at the actual values on these two variables for southern states.

Data File: **STATES**
Task: **Mapping**
Variable 1: **48) UNEMPLMNT**
Variable 2: **42) FEM.HEAD**
➤ *Views:* **List: Alpha**

a. List the *ranking* of each southern state on unemployment and the percentage of female-headed households.

	48) UNEMPLMNT	**42) FEM.HEAD**
ALABAMA	________	________
ARKANSAS	________	________
DELAWARE	________	________
FLORIDA	________	________
GEORGIA	________	________
KENTUCKY	________	________
LOUISIANA	________	________
MARYLAND	________	________
MISSISSIPPI	________	________

	48) UNEMPLMNT	42) FEM.HEAD
NORTH CAROLINA	________	________
OKLAHOMA	________	________
SOUTH CAROLINA	________	________
TENNESSEE	________	________
TEXAS	________	________
VIRGINIA	________	________
WEST VIRGINIA	________	________

b. Using the results from your work above, how many southern states rank in the top ten on the unemployment rate? ________

c. How many southern states rank in the top ten on the percentage of female-headed households? ________

4. Consider another variable that might exhibit regional variation: the percentage of persons who claim no religious affiliation.

   Data File: **STATES**
   Task: **Mapping**
   ➤ *Variable 1:* **64) %NORELIG**
   ➤ *Views:* **Map**

   Describe the pattern of the map for southern states. (circle one of the following)

   a. Southern states tend to be dark (high values).
   b. Southern states tend to be light (low values).
   c. Southern states tend to be neither dark nor light.

5. Let's look at some of the specific values for the religion variable.

   Data File: **STATES**
   Task: **Mapping**
   Variable 1: **64) %NORELIG**
   ➤ *View:* **List: Rank**

List the eight states ranked lowest (41–48) on percentage with no religion and the respective values (data are missing for Alaska and Hawaii).

	STATE	VALUE
41.	____________	________
42.	____________	________
43.	____________	________
44.	____________	________
45.	____________	________
46.	____________	________
47.	____________	________
48.	____________	________

6. So far, you've examined the regional patterning of homicide. What might the maps look like for other offenses? Let's compare maps for an offense that is similar to homicide in that it is a violent crime—assault—and an offense that is different from homicide in that it is a property crime—larceny.

Data File: **STATES**
Task: **Mapping**
➤ *Variable 1:* **5) ASSAULT**
➤ *Variable 2:* **7) LARCENY**
➤ *Views:* **Map**

For which of these offenses, assault or larceny, is there a more pronounced geographic clustering with southern states exhibiting relatively high values? (circle one) ASSAULT LARCENY

7. Now examine the rankings on both variables.

Data File: **STATES**
Task: **Mapping**
Variable 1: **5) ASSAULT**
Variable 2: **7) LARCENY**
➤ *View:* **List: Rank**

a. List the three states ranked highest on assault rates and those ranked highest on larceny rates.

	ASSAULT RATE	LARCENY RATE
1.	______________	______________
2.	______________	______________
3.	______________	______________

b. In terms of regional patterning, are assault rates or larceny rates most similar to homicide rates?(circle one) ASSAULT LARCENY

8. Some proponents of the "southern culture of violence" thesis introduced earlier in this chapter claim that the South is distinctive primarily for high levels of lethal violence. Now, let's do a direct comparison of the maps for two types of violent offenses—homicide and assault—that you've looked at previously.

Data File: **STATES**
Task: **Mapping**
➤ *Variable 1:* **2) HOMICIDE**
➤ *Variable 2:* **5) ASSAULT**
➤ *Views:* **Map**

For which of these offenses is there a more pronounced geographic clustering with southern states exhibiting relatively high values? (circle one) ASSAULT HOMICIDE

ESSAY QUESTION

9. As discussed at the beginning of this chapter, the geographic clustering of homicide rates could reflect cultural differences, but it could also be due to differences among states in social characteristics. On the basis of the results of the mapping exercises above, which of the following social variables is more likely to explain the tendency for southern states to exhibit high homicide rates: the unemployment rate or the percentage of households that are headed by females? Explain the basis of your answer.

CHAPTER 2

VICTIMIZATION SURVEYS

Governments are very keen on amassing statistics. They collect them, raise them to the nth power, take the cube root and prepare wonderful diagrams. But you must never forget that every one of these figures comes in the first instance from the village watchman, who just puts down what he damn pleases.

SIR JOSIAH STAMP (1880–1941), ENGLISH ECONOMIST[1]

Tasks: Historical Trends, Univariate
Data Files: HISTORY, NCVS

Criminologists have long suspected that official crime statistics reported by police agencies do not provide a complete count of all offenses. Most of the "crimes known to the police" come from citizen complaints. Yet citizens might decide not to go to the police to file complaints for a wide range of reasons (e.g., lack of confidence in the police, embarrassment, inconvenience, etc.). Recognizing this possibility, criminologists have developed alternative means of measuring crime. One of the more important of these is the victimization survey. In such a survey, a sample of the general population is selected, and respondents are asked whether they have been victims of different kinds of crimes within a specified period of time. Presumably, many people who are reluctant to report crimes to police officers will nevertheless be willing to mention them to interviewers.

There is an important weakness associated with the victimization survey. Since many crimes are rare, especially the serious crimes that people are most concerned about, huge samples are needed to get even a few victims of such crimes. For example, based on the official rape rate for 1995, we would expect only about 11 rape victims to turn up in a sample of 3,000 respondents. Even if the actual rate of rape is twice the official rate, only about 22 victims would turn up in such a sample. These small numbers imply that victimization surveys will have to be based on very large samples if they are to yield useful information about serious crimes.

Fortunately, the federal government has supported a large-scale, ongoing victimization survey in the United States. The survey, which is referred to as the National Crime Victimization Survey (NCVS), is carried out annually by the Census Bureau in collaboration with the Bureau of Justice Statistics. The NCVS collects information on victimizations from a nationally representative sample of U.S. households. For a given year it includes approximately 50,000 households and covers about 100,000 individ-

[1] Quoted in Gwynn Nettler, *Explaining Crime* (New York: McGraw-Hill, 1974), p. 45.

uals age 12 and over (victimizations of persons under age 12 are not included). The NCVS offers an alternative source for measuring levels of crime that can be compared with the official police statistics. In addition, respondents who report victimizations in the NCVS are asked to provide detailed information about what happened during the incidents. This enables criminologists to describe many of the circumstances surrounding different kinds of crime.

You might be wondering how it is possible to determine the level of crime for the nation at large, or more specifically, for all those age 12 and over, if only some of the people in this age group have been interviewed. Strictly speaking, we can't determine on the basis of the sample data the exact level of victimization for the entire population. We can, however, use probability theory to estimate the range within which the figure for the nation at large is likely to fall. This range is referred to as the **confidence interval**. You have probably seen stories in the press based on surveys that mention that the results are accurate within a particular range (e.g., plus or minus 3 percentage points). The size of this range, or confidence interval, depends largely on the number of people sampled. As the sample size increases, estimates become more accurate, and the confidence interval decreases. For our purposes, it is not necessary to examine confidence intervals for the NCVS data, but you should realize that the crime rates reported in these data are sample estimates and are thus always subject to a certain margin of error.

With this qualification in mind, let's compare crime rates for some of the offenses included in both the UCR and the NCVS. (Note that murder rates are not available in the NCVS; murder victims obviously cannot serve as respondents in victimization surveys!) Consider the offense of aggravated assault. This crime involves a threat to attack someone with a weapon, or an actual attack that results in an injury (regardless of whether there was a weapon or not). In 1995, the aggravated assault rate reported in the UCR was 418 per 100,000 population. The estimated rate from the NCVS, on the other hand, was 950 per 100,000—more than twice as high. The NCVS rates for robbery and rape are also much larger than those in the UCR:

Rates per 100,000

	NCVS	UCR
Robbery	540	221
Rape	170	37

We can see from the surveys that citizens report much more criminal victimization occurring than is reflected in the police statistics.

In addition to considering differences in levels of offending across data sources, we can examine the observed trends in crime. Do the two sources lead to the same conclusions about whether levels of crime are increasing, decreasing, or staying about the same? A comprehensive report by the Bureau of Justice Statistics allows us to compare selected crime rates from the NCVS with those reported in the UCR for the 20-year period following the implementation of the NCVS: 1973–92.[2] We can use the HISTORICAL TRENDS task in ExplorIt to examine trends in assault for these two data sources.

[2] Bureau of Justice Statistics, *Criminal Victimization in the United States: 1973–92* (Washington, D.C.: U.S. Department of Justice, 1994).

➤ *Data File:* **HISTORY**

➤ *Task:* **Historical Trends**

➤ *Variables:* **5) UCRASLT**

9) NCVSASLT

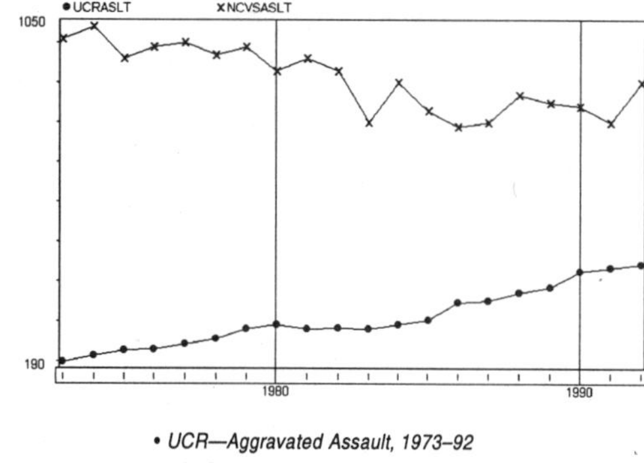

• *UCR—Aggravated Assault, 1973–92*

x *NCVS—Aggravated Assault, 1973–92*

Open the HISTORY data file and select the HISTORICAL TRENDS task. Select 5) UCRASLT and 9) NCVSASLT as your trend variables.

Two important conclusions can be drawn from the graph on your screen. First, as expected, rates of aggravated assault estimated from the NCVS are consistently higher than those reported in the UCR—the NCVS line is always above the UCR line. Second, the trends are quite different. The UCR rates of aggravated assault rose steadily and substantially over the 20-year period, increasing from a rate of about 200 per 100,000 to over 400 per 100,000. The curve for NCVS rates, in contrast, does not display any clear upward trend. Rates went up and down, and if anything, there was a slight drop in the NCVS assault rate over the period.

How can we account for this discrepancy across data sources? The criminologist Robert O'Brien has examined these data along with additional data on trends in violent crime.[3] After extensive analyses, he concludes that the most plausible explanation for the discrepant trends is that the police became much more productive over the 1973–92 period. Local police departments received substantial funding from the Department of Justice to improve their record-keeping, and they were able to expand the number of non-uniformed law enforcement personnel, personnel who are involved in the processing of crime records. Given improved police reporting of crimes, the UCR statistics on assaults would be expected to increase, even if there were no increases in the actual volume of assaults.

O'Brien points to the trend in UCR homicides as further evidence in support of his hypothesis. We might reasonably assume that trends in the "true" levels of assault and homicide will resemble one another, because the motivations for these two offenses are likely to be similar. Indeed, some criminologists argue that homicide can be viewed as a special type of assault, an assault in which the victim dies. In contrast with the official assault rates, however, the official statistics on homicide are likely to be relatively unaffected by changes in police productivity—homicides have always been fairly well recorded. Let's look at the trends in UCR homicide rates.

[3] Robert M. O'Brien, "Police Productivity and Crime Rates: 1973–1992," *Criminology* 34 (1996): 183–207.

Data File: **HISTORY**
Task: **Historical Trends**
➤ *Variables:* **2) UCRHOM**

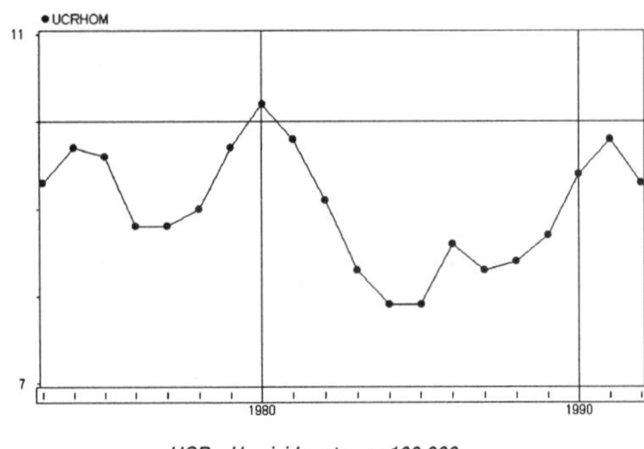

UCR—Homicide rate per 100,000

If you are continuing from the previous example, return to the variable selection screen, click [Clear All] to remove the previously selected variables, and select 2) UCRHOM as your trend variable.

As the graph on your screen indicates, the trend in UCR homicides fluctuates, like the NCVS assault rate, with no discernible upward trend. O'Brien concludes that the 1973–92 period probably was not one of ever-increasing criminal violence. Rather, it was one of improved police productivity in crime recording.

In addition to providing another source for estimating the volume of crime, the NCVS allows us to describe the nature of criminal incidents. For example, let's take a look at selected demographic characteristics of robbery victims. Your data file contains information from the NCVS on attempted and completed robbery incidents over the 1992–94 period.[4] Let's begin by examining the sex of victims using the UNIVARIATE task.

➤ *Data File:* **NCVS**
➤ *Task:* **Univariate**
➤ *Primary Variable:* **1) VICSEX**
➤ *View:* **Pie**

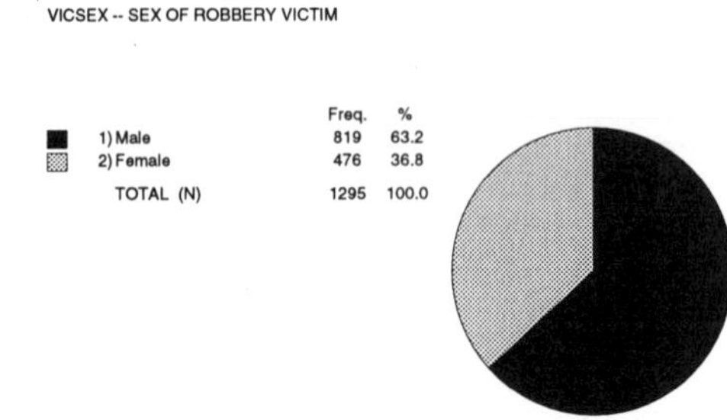

Notice that the NCVS data file must be open.

The data reveal that about 63 percent of robbery victims are male, whereas about 37 percent are female. Males comprise slightly less than half of the total U.S. population (about 49 percent). Hence, males are overrepresented among robbery victims—there are more of them than we would expect on the basis of the relative size in the population at large. Males, in other words, are at greater risk of becoming robbery victims than are females.

---

[4] The NCVS data file used here is based on U.S. Dept. of Justice, Bureau of Justice Statistics, National Crime Victimization Survey, 1992–1994 [Computer file]. Conducted by U.S. Dept. of Commerce, Bureau of the Census. 3rd ICPSR ed. Ann Arbor, MI: Inter-university Consortium for Political and Social Research [producer and distributor], 1997. Study Number: (ICPSR 6406).

We can also examine the racial characteristics of robbery victims.

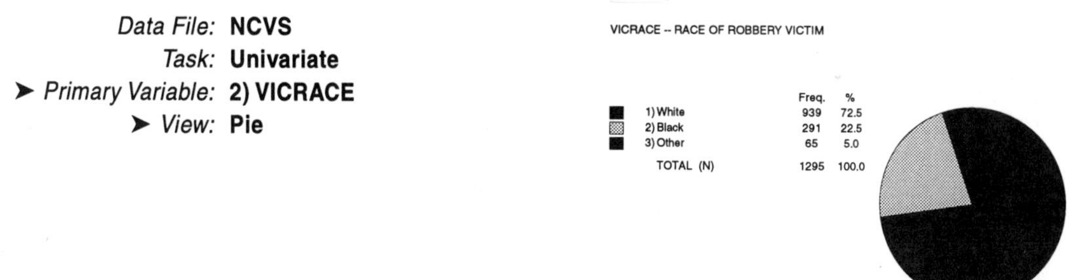

Data File: NCVS
Task: Univariate
➤ Primary Variable: 2) VICRACE
➤ View: Pie
VICRACE -- RACE OF ROBBERY VICTIM
Freq. %
1) White 939 72.5
2) Black 291 22.5
3) Other 65 5.0
TOTAL (N) 1295 100.0

The NCVS data indicate that race is also associated with risk of robbery victimization. African Americans constitute about 12 percent of the total U.S. population, but as the data on your screen show, they comprise about 23 percent of the robbery victims. In contrast, whites make up around 80 percent of the total population but only 73 percent of robbery victims. African Americans experience a comparatively high risk of robbery victimization, while whites experience a comparatively low risk.

Finally, let's look at the relationship between the victim and the offender—whether the victim knew the offender or whether he or she was a stranger to the victim. Robbery is commonly thought of as a "stranger" crime. Is this in fact the case?

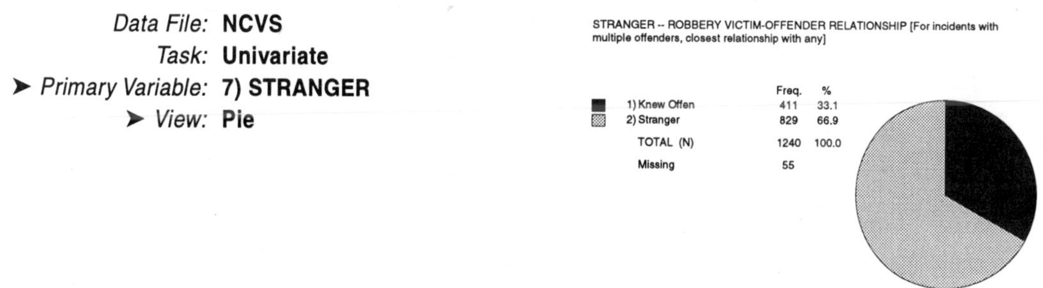

The NCVS data on victim-offender relationships confirm the conventional wisdom about robbery. A substantial majority of robbery incidents (66.9 percent) involve offenders and victims who are unknown to one another.

Now, it's your turn to analyze victimization data.

WORKSHEET	CHAPTER
NAME:	2
COURSE:	
DATE:	

REVIEW QUESTIONS

Based on the first part of this chapter, answer True or False to the following items:

The National Crime Victimization Survey (NCVS) is conducted annually by governmental agencies.	T	F
The trend over the 1973–92 period in levels of aggravated assault as measured in the National Crime Victimization Survey (NCVS) is basically similar to the trend as measured in the FBI's Uniform Crime Reports (UCR).	T	F
Data on homicide rates from the Uniform Crime Reports exhibit a steady upward trend over the 1973–92 period.	T	F
African Americans have a higher risk of robbery victimization than do whites.	T	F
According to the NCVS data on robbery, victims knew their offender in a majority of incidents.	T	F

EXPLORIT QUESTIONS

If you have any difficulties using the software to obtain the appropriate information, or if you want to learn additional features of the HISTORICAL TRENDS or UNIVARIATE tasks, refer to Appendix B.

1. Let's compare NCVS and UCR levels and trends in rape rates.

➤ *Data File:* **HISTORY**
➤ *Task:* **Historical Trends**
➤ *Variables:* **3) UCRRAPE**
7) NCVSRAPE

a. How do the levels of rape rates as measured in the NCVS over the 1973–92 period compare to those reported in the UCR? (circle one of the following)
   1. UCR rates are always higher than NCVS rates.
   2. NCVS rates are always higher than UCR rates.
   3. In some years, UCR rates are higher, in other years, NCVS rates are higher.

b. How do the trends in UCR and NCVS rape rates compare? (circle one of the following)
   1. Both the UCR and the NCVS data reveal increasing rape rates.
   2. Both the UCR and the NCVS data reveal decreasing rape rates.
   3. UCR rape rates have been increasing, while NCVS rates have been decreasing.
   4. UCR rape rates have been decreasing, while NCVS rates have been increasing.

c. In what year of the 1973–92 period do the official police statistics (UCR) yield a rape rate most similar to the NCVS rate? ________

2. Now, let's compare levels and trends in UCR and NCVS robbery rates.

Data File: **HISTORY**
Task: **Historical Trends**
➤ *Variables:* **4) UCRROB**
8) NCVSROB

How do the trends in UCR and NCVS robbery rates compare over the 1973–92 period? (circle one of the following)

   a. Both the UCR and NCVS data reveal generally increasing robbery rates.
   b. Both the UCR and NCVS data reveal generally decreasing robbery rates.
   c. Despite the gap between UCR and NCVS robbery rates, the variation for both sources is fairly similar over time.
   d. UCR robbery rates have been decreasing, while NCVS rates have been increasing.

3. The NCVS asks respondents who say that they have been victims of violent crime whether or not they reported the crimes to the police. We can thus examine any trend in the reporting of criminal violence.

Data File: **HISTORY**
Task: **Historical Trends**
➤ *Variables:* **11) VIORPTED**

Answer the following True/False questions using the NCVS data on the percent of violent crimes reported to the police.

a. The percentage of violent crimes reported to the police between 1973 and 1992 has ranged between 44 percent and 50 percent. T F

b. Citizens have steadily become less willing to report violent crimes to the police over the 1973–92 period. T F

4. Earlier in this chapter, you examined the sex of robbery victims. Now, let's look at the sex of robbery offenders.

   ➤ *Data File:* **NCVS**
   ➤ *Task:* **Univariate**
   ➤ *Primary Variable:* **8) OFFSEX**
   ➤ *View:* **Pie**

   a. Fill in the percentage for *Male* robbery offenders. ________

   b. Fill in the percentage for *Female* robbery offenders. ________

5. Use the UNIVARIATE task to examine the likelihood that weapons are used in robbery incidents.

   Data File: **NCVS**
   Task: **Univariate**
   ➤ *Primary Variable:* **9) WEAPON**
   ➤ *View:* **Pie**

   Most robberies do not involve weapons. T F

6. Use the UNIVARIATE task to examine the likelihood that victims were attacked in robbery incidents.

   Data File: **NCVS**
   Task: **Univariate**
   ➤ *Primary Variable:* **10) ATTACKED**
   ➤ *View:* **Pie**

   Victims are hit or attacked in less than a third of all robberies. T F

7. Use the UNIVARIATE task to examine the likelihood that victims reported robbery incidents to the police.

   Data File: **NCVS**
   Task: **Univariate**
   ➤ *Primary Variable:* **14) REPORTED**
   ➤ *View:* **Pie**

   In a majority of incidents, robberies are reported to the police. T F

8. Use the UNIVARIATE task to examine the likelihood that robbery victims took some type of protective action.

Data File: **NCVS**
Task: **Univariate**
➤ *Primary Variable:* **11) PROTECT**
➤ *View:* **Pie**

In the majority of incidents, robbery victims take some type of self-protective action during the crime. T F

9. The NCVS asks respondents who report having taken self-protective action during a robbery about the consequences of these actions.

a. How likely is it that the self-protective action helped?

Data File: **NCVS**
Task: **Univariate**
➤ *Primary Variable:* **12) HELPED**
➤ *View:* **Pie**

Write in the percentage of robbery victims who took self-protective actions who reported that these actions helped the situation. ________

b. How likely is it that the self-protective action made the situation worse?

Data File: **NCVS**
Task: **Univariate**
➤ *Primary Variable:* **13) WORSE**
➤ *View:* **Pie**

Write in the percentage of robbery victims who took self-protective actions who reported that these actions hurt the situation. ________

10. The NCVS asks robbery victims about the location of the incident.

Data File: **NCVS**
Task: **Univariate**
➤ *Primary Variable:* **4) HOWFAR**
➤ *View:* **Pie**

Describe the distribution of robbery incidents according to closeness to the victim's home. Write in the appropriate percentages.

	PERCENT
AT, NEAR HOME	________
WITHIN 1 MILE	________
WITHIN 5 MILES	________
WITHIN 50 MILES	________
MORE THAN 50 MILES	________

11. The NCVS also asks robbery victims when the robbery occurred.

Data File: **NCVS**
Task: **Univariate**
➤ *Primary Variable:* **5) TIMEDAY**
➤ *View:* **Pie**

Describe the distribution of robbery incidents according to the time of day. Write in the appropriate percentages.

	PERCENT
6 AM TO NOON	________
NOON TO 6 PM	________
6 PM TO MIDNIGHT	________
MIDNIGHT TO 6 AM	________

ESSAY QUESTION

12. On the basis of the ExplorIt questions above, write an essay that describes selected features of the typical robbery incident. Refer to the likely sex of the offender, whether or not a weapon is likely to be used, whether the crime is likely to be reported to the police, and the time of the day during which the crime is most likely to occur. Explain why you think that robberies tend to exhibit these features. Also include statistical evidence to support your claims. (Use the back side of this page for your answer.)

CHAPTER 3

SELF-REPORT SURVEYS

There is nothing so powerful as truth,—and often nothing so strange.

DANIEL WEBSTER (1782–1852)[1]

Tasks: Univariate
Data Files: NYS, COLLEGE

In previous chapters you looked at two methods for getting information about crime. One involves making use of the official records of agencies responsible for controlling crime, and the other involves asking people to describe their experiences as victims of crimes. A third method for getting data on crime—the self-report method—is perhaps the most direct approach of all: we ask people to tell us about their own criminal offending.

The self-report method for measuring offending was pioneered in studies of juvenile delinquency in the 1950s and 60s. Researchers selected samples of youths, typically junior or senior high school students, and presented them with questionnaires asking about involvement in specified types of illegal behavior (e.g., taking somebody else's property, drinking alcohol, using or selling drugs, damaging property, attacking people, etc.). The most important finding to emerge from these studies is that the officially recorded rate of delinquency vastly understates the actual volume of delinquent behavior. Indeed, self-report studies indicate that most young people commit at least some delinquent acts.

As you might expect, criminologists have been concerned about whether self-report data are reliable. Will respondents actually admit to having committed behavior that is socially disapproved of? Through the years a good deal of research has been done to check the accuracy of self-report data to determine if people will, in fact, be truthful in their responses. Some of these studies compared teenagers' self-reports of delinquent behavior against police records. Others reinterviewed a sample of respondents using lie-detector tests. And still others checked answers given by respondents against reports about their behavior given by other informants (friends, parents, teachers). The results of these studies suggest that while there might be a bit of underreporting in self-reports of offending, it is far less than what might be expected. In general, criminologists have concluded that the self-report method is sufficiently trustworthy to use in their research.

Most self-report studies are limited in geographic coverage. These studies typically describe a particular school or local community. This makes it difficult to generalize to the nation at large. An exception, however, is a major study conducted by Delbert Elliott and colleagues called the National Youth Survey (NYS). This research was based on a nationally representative sample of young people in the

[1] Quoted in John Bartlett, *Familiar Quotations: A Collection of Passages, Phrases, and Proverbs Traced to Their Sources in Ancient and Modern Literature*. On-line edition: Columbia University Academic Information Systems [http://www.cc.columbia.edu/acis/bartleby/bartlett/358.html].

United States. Respondents in the study were first interviewed in 1976 and asked about involvement in various forms of delinquency, including fairly serious delinquent acts. The same respondents were then reinterviewed in subsequent "waves" of the study in later years as they grew older.

You have a data file based on the seventh wave of the National Youth Survey.[2] This wave was conducted in 1987, when respondents had reached the stage of young adulthood (age 21–29). One question on the survey asked whether the respondent had been arrested over a recent, three-year time period (1984–86). Let's look at how frequent the experience of a recent arrest is for young adults in the United States.

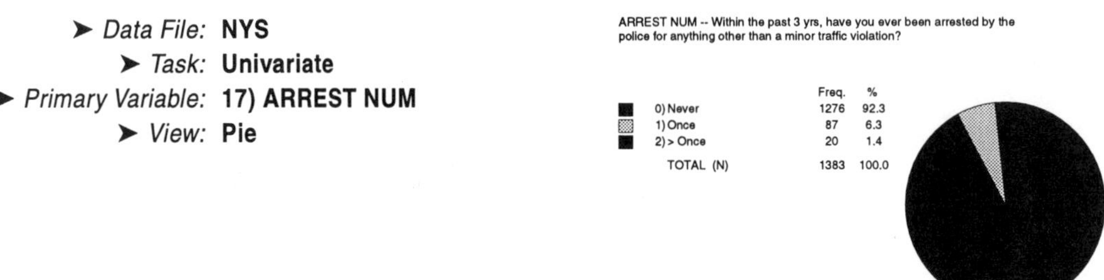

As you can see from the univariate statistics, the experience of a formal arrest over the specified time period was relatively rare. Only about 8 percent of the respondents reported any arrest, and very few were arrested more than once (less than 2 percent). These figures on arrest are interesting when contrasted with the following reports on the use of marijuana. The specific question here refers to the frequency of marijuana use (if any) during the year preceding the survey.

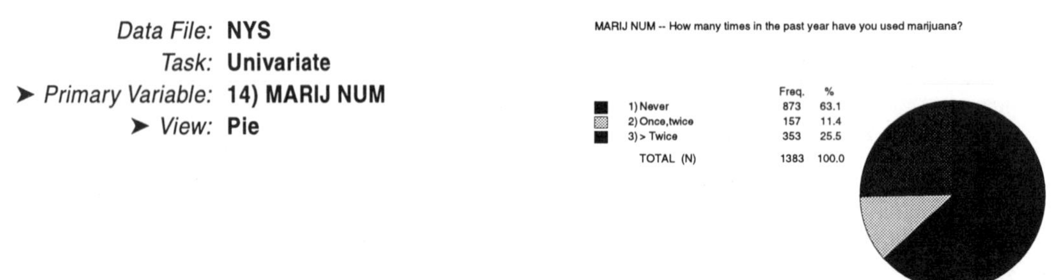

We see that over a third of the respondents (about 37 percent) reported that they had used marijuana during the past year. About one out of four stated that they had used marijuana more than twice in the past year. Thus, consistent with the general literature on self-reported crime, the NYS suggests that there is a fair amount of law breaking among the general population that never results in formal legal sanctioning.

[2] The MicroCase NYS data file is based on Delbert Elliott *National Youth Survey [United States]: Wave VII, 1987* [Computer file]. ICPSR version. Boulder, CO: Behavioral Research Institute [producer], 1995. Ann Arbor, MI: Inter-university Consortium for Political and Social Research [Distributor], 1996.

Of course, many people do not regard smoking marijuana as a serious crime, and some do not think it should be illegal at all. The NYS also asks about more serious infractions, such as stealing a motor vehicle. How common is this kind of offense?

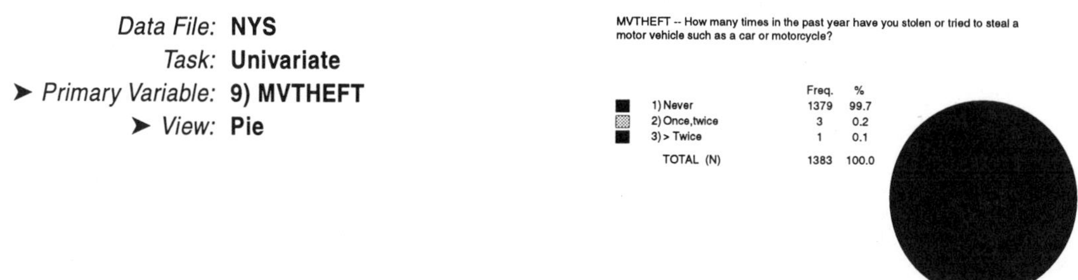

Data File: **NYS**
Task: **Univariate**
➤ *Primary Variable:* **9) MVTHEFT**
➤ *View:* **Pie**
MVTHEFT -- How many times in the past year have you stolen or tried to steal a motor vehicle such as a car or motorcycle?
Freq. %
1) Never 1379 99.7
2) Once,twice 3 0.2
3) > Twice 1 0.1
TOTAL (N) 1383 100.0

The survey results suggest that this is a very infrequent activity. Only 4 of the 1,383 respondents (less than 1 percent) admitted to motor vehicle theft within the past year. In general, the number of respondents who report very serious criminal acts in any given year tends to be small in self-report studies because the rates for these behaviors are relatively low, and most self-report studies are limited in size, at least in comparison with the National Crime Victimization Survey (which we discussed in Chapter 2).

In addition to asking for reports about offending within the past year, the NYS contains items indicating whether or not the respondent had *ever* engaged in certain kinds of crime. One such item asks about serious theft, that is, stealing property worth more than $50. What do these responses look like?

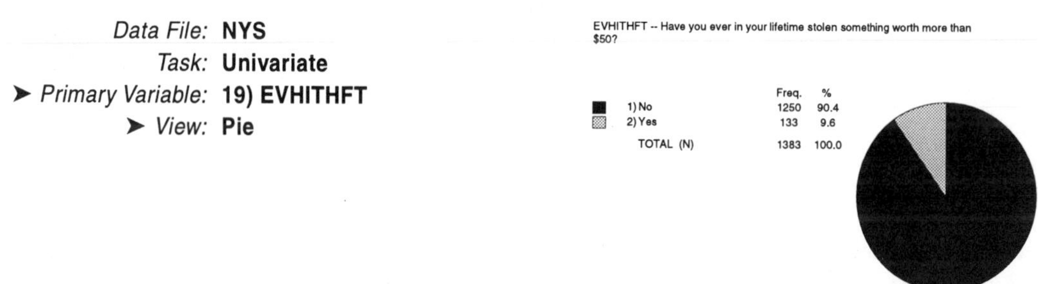

The table indicates that just under 10 percent of the young adults in the sample admitted to having committed a serious theft at some point in their lifetime. If we regard a person who has committed such an act as a "serious thief," the NYS data imply that about one out of ten young adults are serious thieves!

You also have a file containing self-reports of college students. The file is based on surveys conducted during the 1995–96 academic year of first-year students attending a large university. A combined total of 761 respondents participated in the surveys. The results of the surveys are very similar to those obtained at many other schools. But, because the data reveal rather high levels of involvement in crime and illegal alcohol and drug use, it would be unfair to identify the school and subject it to unjustified bad publicity.

One of the questions on the survey asks students about traffic violations: "Have you ever received a ticket, or been charged by the police, for a traffic violation—other than illegal parking?" Let's look at the responses to this question.

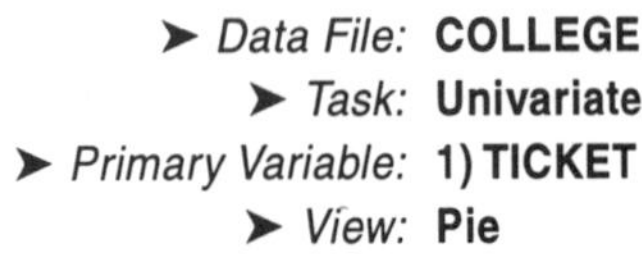

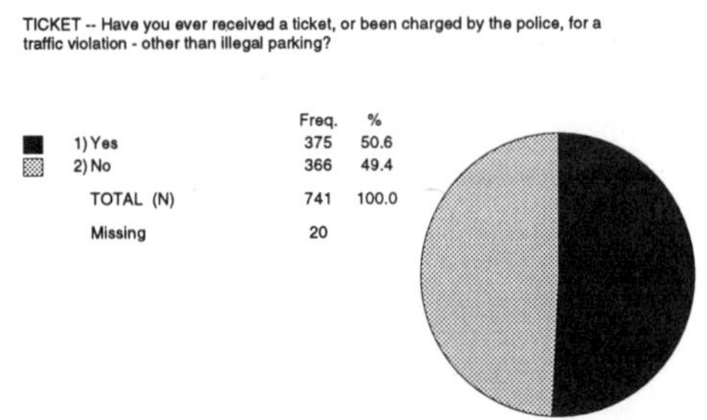

The results of the univariate analysis show that about half (50.6 percent) of these college students admitted having been ticketed for a traffic violation. However, criminologists who designed this question (it is widely used) weren't all that interested in traffic violations. Instead, they used this question as a filter to set up the following question: "Were you ever picked up, or charged, by the police *for any other reason*, whether or not you were guilty?" Let's examine responses to this item.

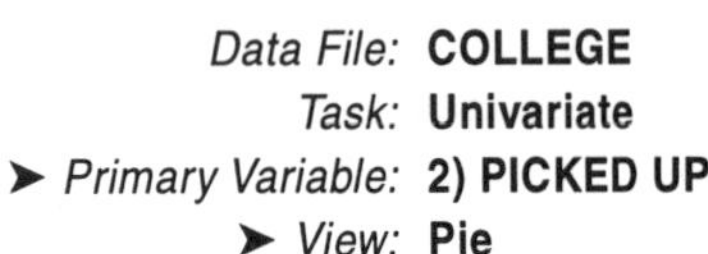

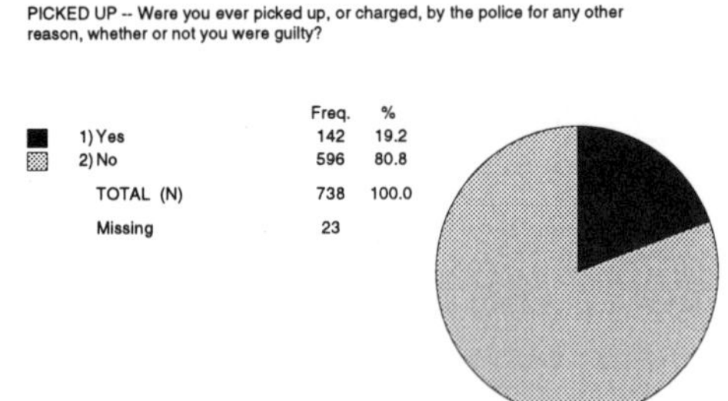

About one out of five (19.2 percent) of the college students in the sample admitted to having been picked up by the police. Although we don't know what they got picked up for, we do know that they were not reporting traffic stops. This might strike you as rather high for students at a good university, but it is actually typical for college students around the nation. Moreover, college students are about as likely to report having been picked up by the police as are all Americans of college age. When a similar question was asked as part of the General Social Survey, 24 percent of persons age 18–23 said they had been picked up by the police.

Now, it's your turn to examine self-report data.

WORKSHEET	CHAPTER
NAME:	3
COURSE:	
DATE:	

REVIEW QUESTIONS

Based on the first part of this chapter, answer True or False to the following items:

Research has shown that respondents are willing to admit to having committed illegal behavior on questionnaires.	T	F
Criminologists have not yet conducted a nationally representative survey of self-reported criminal offending.	T	F
According to the National Youth Survey (NYS), a slight majority of young adults report being arrested over the past three years.	T	F
The National Youth Survey does not include any serious forms of offending on its self-report checklist.	T	F
Survey data indicate that about one out of five college students report having been picked up by the police for reasons other than traffic violations.	T	F

EXPLORIT QUESTIONS: PART I

Use data on young adults (age 21–29) from WAVE VII of the National Youth Survey to answer the following questions.

1. Let's begin by examining involvement in property crime. Fill in the appropriate numbers indicating how many times within the past year the respondent has knowingly bought, sold, or held stolen goods.

➤ *Data File:* **NYS**
➤ *Task:* **Univariate**
➤ *Primary Variable:* **6) HOTGOODS**
➤ *View:* **Pie**

	FREQUENCY	PERCENT
NEVER	______	______
ONCE OR TWICE	______	______
MORE THAN TWICE	______	______

2. Now consider an item for carrying a weapon. Fill in the appropriate numbers indicating how many times within the past year a respondent has carried a hidden weapon other than a pocket knife.

Data File: **NYS**
Task: **Univariate**
➤ *Primary Variable:* **7) HIDWEAP**
➤ *View:* **Pie**

	FREQUENCY	**PERCENT**
NEVER	________	________
ONCE OR TWICE	________	________
MORE THAN TWICE	________	________

3. The NYS also asks about relatively minor infractions, such as public drunkenness. Fill in the appropriate numbers indicating how many times within the past year a respondent has been drunk in a public place.

Data File: **NYS**
Task: **Univariate**
➤ *Primary Variable:* **12) DRUNK NUM**
➤ *View:* **Pie**

	FREQUENCY	**PERCENT**
NEVER	________	________
ONCE OR TWICE	________	________
MORE THAN TWICE	________	________

4. Rank the above three offenses—buying stolen goods, carrying a hidden weapon, and being drunk in public places—in terms of how serious you think they are. Then, rank these offenses in terms of how rare they are (use the percentage who respond "never" to indicate how rare an offense is).

   a. Rank the seriousness of the offense.

      MOST SERIOUS ________

      INTERMEDIATE ________

      LEAST SERIOUS ________

b. Rank the offenses in terms of how rare they are.

RAREST ____________

INTERMEDIATE ____________

MOST COMMON ____________

c. How do the two rankings compare?

5. Now let's examine some of the questions asking about the respondent's involvement in misbehaviors at any time, not just within the past year. Fill in the appropriate numbers indicating whether the respondent has ever in his or her lifetime stolen a motor vehicle.

Data File: **NYS**
Task: **Univariate**
➤ *Primary Variable:* **18) EVERMV**
➤ *View:* **Pie**

	FREQUENCY	PERCENT
NO	____________	____________
YES	____________	____________

6. Consider the offense of assault. Fill in the appropriate numbers indicating whether the respondent has ever in his or her lifetime attacked someone with the idea of seriously hurting them.

Data File: **NYS**
Task: **Univariate**
➤ *Primary Variable:* **20) EVATTACK**
➤ *View:* **Pie**

	FREQUENCY	PERCENT
NO	____________	____________
YES	____________	____________

7. Let's look at burglary. Fill in the appropriate numbers indicating whether the respondent has ever in his or her lifetime broken into a building to steal something.

Data File: **NYS**
Task: **Univariate**
➤ *Primary Variable:* **21) EVBREAKN**
➤ *View:* **Pie**

	FREQUENCY	**PERCENT**
NO	______	______
YES	______	______

8. On the basis of your answers to Questions 5–7, answer True or False to the following item:

Relatively fewer young adults have committed assaults than have committed the property crimes of motor vehicle theft or burglary. T F

9. The National Youth Survey also collected information about domestic conflict and violence. Respondents who were married or were living with a partner were asked if in the past year they had done any of a list of "things which couples may do in an effort to deal with their frustrations and settle differences."

One such item deals with verbal conflict. Fill in the appropriate numbers indicating how many times in the past year a respondent swore at or insulted his or her partner.

Data File: **NYS**
Task: **Univariate**
➤ *Primary Variable:* **23) SWORE PRT**
➤ *View:* **Pie**

	FREQUENCY	**PERCENT**
NEVER	______	______
ONCE	______	______
MORE THAN ONCE	______	______

10. Now consider acts involving physical force. Fill in the appropriate numbers indicating how many times in the past year a respondent pushed, grabbed, or shoved his or her partner.

Data File: **NYS**
Task: **Univariate**
➤ *Primary Variable:* **26) SHOVED PRT**
➤ *View:* **Pie**

	FREQUENCY	PERCENT
NEVER	______	______
ONCE	______	______
MORE THAN ONCE	______	______

11. Let's also consider an item reflecting other forms of physical force. Fill in the appropriate numbers indicating how many times in the past year a respondent kicked, bit, or hit his or her partner.

Data File: **NYS**
Task: **Univariate**
➤ *Primary Variable:* **28) HIT PRT**
➤ *View:* **Pie**

	FREQUENCY	PERCENT
NEVER	______	______
ONCE	______	______
MORE THAN ONCE	______	______

12. How common do you think it is for someone to pull a gun on his or her partner? Fill in the appropriate numbers indicating how many times in the past year a respondent threatened his or her partner with a gun.

Data File: **NYS**
Task: **Univariate**
➤ *Primary Variable:* **31) GUN PRT**
➤ *View:* **Pie**

	FREQUENCY	PERCENT
NEVER	______	______
ONCE	______	______
MORE THAN ONCE	______	______

13. Which of the following statements best supports your analyses for Questions 9–12? (circle one of the following)

    a. Verbal conflict between partners (e.g., swearing, insults) is fairly common.

    b. More than one out of four (25 percent) respondents report having committed some form of physical aggression (e.g., pushing, shoving) against their partner within the past year.

    c. The use of weapons by one partner against another is very rare.

    d. All of the above.

EXPLORIT QUESTIONS: PART II

Use data from the sample of first-year college students to answer the following questions.

14. Let's examine self-reports of shoplifting.

    ➤ *Data File:* **COLLEGE**
    ➤ *Task:* **Univariate**
    ➤ *Primary Variable:* **3) SHOPLIFT**
    ➤ *View:* **Pie**

    a. Fill in the appropriate numbers indicating whether a respondent engaged in shoplifting in the past year.

	FREQUENCY	PERCENT
YES	______	______
NO	______	______

    b. Suppose students at your school were asked this question. Do you think the responses would be similar? (circle one of the following)

        1. Similar
        2. Less shoplifting here
        3. More shoplifting here

15. Now, consider the consumption of alcohol.

Data File:	**COLLEGE**
Task:	**Univariate**
➤ *Primary Variable:*	**4) DRINK**
➤ *View:*	**Pie**

a. Fill in the appropriate numbers indicating whether a respondent currently drinks alcohol or is a total abstainer.

	FREQUENCY	**PERCENT**
DRINK NOW	________	________
ABSTAIN	________	________

b. Suppose students at your school were asked this question. Do you think the responses would be similar? (circle one of the following)

1. Similar
2. Less drinking here
3. More drinking here

16. How common do you think the abuse of alcohol or drugs is?

Data File:	**COLLEGE**
Task:	**Univariate**
➤ *Primary Variable:*	**8) THROW UP**
➤ *View:*	**Pie**

a. Fill in the appropriate numbers indicating whether a respondent has been nauseated or vomited from drinking or drug use during the past year.

	FREQUENCY	**PERCENT**
YES	________	________
NO	________	________

b. Suppose students at your school were asked this question. Do you think the responses would be similar? (circle one of the following)

1. Similar
2. Less abuse here
3. More abuse here

17. Let's examine the frequency of marijuana use among college students.

Data File:	**COLLEGE**
Task:	**Univariate**
➤ *Primary Variable:*	**5) FREQ MARIJ**
➤ *View:*	**Pie**

a. Fill in the appropriate numbers indicating how often the respondent has used marijuana.

	FREQUENCY	**PERCENT**
YES, IN PAST YR	_______	_______
YES, NOT IN PAST YR	_______	_______
NEVER	_______	_______

b. Suppose students at your school were asked this question. Do you think the responses would be similar? (circle one of the following)

1. Similar
2. Less use here
3. More use here

18. How common do you think cocaine use is among college students?

Data File:	**COLLEGE**
Task:	**Univariate**
➤ *Primary Variable:*	**7) FREQ COKE**
➤ *View:*	**Pie**

a. Fill in the appropriate numbers indicating how often the respondent has used cocaine.

	FREQUENCY	**PERCENT**
YES, IN PAST YR	_______	_______
YES, NOT IN PAST YR	_______	_______
NEVER	_______	_______

b. Suppose students at your school were asked this question. Do you think the responses would be similar? (circle one of the following)
   1. Similar
   2. Less use here
   3. More use here

19. Now let's consider academic dishonesty.

Data File: **COLLEGE**
Task: **Univariate**
➤ *Primary Variable:* **9) CHEAT**
➤ *View:* **Pie**

a. Fill in the appropriate numbers indicating how often the respondent has cheated on an exam.

	FREQUENCY	PERCENT
YES, OFTEN	______	______
ONCE OR TWICE	______	______
NO	______	______

b. Suppose students at your school were asked this question. Do you think the responses would be similar? (circle one of the following)
   1. Similar
   2. Less cheating here
   3. More cheating here

20. Now let's look at the socioeconomic status of the respondents in the college sample.

Data File: **COLLEGE**
Task: **Univariate**
➤ *Primary Variable:* **24) FAMILY $**
➤ *View:* **Pie**

Fill in the appropriate numbers indicating the respondent's perception of his or her family income.

	FREQUENCY	PERCENT
FAR BELOW AV	______	______
BELOW AV	______	______
AVERAGE	______	______
ABOVE AV	______	______
FAR ABOVE AV	______	______

21. Consider the following hypothesis:

Crime, alcohol, and drug use are concentrated exclusively among the poor, uneducated segments of the population.

What are the implications of the results of the survey of college students for this hypothesis? (Circle one).

a. The hypothesis is supported.

b. The hypothesis is not supported.

ESSAY QUESTION

22. Self-reports indicate that wrongdoing is much more widespread than would be suggested by the official crime statistics. Criminologists caution, however, that the seriousness of infractions needs to be considered when drawing conclusions about how common involvement in deviant behavior is among the general population. Explain the reason for this caution by referring specifically to some of the results from the ExplorIt questions above. Given these findings, how might you account for some of the discrepancies between official crime statistics and self-report data on crime? Your essay should include statistical evidence to support your conclusions.

CHAPTER 4

CRIME AND PUBLIC OPINION

Wicked people exist. Nothing avails except to set them apart from innocent people. And many people, neither wicked nor innocent, but watchful, dissembling, and calculating of their opportunities, ponder our reaction to wickedness as a cue to what they might profitably do. We have trifled with the wicked, made sport of the innocent, and encouraged the calculators.

JAMES Q. WILSON,
POLITICAL SCIENTIST AND
CRIMINOLOGIST[1]

Tasks: Univariate, Historical Trends
Data Files: GSS, HISTORY

It is hardly an exaggeration to state that people in our society are bombarded with information about crime and the criminal justice system. The media, in particular, provide a fairly steady diet of crime stories to the public in both entertainment and news programming. The social scientist Ray Surette has conducted extensive studies of the relationship between the media and attitudes about crime-related issues. Surette argues that people take the knowledge they acquire from the media and use it to create a general world view of the "crime situation" in the nation. Consistent with the quotation cited above, the public learns that "the criminal justice system is not effective and that its improvement is the best solution to crime."[2] These messages, Surette maintains, promote a "law and order" approach to crime problems. Whether or not we agree with the specifics of Surette's analysis, it seems clear that people think very seriously about crime. They form strong opinions about what is currently being done to combat crime and, also, what should be done.

Social scientists interested in studying attitudes held by the general American public often turn to the General Social Survey (GSS). The GSS is an ongoing survey of U.S. households conducted by the National Opinion Research Center (NORC) at the University of Chicago. It is based on personal interviews of a nationally representative sample of respondents age 18 and over. The GSS began in 1972 and, with the exception of a few years, was conducted annually through 1993. The survey became biennial in 1994. Recent surveys have included approximately 3,000 respondents. However, some questions are asked only of randomly selected subsets of the sample, resulting in smaller numbers of cases for analysis of these questions.

---

[1] James Q. Wilson, *Thinking About Crime*, (New York: Vintage Books, 1975), pp. 235–236.

[2] Ray Surette, *Media, Crime, and Criminal Justice: Images and Realities*, (Pacific Grove, CA: Brooks/Cole, 1992), p. 76.

The GSS contains a wealth of information on the attitudes, selected behaviors, and characteristics of the U.S. population. Standard demographic variables are recorded, such as age, sex, race, and marital status of respondents. In addition, the GSS asks about a variable of particular interest to social scientists—perceived social class. The specific wording of the questions is: "If you were asked to use one of four names for your social class, which would you say you belong in: the lower class, the working class, the middle class, or the upper class?" Look at how respondents perceive their own social class.

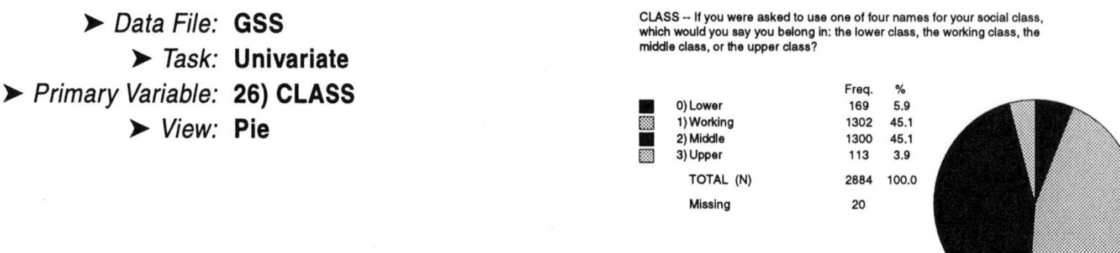

As your univariate analysis reveals, most respondents consider themselves to be in either the working or middle class (about 45 percent each), with relatively small numbers placing themselves in the other two categories.

The GSS also asks about various forms of behavior, such as religious behavior. For example, one such item asks respondents whether they attended a religious service in the last seven days.

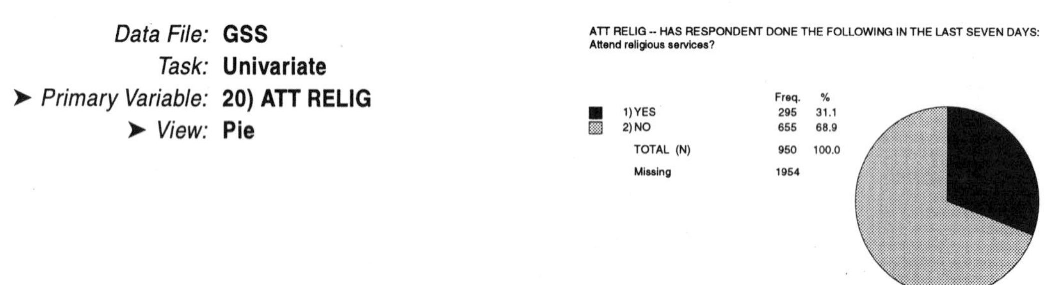

Only about a third of GSS respondents indicate that they attended a religious service within the past week. Even the percentage answering "yes" is slightly inflated because it includes those people who may have attended a religious service such as a wedding or baptism, rather than a regular worship service.

One of the most important items in the GSS for criminological inquiry deals with the fear of crime. The specific question is this: "Is there any area right around here—that is, within a mile—where you would be afraid to walk alone at night?" Although the question does not explicitly refer to crime, criminologists generally agree that responses can be interpreted as reflecting fear of crime, given the context of the question in the survey. Let's look at levels of fear in the United States.

Data File: **GSS**
Task: **Univariate**
➤ *Primary Variable:* **1) FEAR WALK**
➤ *View:* **Pie**

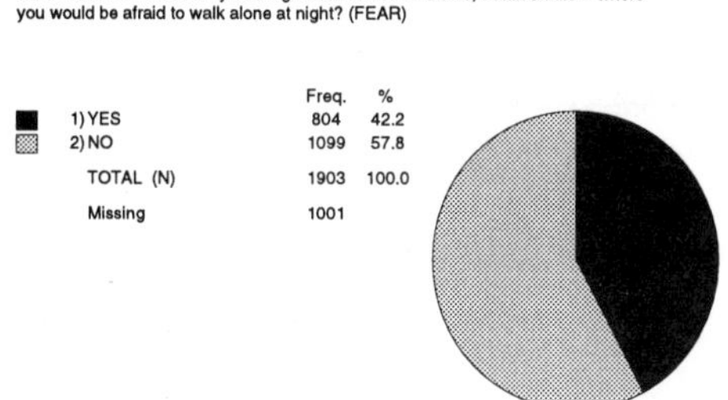

FEAR WALK -- Is there any area right around here -- that is, within a mile -- where you would be afraid to walk alone at night? (FEAR)
Freq. %
1) YES 804 42.2
2) NO 1099 57.8
TOTAL (N) 1903 100.0
Missing 1001

You can see from the univariate analysis of the responses to this item that in 1996 about 42 percent of all respondents answered that they would be afraid to walk around their neighborhood alone at night. Is this a relatively recent phenomenon? The fear of crime item was asked in the first GSS survey in 1972, and it has been repeated in many of the subsequent surveys. You can thus look at responses over an extended period of time using the HISTORICAL TRENDS task.

➤ *Data File:* **HISTORY**
➤ *Task:* **Historical Trends**
➤ *Variables:* **12) GSSFEAR**

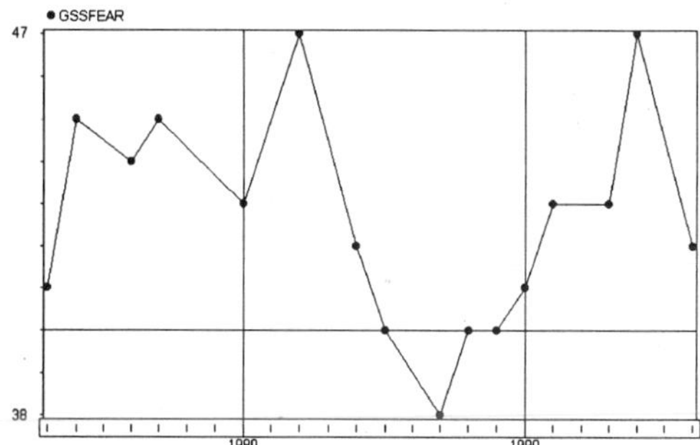

Percent who fear walking alone in their neighborhood at night, 1972–1996

The percentage responding "yes" to this item has fluctuated somewhat over the 1972–96 period, ranging from a low of 38 percent in 1987 to a high of 47 percent in 1982 and 1994. In general, the pattern shows appreciable levels of fear among the general public. In surveys over approximately 25 years, somewhere around 40 percent of U.S. citizens report that they are afraid to walk alone at night in their neighborhood.

To what extent are people willing to sacrifice basic civil liberties to secure the safety of their person and belongings? In other words, does fairly widespread fear of crime in the United States lead to a "law and order" mentality that allows the police to do virtually anything they want to control crime? The GSS includes a series of items which ask the respondent to indicate whether he or she would approve of a police officer striking a citizen under different circumstances. Consider the situation where the citizen is attacking the police officer with his or her fists.

➤ *Data File:* **GSS**
➤ *Task:* **Univariate**
➤ *Primary Variable:* **8) COP:ATT**
➤ *View:* **Pie**

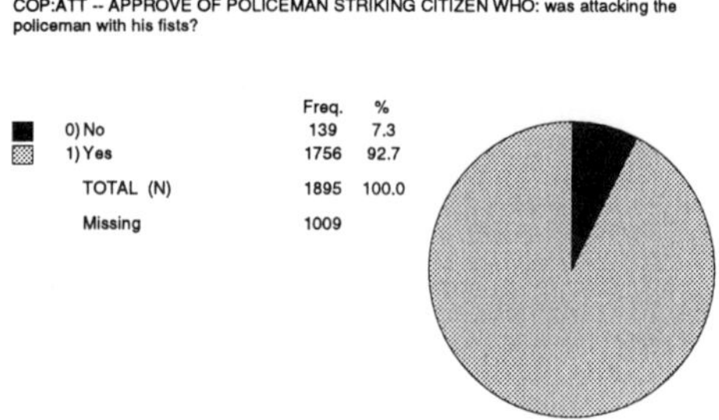

COP:ATT -- APPROVE OF POLICEMAN STRIKING CITIZEN WHO: was attacking the policeman with his fists?
Freq. %
0) No 139 7.3
1) Yes 1756 92.7
TOTAL (N) 1895 100.0
Missing 1009

The vast majority of respondents—almost 93 percent—would approve of the police officer's use of physical force under this circumstance. This is not very surprising. The right to defend oneself when under attack has long been recognized in both the law and the general culture, and people evidently accord this right to on-duty police officers as well.

Another circumstance mentioned in the GSS is when the citizen is attempting to escape from custody. How do survey respondents answer this question?

Data File: **GSS**
Task: **Univariate**
➤ *Primary Variable:* **7) COP:ESC**
➤ *View:* **Pie**

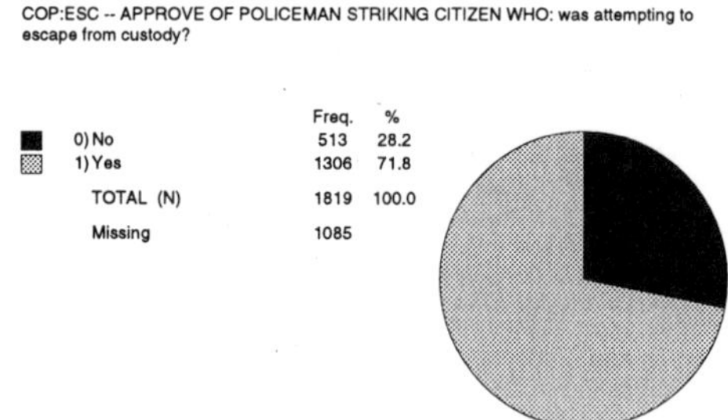

COP:ESC -- APPROVE OF POLICEMAN STRIKING CITIZEN WHO: was attempting to escape from custody?
Freq. %
0) No 513 28.2
1) Yes 1306 71.8
TOTAL (N) 1819 100.0
Missing 1085

Under this situation, about 72 percent of respondents approve of a police officer striking the citizen, whereas about 28 percent disapprove. The police are generally empowered by law to use "reasonable force" in effecting an arrest. Evidently, most respondents see striking a person as a reasonable exercise of force to effect an arrest when a suspect is trying to get away, although a fairly substantial proportion—more than 1 out of 4—disagrees.

Tolerance for use of physical force by the police does not extend, however, to instances of verbal abuse. You can see this by examining responses to the item asking if the respondent approves of a police officer striking a citizen who had said vulgar and obscene things to the officer.

Data File: **GSS**
Task: **Univariate**
➤ *Primary Variable:* **5) COP:CUSS**
➤ *View:* **Pie**

COP:CUSS -- APPROVE POLICEMAN STRIKING CITIZEN WHO: had said vulgar and obscene things to the policeman?

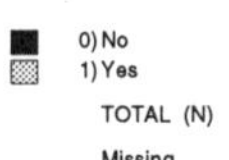

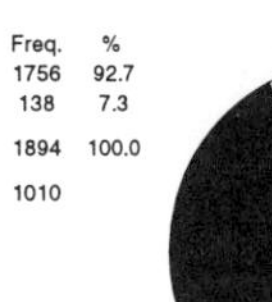

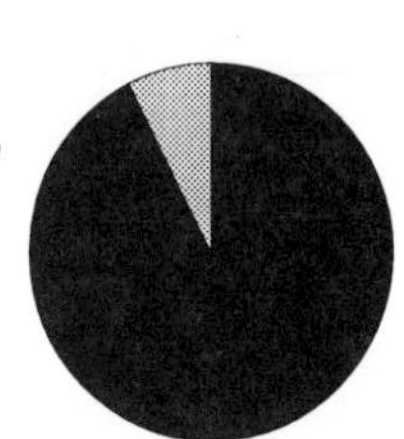

Only about 7 percent of respondents approve of a police officer striking a citizen who had been verbally abusive.

Finally, let's consider support for the police use of violence as an investigative tool in the most serious of criminal cases—murder. The GSS item asks if it's acceptable for a police officer to strike a suspect being questioned in a murder case.

Data File: **GSS**
Task: **Univariate**
➤ *Primary Variable:* **6) COP:KILL**
➤ *View:* **Pie**

COP:KILL -- APPROVE POLICEMAN STRIKING CITIZEN WHO: was being questioned as a suspect in a murder case?

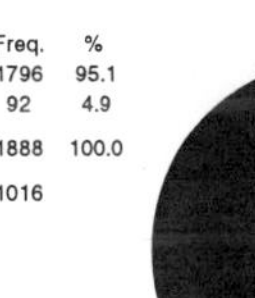

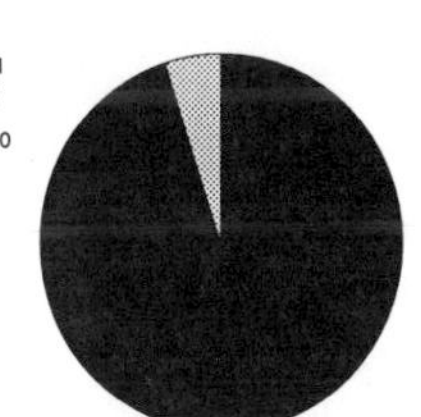

Just less than 5 percent of respondents approve of a police officer striking a citizen as part of the questioning of a murder suspect.

Recall that the GSS is based on a representative sample of the adult population in the United States, and so the figures reported above presumably indicate the mood of the country (given, of course, the limitations of all survey data). How do your attitudes on these topics compare with those for the population at large?

WORKSHEET	CHAPTER
NAME:	4
COURSE:	
DATE:	

REVIEW QUESTIONS

Based on the first part of this chapter, answer True or False to the following items:

A major limitation of the General Social Survey (GSS) is that the sample is not representative of adults 18 and over for the nation at large.	T	F
In addition to asking about demographic characteristics, the GSS asks people to report their perceived social class.	T	F
The 1996 GSS indicates that over half of adult U.S. citizens attend religious services every week.	T	F
An item commonly used to measure fear of crime in the GSS is a question asking respondents if they would be afraid to walk alone at night within a mile of where they live.	T	F
According to the 1996 GSS, a very small proportion of adults in the United States (less than one out of ten) approves of a police officer striking a citizen who said vulgar and obscene things to the officer.	T	F

EXPLORIT QUESTIONS: PART I

The following questions require you to analyze the responses to several questions contained in the General Social Survey (GSS). For each question, you are required to do the following:

a. Write down the complete survey question that was asked. To do this you need to open the GSS file, select the UNIVARIATE task, use your mouse to highlight the survey question being examined, and then write down the wording of the question that appears in the variable description window.

b. Estimate (i.e., guess) what the percentage distributions will be for each answer category. Also, indicate whether you think the percent of respondents who give the specified response has increased over time, decreased, or stayed about the same. (Note: Fill in your estimates/guesses before you do the analyses themselves—there are no right or wrong answers for these.)

c. Report how you would answer the survey question.

d. Conduct univariate analysis of the variable and fill in the actual percentages in the table.

e. Switch to the HISTORY file and select the comparable variable to determine whether survey responses have changed over time. As a rule of thumb, regard a difference of 5 percentage points or less over the entire period as “staying about the same.”

1. The first question we'll examine in the GSS file is 2) CAPPUN.

   a. Write down the question wording. ____

   ____

   b. Estimate (guess) what the percentage will be for each answer category.

   Favor: _________%

   Oppose: _________%

   c. What response would you give to this question? Favor Oppose

   d. Conduct the univariate analysis of this survey question and fill in the actual percentages.

   Data File: **GSS**
   Task: **Univariate**
   ➤ *Primary Variable:* **2) CAPPUN**
   ➤ *View:* **Pie**

   Favor: _________%

   Oppose: _________%

   e. Over the past 25 years or so, do you think that the percentage of people who favor the death penalty has increased, decreased, or stayed the same? (circle one of the following)

      1. Increased
      2. Decreased
      3. Stayed the same

   f. Open the HISTORY file and select the HISTORICAL TRENDS task. Choose 13) CAPPUNGSS as the variable. Has the percentage of people who favor the death penalty increased, decreased, or stayed the same? (circle one of the following)

      1. Increased
      2. Decreased
      3. Stayed the same

2. The next question we'll examine in the GSS file is 3) COURTS.

   a. Write down the question wording. ____

   ____

   ____

b. Estimate (guess) what the percentage will be for each answer category.

Too Harsh: ________%

Not Enough: ________%

About Right: ________%

c. What response would you give to this question?

Too Harsh

Not Enough

About Right

d. Conduct the univariate analysis of this survey question and fill in the actual percentages.

Data File: **GSS**
Task: **Univariate**
➤ *Primary Variable:* **3) COURTS**
➤ *View:* **Pie**

Too Harsh: ________%

Not Enough: ________%

About Right: ________%

e. Over the past 25 years or so, do you think that the percentage of people who believe that the courts are not harsh enough with criminals has increased, decreased, or stayed the same? (circle one of the following)

1. Increased
2. Decreased
3. Stayed the same

f. Open the HISTORY file and examine the HISTORICAL TRENDS task for 14) COURTSGSS. Has the percentage of people who believe that the courts are not harsh enough increased, decreased, or stayed the same? (circle one of the following)

1. Increased
2. Decreased
3. Stayed the same

3. Now let's examine 12) GUNLAW.

a. Write down the question wording. ____________________

____

____

b. Estimate (guess) what the percentage will be for each answer category.

Favor: __________%

Oppose: __________%

c. What response would you give to this question? Favor Oppose

d. Conduct the univariate analysis of this survey question and fill in the actual percentages.

Data File: **GSS**
Task: **Univariate**
➤ *Primary Variable:* **12) GUNLAW**
➤ *View:* **Pie**

Favor: __________%

Oppose: __________%

e. Over the past 25 years or so, do you think that the percentage of people who favor a gun law has increased, decreased, or stayed the same? (circle one of the following)

1. Increased
2. Decreased
3. Stayed the same

f. Open the HISTORY file and examine the trend for 15) GUNLAWGSS. Has the percentage of people who favor a gun law increased, decreased, or stayed the same? (circle one of the following)

1. Increased
2. Decreased
3. Stayed the same

4. The next question from the GSS file that we will examine is 22) OWNGUN.

a. Write down the question wording. ____

____

b. Estimate (guess) what the percentage will be for each answer category.

Yes: __________%

No: __________%

c. What response would you give to this question? Yes No

d. Conduct the univariate analysis of this survey question and fill in the actual percentages.

Data File: **GSS**
Task: **Univariate**
➤ *Primary Variable:* **22) OWNGUN**
➤ *View:* **Pie**

Yes: __________%

No: __________%

e. Over the past 25 years or so, do you think that the percentage of people who own guns has increased, decreased, or stayed the same? (circle one of the following)

1. Increased
2. Decreased
3. Stayed the same

f. Open the HISTORY file and examine the trend for 16) OWNGUNGSS. Has the percentage of people who own guns increased, decreased, or stayed the same? (circle one of the following)

1. Increased
2. Decreased
3. Stayed the same

5. Now let's look at the popularity of hunting using the GSS variable 23) HUNT.

a. Write down the question wording. ____

____

b. Estimate (guess) what the percentage will be for each answer category.

Hunts: __________%

Not Hunts: __________%

c. What response would you give to this question? Hunt Don't Hunt

d. Conduct the univariate analysis of this survey question and fill in the actual percentages.

Data File: **GSS**
Task: **Univariate**
➤ *Primary Variable:* **23) HUNT**
➤ *View:* **Pie**

Hunts: __________%

Not Hunts: __________%

e. Over the past 25 years or so, do you think that the percentage of people who hunt has increased, decreased, or stayed the same? (circle one of the following)

   1. Increased
   2. Decreased
   3. Stayed the same

f. Open the HISTORY file and examine the trend for 17) HUNTGSS. Has the percentage of people who hunt increased, decreased, or stayed the same? (circle one of the following)

   1. Increased
   2. Decreased
   3. Stayed the same

6. The next question in the GSS file that we will examine is 9) CRIME$.

a. Write down the question wording. ____

____

b. Estimate (guess) what the percentage will be for each answer category.

Too Little: __________%

Right: __________%

Too Much: __________%

c. What response would you give to this question?

Too Little

Right

Too Much

d. Conduct the univariate analysis of this survey question and fill in the actual percentages.

Data File: **GSS**
Task: **Univariate**
➤ *Primary Variable:* **9) CRIME$**
➤ *View:* **Pie**

Too Little: __________%

Right: __________%

Too Much: __________%

e. Over the past 25 years or so, do you think that the percentage of people who believe that too little is being spent on halting the rising crime rate has increased, decreased, or stayed the same? (circle one of the following)

1. Increased
2. Decreased
3. Stayed the same

f. Open the HISTORY file and examine the trend for 18) CRIME$GSS. Has the percentage of people who believe that too little is being spent on halting the rising crime rate increased, decreased, or stayed the same? (circle one of the following)

1. Increased
2. Decreased
3. Stayed the same

7. How do people feel about the regulation of pornography? Let's examine this question using the GSS variable 13) PORNLAW.

a. Write down the question wording. ____

____

____

____

____

b. Estimate (guess) what the percentage will be for each answer category.

Yes, all: __________%

Yes, <18: __________%

No Laws: __________%

c. What response would you give to this question?

Yes, all

Yes, <18

No laws

d. Conduct the univariate analysis of this survey question and fill in the actual percentages.

Data File: **GSS**
Task: **Univariate**
➤ *Primary Variable:* **13) PORNLAW**
➤ *View:* **Pie**

Yes, all: __________%

Yes, <18: __________%

No Laws: __________%

e. Over the past 25 years or so, do you think that the percentage of people who believe that there should be laws against the distribution of pornography, whatever the age, has increased, decreased, or stayed the same? (circle one of the following)

   1. Increased
   2. Decreased
   3. Stayed the same

f. Open the HISTORY file and examine the trend for 20) PORNLAWGSS. Has the percentage of people who believe that there should be laws against the distribution of pornography, whatever the age, increased, decreased, or stayed the same? (circle one of the following)

   1. Increased
   2. Decreased
   3. Stayed the same

8. Now let's examine beliefs about the legalization of marijuana using variable 11) GRASS from the GSS.

   a. Write down the question wording. ____

   ____

   b. Estimate (guess) what the percentage will be for each answer category.

   Should: __________%

   Shouldn't: __________%

   c. What response would you give to this question? Should Shouldn't

   d. Conduct the univariate analysis of this survey question and fill in the actual percentages.

   Data File: **GSS**
   Task: **Univariate**
   ➤ *Primary Variable:* **11) GRASS**
   ➤ *View:* **Pie**

   Should: __________%

   Shouldn't: __________%

e. Over the past 25 years or so, do you think that the percentage of people who think that the use of marijuana should be made legal has increased, decreased, or stayed the same? (circle one of the following)

 1. Increased
 2. Decreased
 3. Stayed the same

f. Open the HISTORY file and examine the trend for 21) GRASSLAW. Has the percentage of people who think that marijuana should be made legal steadily increased, steadily decreased, or had periods of both increase and decrease? (circle one of the following)

 1. Steadily increased
 2. Steadily decreased
 3. Had periods of increase and decrease

ESSAY QUESTION

9. Summarize the results of the analyses above, describing how the results were either similar to what you expected or different from what you expected. In instances where the differences are pronounced, explain why you think your expectations were so different from the actual results.

CHAPTER 5

FEAR OF CRIME

... the preoccupation with crime is not a national past-time in more countries than one [the United States]. Neither the design of doors and windows, nor the front page stories in the national press, nor the budgetary allocations of municipal and national governments, indicate any obsession with crime, the fear of crime, the fear of victimization, or indeed, the national destiny.

FREDA ADLER,
COMPARATIVE CRIMINOLOGIST
AND PAST PRESIDENT OF THE
AMERICAN SOCIETY OF
CRIMINOLOGY[1]

Tasks: Cross-tabulation, Auto-Analyzer
Data Files: GSS

In the previous chapter, we discovered that the proportion of respondents in the 1996 General Social Survey (GSS) who reported that they were afraid to walk in their neighborhoods alone at night is rather substantial—about 42 percent of all respondents. Many other national surveys have been conducted asking people about their concern over crime, and not surprisingly, the exact degree of fear detected varies depending on the wording of the questions. For example, a national poll by the Princeton Survey Research Associates asked respondents the following question: "How concerned are you, if at all, about becoming a victim of crime?" Slightly over half of the respondents (50.6 percent) reported that they were "very concerned"; another 29.4 percent were "somewhat concerned;" the remaining 19.7 percent were either "not too concerned" or "not concerned at all."[2] Figures for other polls sometimes indicate higher or lower levels of fear of crime, but the survey evidence considered as a whole clearly indicates that the risk of becoming a crime victim is a salient concern among the general public in the United States.

Documenting the overall level of fear of crime in the nation at large is certainly a useful task. However, as explained in Chapter 1, the principal objective of social science is to *explain variation*. We would like to know not only how common fear of crime is among the general population, but also who is afraid and why.

---

[1] Freda Adler, *Nations Not Obsessed With Crime*, (Littleton, CO: Fred B. Rothman & Co, 1983), p. xix.

[2] Kathleen Maguire and Ann L. Pastore (eds.). *Bureau of Justice Statistics Sourcebook of Criminal Justice Statistics—1995*, U.S. Department of Justice, Bureau of Justice Statistics (Washington, D.C.: U.S. Government Printing Office, 1996), p. 156.

What kinds of people are most likely to be fearful? Perhaps fear of crime is related to the kinds of communities in which people were raised. We might hypothesize, for example, that people who grew up in large cities tend to be more fearful of crime than those who were raised in smaller cities and in rural areas, because common forms of street crime are generally higher in urban areas. This hypothesis can be tested with the GSS data by comparing responses to the question about being afraid to walk alone at night for people who grew up in communities of varying sizes.

The ExplorIt procedure that enables us to test this hypothesis is called **cross-tabulation**. Here's how a cross-tabulation between fear of crime and place of residence looks.

➤ *Data File:* **GSS**
➤ *Task:* **Cross-tabulation**
➤ *Row Variable:* **1) FEAR WALK**
➤ *Column Variable:* **29) HOME AT 16**
➤ *View:* **Tables**
➤ *Display:* **Frequency**

FEAR WALK by HOME AT 16
Cramer's V: 0.065 *

FEAR WALK	RURAL/FARM	SMALL CITY	MEDIUM/LAR	Missing	TOTAL
YES	174	244	385	1	803
NO	283	356	458	2	1097
Missing	250	322	426	3	1001
TOTAL	457	600	843	6	1900

To construct this table, open the GSS data file and select the CROSS-TABULATION task. Then select 1) FEAR WALK as the row variable and 29) HOME AT 16 as the column variable. Click the [OK] button. The table automatically displays the [Frequency] option.

In this analysis, the cross-tabulation separates the total population into three different categories depending upon where the respondent lived at age 16: rural/farm communities, small cities, or medium/large cities. The respondents from rural/farm areas are listed in the first column; the respondents from small cities are listed in the second column; and the respondents from medium/large cities are listed in the third column. (The fourth column reports cases with missing information on residence.) The numbers within the table reflect the numbers within each column who said "yes" in response to the fear of crime question or "no." The question was not asked of all respondents; hence 1,001 respondents are classified as missing on fear of crime. (These numbers are presented in the third row of the table, but they are not used in computations.)

Looking at the table we see that 174 respondents from rural backgrounds said that they were afraid to walk alone at night and 283 said they were not afraid. Looking at the next column we see that more respondents from small cities than from rural areas said yes to the question about walking alone at night—244. The number of respondents from medium/large cities who said yes is even larger—385. However, there were also more people in the sample from medium/large cities than from small cities (843 vs. 600), and more from small cities than from rural/farm areas (600 vs. 457). This implies that, if we are interested in comparing the *likelihood* of saying yes, we can't simply look at the raw numbers of respondents; rather, we must take differences in the size of the populations into account.

To do so, we can calculate the percentage who said yes and no in each group. If you select the column percentaging option, the new screen looks like this:

Data File: **GSS**
Task: **Cross-tabulation**
Row Variable: **1) FEAR WALK**
Column Variable: **29) HOME AT 16**
View: **Tables**
➤ *Display:* **Column %**

FEAR WALK by HOME AT 16
Cramer's V: 0.065 *

FEAR WALK	HOME AT 16				
	RURAL/FARM	SMALL CITY	MEDIUM/LAR	Missing	TOTAL
YES	174	244	385	1	803
	38.1%	40.7%	45.7%		42.3%
NO	283	356	458	2	1097
	61.9%	59.3%	54.3%		57.7%
Missing	250	322	426	3	1001
TOTAL	457	600	843	6	1900
	100.0%	100.0%	100.0%		

If you are continuing from the previous example, simply click the [Column %] option to view the new display.

The data show that respondents raised in the bigger cities are in fact more likely to be afraid than those raised elsewhere: 45.7 percent of medium/large-city respondents answered yes, compared with 40.7 percent of small-city respondents, and 38.1 percent of rural respondents. Or, comparing across the lower row of the table, we see that 61.9 percent of the rural respondents said they were not afraid, compared with 59.3 percent of the small-city respondents, and 54.3 percent of the medium/large-city respondents.

The general pattern of results is thus consistent with the hypothesis that people who grew up in large cities tend to be more fearful of crime than those who were raised in smaller cities and in rural areas. However, before we accept the hypothesis, we must remember an important limitation of sample data that we discussed briefly in Chapter 2. Estimates from samples are not necessarily exactly the same as the figures that would be obtained if data were collected for the entire population. There is always the possibility of some distortion or **sampling error**. But if the sample has been selected randomly, the laws of probability allow us to calculate the **odds** that something observed in the sample accurately reflects a feature of the population sampled.

The calculation of these odds depends upon two features of the sample. One is the sample size. The larger the sample, the more accurate it is. Sampling is surprisingly efficient, and unless we are studying very rare attributes or events, a sample of about 1,000 cases is adequate for describing a population as large as that of the United States—a population of about 270 million persons.

The other feature of sample results that affects our capacity to draw conclusions is the magnitude (or size) of the difference observed in the table. Because some random sampling error is always possible, small differences might appear in a sample table even if there is no real difference among the population at large, which is what we would find if data were available for everyone. Experienced analysts are thus skeptical of small differences in sample results, because these differences might reflect random fluctuations.

Fortunately, there are mathematical techniques for calculating the odds that a given difference is likely to be real or random. These techniques are called **tests of statistical significance**. Differences observed in samples are said to be statistically significant when the *odds against* random results are high enough to satisfy the researcher. There are no mathematical rules to determine just how high is high enough. Over the years, social scientists have settled on the rule of thumb that they will ignore all differences unless the odds are at least **20** to **1** against their being random. Put another way, social scientists usually dismiss all findings when the probability that they are random is greater than .05, or 5 in 100. This standard is referred to as a **level of significance** (or the probability level). What this level of significance means is that if 100 random samples were drawn independently from the same population, a difference this large would not turn up more that 5 times purely by chance. Although the .05 standard is the conventional rule of thumb, social scientists sometimes use more stringent standards (e.g., a level of .01, or 1 in 100). Whatever the precise level of significance might be, it provides the researcher with a means of deciding whether an observed difference for a sample can be regarded as an indication of a real difference in the larger population.

The cross-tabulation procedure for ExplorIt provides a number of statistics. Let's look at a particularly important statistic, **chi square** (often written as χ^2).

Data File: **GSS**
Task: **Cross-tabulation**
Row Variable: **1) FEAR WALK**
Column Variable: **29) HOME AT 16**
➤ *View:* **Statistics (Summary)**

FEAR WALK by HOME AT 16

Nominal Statistics

Chi-Square: 7.923 (DF = 2; Prob. = 0.019)

V:	0.065	C:	0.064		
Lambda: (DV=29)	0.000	Lambda: (DV=1)	0.000	Lambda:	0.000

Ordinal Statistics

Gamma:	-0.109	Tau-b:	-0.061	Tau-c:	-0.068
s.error	0.039	s.error	0.022	s.error	0.024
Dyx:	-0.053	Dxy:	-0.070		
s.error	0.019	s.error	0.025		
Prob. =	0.005				

If you are continuing from the previous example, you can reproduce this graphic by switching from the [Tables] display option to the [Statistics] view.

For now, you can ignore everything on the screen except the text in the chi-square row that reads: Prob. = 0.019. This number indicates the probability that the differences in the table are due simply to random sampling error. Put another way, the number means that if there really are no differences in fear across types of communities in the population as a whole, we would expect the observed differences to occur by sheer chance only 19 times out of every 1,000 random samples. This is a highly unlikely occurrence, suggesting that there really are differences across communities in fear of crime. In any event, the level of significance is much lower than the minimal .05 level. We shall regard a sample result as significant whenever the probability of it being a random result is smaller than .05. If the chi-square test had yielded a probability level of .051 or greater, we would have rejected the hypothesis and concluded that people raised in different types of communities do not differ in their fear of walking alone in their neighborhoods at night.

We can also assess statistical significance quickly by examining the coefficient for Cramer's V. To see this, let's switch from the [Statistics] view back to the [Tables] view.

Data File: **GSS**
Task: **Cross-tabulation**
Row Variable: **1) FEAR WALK**
Column Variable: **29) HOME AT 16**
➤ *View:* **Tables**
➤ *Display:* **Column %**

FEAR WALK by HOME AT 16
Cramer's V: 0.065 *

FEAR WALK	HOME AT 16				
	RURAL/FARM	SMALL CITY	MEDIUM/LAR	Missing	TOTAL
YES	174	244	385	1	803
	38.1%	40.7%	45.7%		42.3%
NO	283	356	458	2	1097
	61.9%	59.3%	54.3%		57.7%
Missing	250	322	426	3	1001
TOTAL	457	600	843	6	1900
	100.0%	100.0%	100.0%		

ExplorIt reports Cramer's V above the table. The meaning of Cramer's V will be explained later, but for now you can simply look to see if an asterisk is reported alongside the number. A single asterisk signifies that the chi square is significant at the .05 level (the probability of a random result is 5 out of 100 or less). Two asterisks signify that the chi square is significant at the .01 level (the probability of a random result is 1 out of 100 or less). In this example, a single asterisk follows the V coefficient, indicating significance at the .05 level.

There is a special feature of the ExplorIt CROSS-TABULATION task worth mentioning at this point. Sometimes the researcher might want to combine categories of a variable, perhaps to simplify the interpretation of the results. For example, in analyzing the relationship between residence while growing up and fear of crime, we might want to compare rural/farm respondents with all others. ExplorIt provides an easy way to temporarily "collapse" categories in a cross-tabulation result. Let's use the table you just created that should still be on your screen as an illustration (if you have cleared the screen, simply repeat the ExplorIt commands directly above).

With the table showing on your screen, click on the category label "SMALL CITY" located at the top of the second column. This will cause the entire column to be highlighted. Then click the label for the next column, "MEDIUM/LAR," so that it too is highlighted. With both columns highlighted, click the button labeled [Collapse]. You are given two choices at this point: you can "drop" the highlighted categories which would temporarily turn the values to missing data, or you can combine the categories and type in a new name to represent the combined values. Since we want to combine the highlighted categories, type "NON-RURAL" as the new label and click [OK]. These two columns have been combined and the table has been updated. (Don't worry, you have not permanently modified the variable—the next time you use it in an analysis all three categories will appear.) The table looks like this:

FEAR WALK by HOME AT 16
Cramer's V: 0.048 *

FEAR WALK	HOME AT 16			
	RURAL/FARM	NON-RURAL	Missing	TOTAL
YES	174	629	1	803
	38.1%	43.6%		42.3%
NO	283	814	2	1097
	61.9%	56.4%		57.7%
Missing	250	748	3	1001
TOTAL	457	1443	6	1900
	100.0%	100.0%		

Social scientists often begin their analyses of a given attitude or behavior by examining the relationship with various sociodemographic variables, such as age, race, sex, and so on. These variables tend to be very "fertile" in the sense that they are related to a wide variety of social phenomena. For example, we might hypothesize that race is related to fear of crime using similar reasoning to that for place of upbringing. African Americans are more likely than whites to reside in the inner-city communities that exhibit high crime rates. Hence, we might expect that African Americans will be more likely than whites to be afraid to walk alone at night in their neighborhoods.

To test this hypothesis, let's use another ExplorIt task called AUTO-ANALYZER. This task in effect combines the univariate and cross-tabulation tasks you've already used. It first shows you the distribution of a *primary variable* you select and then allows you to choose one of nine demographic variables—sex, race, political party, marital status, religious preference, region, age, education, and income—to see what difference, if any, each demographic variable makes. It then presents the requested cross-tabulation and actually tells you what is happening in the table. Let's see how it works.

Data File: **GSS**
➤ *Task:* **Auto-Analyzer**
➤ *Variable:* **1) FEAR WALK**
➤ *View:* **Univariate**

FEAR WALK -- Is there any area right around here -- that is, within a mile -- where you would be afraid to walk alone at night? (FEAR)

	%
YES	42.2%
NO	57.8%
Number of cases	1903

Among all respondents, 42.2% of the sample fear walking alone at night.

To obtain these results, return to the main menu and select the AUTO-ANALYZER task. Then select 1) FEAR WALK as your variable and click [OK].

Here's the univariate distribution for 1) FEAR WALK. These percentages are the same as those observed in an earlier chapter using the UNIVARIATE task from the main menu. Now let's see how the percentages vary by race.

Data File: **GSS**
Task: **Auto-Analyzer**
Variable: **1) FEAR WALK**
➤ *View:* **Race**

FEAR WALK -- Is there any area right around here -- that is, within a mile -- where you would be afraid to walk alone at night? (FEAR)

	White	Black
YES	40.1%	55.8%
NO	59.9%	44.2%
Number of cases	1530	269

Among African-Americans, 55.8% fear walking alone at night. Among whites, this percentage was only 40.1%. The difference is statistically significant.

If continuing from the previous example, simply select [Race] to see the results.

Selecting [Race] as the view option calls up a new screen with the cross-tabulation for fear of crime and race, along with the following summary interpretation of the results: "Among African-Americans, 55.8 percent fear walking alone at night. Among whites, this percentage was only 40.1 percent. The difference is statistically significant."[3] These data, therefore, support the hypothesis about racial differences in fear of crime. Note that when testing a specific hypothesis, it is very important to check to see

[3] In some cases, the significance given in Auto-Analyzer may be slightly different from the significance of chi square given in the CROSS-TABULATION task. Chi square summarizes the entire table, whereas Auto-Analyzer relies on column by column comparisons in an attempt to uncover patterns of interest. These two tasks focus on slightly different aspects of the results and may thus lead to different interpretations.

not only whether there is a difference in percentages, but whether the difference is in the expected direction. If the numbers in the columns of this table were switched around, the difference in percentages would be exactly the same, but the interpretation would be quite different indeed!

What about the association between gender and fear? Males are much more likely than females to be the victims of conventional street crimes. For this reason, we might expect that males, like African Americans and those brought up in big cities, will be especially fearful of crime. Let's use the AUTO-ANALYZER task to assess this hypothesis.

Data File: **GSS**
Task: **Auto-Analyzer**
Variable: **1) FEAR WALK**
➤ *View:* **Sex**

FEAR WALK -- Is there any area right around here -- that is, within a mile -- where you would be afraid to walk alone at night? (FEAR)

	Male	Female
YES	25.8%	55.4%
NO	74.2%	44.6%
Number of cases	846	1057

Among females, 55.4% fear walking alone at night. Among males, this percentage was only 25.8%. The difference is statistically significant.

The cross-tabulation for sex and fear of crime contradicts this hypothesis. Females are much more likely to be fearful than males, a difference that is statistically significant. Why should females be more fearful of victimization than males, when their objective risks are lower? Mark Warr has formulated a plausible explanation that centers around gender differences in *sensitivity to risk*. He proposes that women are more likely than men to make linkages among victimizations, assuming that relatively minor and common offenses are likely to lead to more serious harm. For example, women are more likely to believe that a minor property crime (e.g., a purse snatching) will result not only in the loss of property but also in physical harm: the offender may proceed to assault the victim. Women are particularly fearful that a wide variety of criminal offenses might ultimately lead to a sexual attack. As a result of these cognitive linkages between different types of crime, women perceive situations that men view as relatively innocuous as threatening, and they accordingly exhibit greater levels of fear of crime.[4]

So far, we have been trying to explain the variation in fear of crime by comparing levels of fear across categories of other variables. In the jargon of the social sciences, we have been treating fear of crime as a dependent variable—something that depends on, or is predicted by, something else (e.g., residence, race, sex). The other variables—the predictor variables—are often referred to as independent variables in these analyses. It also seems likely that fear of crime affects people's attitudes and behaviors. In other words, fear of crime is also likely to be a useful independent variable for predicting other, dependent variables.

Criminologists have conducted a good deal of research on the consequences of fear of crime and the actual experience of victimization. Terance Miethe has reviewed this literature and has organized the ways in which people respond to crime and fear of crime in terms of four general categories: avoidance behavior, protective actions, general behavioral and lifestyle changes, and collective reactions.[5] Avoidance behavior refers to efforts to avoid certain places (e.g., parking lots, "bad" neighborhoods,

---

[4] Mark Warr, "Public Perceptions of Crime and Punishment," in *Criminology: A Contemporary Handbook*, 2nd ed., edited by Joseph F. Sheley (Belmont, CA: Wadsworth, 1995), pp. 15–31.

[5] Terance D. Miethe, "Fear and Withdrawal from Urban Life." *The Annals of the American Academy of Political and Social Science* 536 (1995): 14–27.

secluded parks, etc.) and certain kinds of persons (e.g., groups of unsupervised juveniles or strangers). Protective actions encompass activities that are designed to reduce the risk of victimization by making persons and property more difficult to victimize (e.g., replacing locks, improving lighting, taking courses in self-defense). General behavioral and lifestyle changes refer to major shifts in the structure of social life, such as leaving a particular job, transferring to a different school, or moving to a new residence. Finally, collective reactions involve efforts to mobilize people to combat the problem of crime. These might involve the activities of private groups and organizations (e.g., neighborhood watches, self-help groups) or efforts to improve the performance of public agencies with responsibility for crime control (e.g., the police, courts, corrections).

We can explore some of the possible effects of fear of crime on attitudes and behaviors with the data from the GSS. Consider attitudes toward the criminal justice system. As you discovered in the previous chapter, the GSS asks respondents how they feel about the way the courts treat criminals, whether the courts are not harsh enough or too harsh with them. Recall that the vast majority of respondents feel that the courts are not harsh enough in their dealings with criminals, while only relatively small numbers feel that the courts are too harsh. Perhaps these feelings vary depending on fear of crime. We might hypothesize that those who are unafraid will be more likely to criticize the courts for being too harsh, while those who are afraid will be more likely to desire even harsher punishment of offenders. Let's look at the relationship between attitude toward the courts and fear of crime.

Data File: **GSS**
➤ *Task:* **Cross-tabulation**
➤ *Row Variable:* **4) COURTS2**
➤ *Column Variable:* **1) FEAR WALK**
➤ *View:* **Tables**
➤ *Display:* **Column %**

COURTS2 by FEAR WALK
Cramer's V: 0.045

COURTS2	FEAR WALK: YES	NO	Missing	TOTAL
Too harsh	30	56	49	86
	4.3%	6.4%		5.5%
Not enough	662	822	762	1484
	95.7%	93.6%		94.5%
Missing	112	221	190	523
TOTAL	692	878	1001	1570
	100.0%	100.0%		

To reproduce this screen, you must return to the main menu and select the CROSS-TABULATION task.

The table indicates that respondents who are unafraid (those who answered no) are in fact more likely to feel that the courts are too harsh on criminals than those who are afraid (those who answered yes). The difference, however, is very small: 6.4 percent versus 4.3 percent. You know now that social scientists are suspicious of small differences with sample data because of the possibility of random sampling error. In the present case, the V coefficient is not accompanied by an asterisk, indicating that the relationship is not statistically significant at the .05 level. We can confirm this conclusion by examining the results of the chi-square test.

Data File: **GSS**
Task: **Cross-tabulation**
Row Variable: **4) COURTS2**
Column Variable: **1) FEAR WALK**
➤ View: **Statistics (Summary)**

COURTS2 by FEAR WALK

Nominal Statistics

Chi-Square: 3.119 (DF = 1; Prob. = 0.077)

V:	0.045	C:	0.045		
Lambda: (DV=1)	0.000	Lambda: (DV=4)	0.000	Lambda:	0.000

Ordinal Statistics

Gamma:	-0.201	Tau-b:	-0.045	Tau-c:	-0.020
s.error	0.111	s.error	0.025	s.error	0.011
Dyx:	-0.020	Dxy:	-0.097		
s.error	0.011	s.error	0.054		
Prob. =	0.071				

The probability level for chi square is .077. This value exceeds the conventional criterion of .05, suggesting that the small, observed difference might reflect random fluctuation. We therefore conclude that the hypothesis is **not** supported: the relationship between fear of crime and attitude toward the courts is not statistically significant.

The GSS also contains an item asking the respondent for his or her views about the adequacy of the amount of money being spent to halt the rising crime problem. Perhaps fear of crime is related to this attitude. Consider the following hypothesis: people who fear walking in their neighborhoods alone at night will be more likely than those who aren't to feel that the government is spending too little on crime control.

Data File: **GSS**
Task: **Cross-tabulation**
➤ Row Variable: **9) CRIME$**
➤ Column Variable: **1) FEAR WALK**
➤ View: **Tables**
➤ Display: **Column %**

CRIME$ by FEAR WALK
Cramer's V: 0.098 *

CRIME$	FEAR WALK: YES	NO	Missing	TOTAL
Too Little	281	349	335	630
	75.3%	66.3%		70.1%
Right	71	141	118	212
	19.0%	26.8%		23.6%
Too much	21	36	40	57
	5.6%	6.8%		6.3%
Missing	431	573	508	1512
TOTAL	373	526	1001	899
	100.0%	100.0%		

The table shows that fearful respondents are in fact more likely to feel that the government is spending too little—75.3 percent versus 66.3 percent. The asterisk by the V coefficient signifies that this difference is statistically significant at the .05 level. Hence, we conclude that our hypothesis about the relationship between fear of crime and attitude on government spending to control crime is supported by the data.

Now, it's your turn to examine fear of crime.

WORKSHEET — CHAPTER 5

NAME:

COURSE:

DATE:

REVIEW QUESTIONS

Based on the first part of this chapter, answer True or False to the following items:

A sample of 1,000 respondents is generally too small to provide an accurate representation of a population as large as that of the contemporary U.S. T F

The level of statistical significance indicates the probability that a given sample result would occur purely by chance. T F

According to the GSS, African-American respondents are significantly more likely than are whites to report they are afraid to walk alone at night in their neighborhoods. T F

Because they engage in riskier lifestyles, males are more likely than females to express fear about walking alone at night in their neighborhoods. T F

Criminologists have studied fear of crime both as a dependent variable (something that is caused by other factors) and as an independent variable (something that causes other factors). T F

The significance level of .077 for the relationship between fear of crime and attitudes toward the courts is statistically significant at conventional levels. T F

EXPLORIT QUESTIONS

Let's look at some additional sociodemographic characteristics that might affect fear of crime.

1. First, consider occupation. Answer True or False to the following questions:

➤ *Data File:* **GSS**
➤ *Task:* **Cross-tabulation**
➤ *Row Variable:* **1) FEAR WALK**
➤ *Column Variable:* **27) OCCUPATN**
➤ *View:* **Tables**
➤ *Display:* **Column %**

a. Blue-collar workers are the most likely to fear walking alone in their neighborhoods at night. T F

b. Farmers and forest workers are least likely to fear walking alone in their neighborhoods at night. T F

c. The relationship between occupation and fear of crime is statistically significant. T F

2. Next, let's look at marital status. Answer True or False to the following questions:

Data File: **GSS**
Task: **Cross-tabulation**
Row Variable: **1) FEAR WALK**
➤ *Column Variable:* **37) MARITAL**
➤ *View:* **Tables**
➤ *Display:* **Column %**

a. Never-married people are the most likely to fear walking alone in their neighborhoods at night. T F

b. Married people are least likely to fear walking alone in their neighborhoods at night. T F

c. The relationship between marital status and fear of crime is statistically significant. T F

3. How is the fear of crime related to education level? Answer True or False to the following questions:

Data File: **GSS**
Task: **Cross-tabulation**
Row Variable: **1) FEAR WALK**
➤ *Column Variable:* **41) EDUCATION**
➤ *View:* **Tables**
➤ *Display:* **Column %**

a. Those without a high school degree are most likely to fear walking alone in their neighborhoods at night. T F

b. Those with only a high school degree are least likely to fear walking alone in their neighborhoods at night. T F

c. The relationship between education and fear of crime is statistically significant. T F

4. Now let's use the AUTO-ANALYZER task. Describe the kind of person who is most likely to fear walking alone in their neighborhood at night with reference to their income, political party, and their religion.

Data File: **GSS**
➤ *Task:* **Auto-Analyzer**
➤ *Variable:* **1) FEAR WALK**

To conduct these analyses, return to the main menu. Select the AUTO-ANALYZER task. Select 1) FEAR WALK as your variable. Select each of the demographic views.

5. Earlier in the chapter, you discovered that fear of crime is not related to attitudes about whether the courts are treating criminals too harshly or not harshly enough. Perhaps no variables can predict this particular attitude. To assess this possibility, use the AUTO-ANALYZER task to examine the relationships between attitude toward the courts and the age, race, sex, and income of the respondent. For those characteristics that exhibit a significant relationship with attitudes toward the treatment of criminals (if any), briefly summarize the observed patterns.

Data File: **GSS**
Task: **Auto-Analyzer**
➤ *Variable:* **4) COURTS2**

a. AGE:

b. RACE:

c. SEX:

d. INCOME:

6. Consider the following hypothesis: *People who are afraid to walk alone in their neighborhoods at night will be less likely than those who aren't to have eaten at a restaurant within the past week.*

   Answer the following questions using the cross-tabulation between EAT OUT and FEAR WALK.

   Data File: **GSS**
   ➤ *Task:* **Cross-tabulation**
   ➤ *Row Variable:* **24) EAT OUT**
   ➤ *Column Variable:* **1) FEAR WALK**
   ➤ *View:* **Tables**
   ➤ *Display:* **Column %**

   a. Is the pattern for the percentages consistent with the hypothesis (i.e., are the high and low categories the ones that were predicted)? Yes No

   b. Is the difference in percentages statistically significant? Yes No

   c. Is this hypothesis supported? Yes No

7. Consider the following hypothesis: *People who are afraid to walk alone in their neighborhoods at night will be more likely than those who aren't to own a gun.*

   Answer the following questions using the cross-tabulation between OWNGUN and FEAR WALK.

   Data File: **GSS**
   Task: **Cross-tabulation**
   ➤ *Row Variable:* **22) OWNGUN**
   ➤ *Column Variable:* **1) FEAR WALK**
   ➤ *View:* **Tables**
   ➤ *Display:* **Column %**

   a. Is the pattern for the percentages consistent with the hypothesis (i.e., are the high and low categories the ones that were predicted)? Yes No

   b. Is the difference in percentages statistically significant? Yes No

   c. Is this hypothesis supported? Yes No

8. Consider the following hypothesis: *People who are afraid to walk alone in their neighborhoods at night will be less likely than those who aren't to report that they are very happy.*

   Answer the following questions using the cross-tabulation between HAPPY and FEAR WALK.

   Data File: **GSS**
   Task: **Cross-tabulation**
   ➤ *Row Variable:* **25) HAPPY**
   ➤ *Column Variable:* **1) FEAR WALK**
   ➤ *View:* **Tables**
   ➤ *Display:* **Column %**

   a. Is the pattern for the percentages consistent with the hypothesis (i.e., are the high and low categories the ones that were predicted)? Yes No

   b. Is the difference in percentages statistically significant? Yes No

   c. Is this hypothesis supported? Yes No

ESSAY QUESTION

9. Review your answer about the relationship between sociodemographic characteristics and attitudes toward the courts given in Question 5. Describe the demographic profile of a person who is likely to believe that the courts are too harsh in treating criminals (refer only to demographic characteristics that exhibit a statistically significant relationship with attitudes toward the courts). Explain why you think that this kind of person holds these beliefs about the courts.

CHAPTER 6

MOTOR VEHICLE THEFT

Follow this car! I'm being stolen!

REFERENCE TO A HIGH-TECH OPTION FOR CAR PROTECTION, INVOLVING ELECTRONIC TRANSMITTERS WHICH EMIT HOMING SIGNALS THAT POLICE COMPUTERS CAN TRACK.[1]

Tasks: Historical Trends, Mapping, Scatterplot, Correlation
Data Files: HISTORY, STATES

One of the major categories of property crime recorded annually in the *Uniform Crime Reports* (UCR) is motor vehicle theft. Technically, this refers to the stealing or attempted stealing of a "self-propelled" vehicle that "runs on the surface and not on rails" (from Appendix II of the UCR). The vast bulk of motor vehicle thefts involve automobiles, and thus the category is sometimes referred to loosely as "auto" or "car" theft.

Approximately 1.5 million motor vehicle thefts are reported to the police every year. Criminologists believe that the police statistics on this offense are not subject to as much undercounting as is the case for most other offenses, because people must report vehicles as stolen to receive insurance benefits. The National Crime Victimization Survey reveals, for example, that slightly over 90 percent of victims of completed motor vehicle theft in 1994 reported the crime to the police.[2]

Research on motor vehicle theft has revealed different motivations for the crime. For many young offenders, stealing a car or other vehicle is often done for the thrill of it or to impress peers ("joyriding"). Other motor vehicle thefts are committed to provide the offender with transportation, either on a long-term basis or for purposes of committing another offense. Still another motivation for motor vehicle theft is for economic gain—to sell the vehicle or its parts. Whatever the motivation, motor vehicle thefts inflict a significant financial cost on the victim. The average loss in such a theft is about $5,000, which is higher than most other losses due to common "street" crimes.[3] Let's look at trends in the rates of UCR motor vehicle thefts since 1960.

[1] Quoted in Freda Adler, Gerhard O. W. Mueller, and William S. Laufer, *Criminology*, 3rd ed. (Boston, MA: McGraw-Hill, 1998), p. 269.

[2] Kathleen Maguire and Ann L. Pastore (eds.), *Bureau of Justice Statistics Sourcebook of Criminal Justice Statistics—1995*, U.S. Department of Justice, Bureau of Justice Statistics (Washington, DC: U.S. Government Printing Office, 1996), p. 250.

[3] Ibid, p. 349.

➤ *Data File:* **HISTORY**
➤ *Task:* **Historical Trends**
➤ *Variables:* **6) UCRMOTOR**

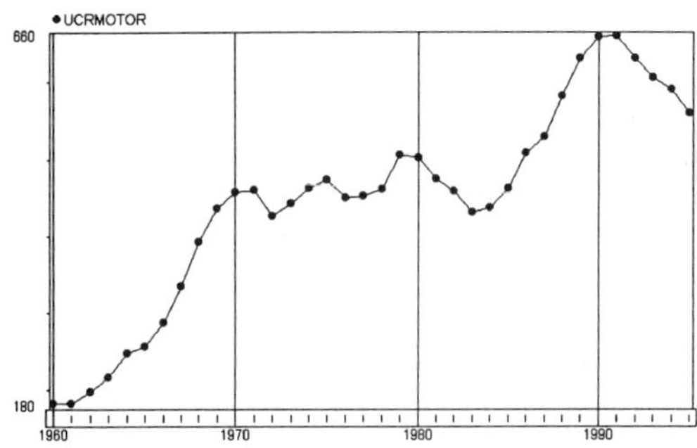

Trends in UCR motor vehicle thefts since 1960

The UCR data show that the rates of this offense were relatively low in 1960 (183 per 100,000). These rates steadily rose through the 1960s and leveled off, with some fluctuation, in the 1970s and early 80s. Rates once again climbed rather steeply in the late 1980s and reached a peak of 659 per 100,000 in 1991. Since then, there has been a fairly steady decline in levels of motor vehicle theft.

Recall from the previous chapter that a major task of criminological research is to explain variation. We want to know why crime rates are high or low at some times and in some places, in comparison with other times and other places. Explaining variation in criminological research entails the identification of relationships between variables. Let's begin by looking at the geography of the UCR rates of motor vehicle theft.

➤ *Data File:* **STATES**
➤ *Task:* **Mapping**
➤ *Variable 1:* **8) MV.THEFT**
➤ *View:* **Map**

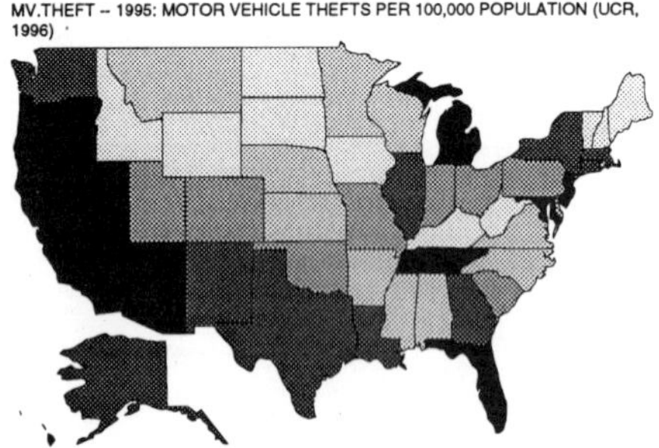

You see dark colors signifying high rates in the West and light colors indicating low rates in the upper plains and northern New England states. Select the [List: Rank] option to view a listing of the values and ranking for different states.

Data File: **STATES**
Task: **Mapping**
Variable 1: **8) MV.THEFT**
➤ *View:* **List: Rank**

MV.THEFT: 1995: Motor vehicle thefts per 100,000 population

RANK	CASE NAME	VALUE
1	Arizona	1157.7
2	California	887.9
3	Florida	785.8
4	Nevada	745.4
5	Maryland	717.6
6	Oregon	702.0
7	Hawaii	690.7
8	Tennessee	648.5
9	Michigan	645.5
10	New Jersey	631.6

In 1995, Arizona had the highest rate—1157.7, followed by California (887.9), Florida (785.8), Nevada (745.4), and Maryland (717.6). Move down to the bottom of the screen to see states with very low rates. The five lowest-ranking states were West Virginia (166.3), New Hampshire (145.1), Vermont (135.7), Maine (134.8), and South Dakota (120.9).

Now, let's compare the map for motor vehicle theft rates with the map for another variable, the percentage of a state's population living in urban areas.

Data File: **STATES**
Task: **Mapping**
Variable 1: **8) MV.THEFT**
➤ *Variable 2:* **31) %URBAN**
➤ *Views:* **Map**

MV.THEFT -- 1995: MOTOR VEHICLE THEFTS PER 100,000 POPULATION (UCR, 1996)

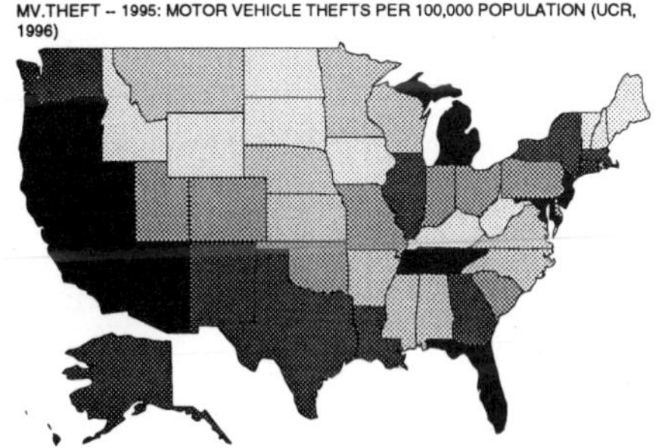

r = 0.743**

%URBAN -- 1990: PERCENT URBAN (CENSUS)

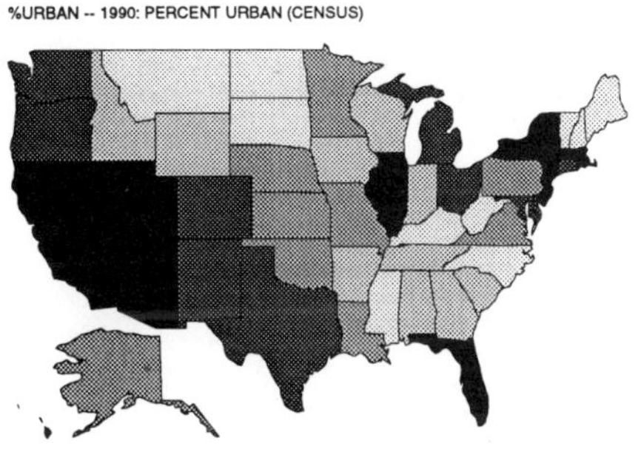

Notice how similar the two maps are, with high rates in the West and low rates in the upper plains and northern New England. Look at the ranking of the states on 8) MV.THEFT and 31) %URBAN.

Data File: **STATES**
Task: **Mapping**
Variable 1: **8) MV.THEFT**
Variable 2: **31) %URBAN**
➤ *Views:* **List: Rank**

MV.THEFT: 1995: Motor vehicle thefts per 100,000 population

RANK	CASE NAME	VALUE
1	Arizona	1157.7
2	California	887.9
3	Florida	785.8
4	Nevada	745.4
5	Maryland	717.6

%URBAN: 1990: Percent urban

RANK	CASE NAME	VALUE
1	California	92.6
2	New Jersey	89.4
3	Hawaii	89.0
4	Nevada	88.3
5	Arizona	87.5

Notice that three of the top five states in the ranking on motor vehicle thefts are also among the top five in the ranking on percentage urban (Arizona, California, and Nevada). Similarly, if you look down to the last page for both rankings, you'll see that three of the bottom five states on percentage urban are among the bottom five on motor vehicle theft (South Dakota, Maine, and Vermont). The similarities in the maps and the rankings for these two variables suggest that they are related to one another.

In this instance it is rather easy to detect a pattern for the two maps. It becomes more difficult to say how alike any two maps are when the maps are very complex. For example, it would be much harder to compare two maps based on the 3,142 counties of the United States than two maps based on the 50 states. The same is true of attempts to compare lists. It is not too hard to compare the distributions of the motor vehicle theft rates and the percent urban and to notice that the same states tend to be high or low for both. But it would have been much harder to do this with a longer list. Thus it was a considerable achievement when, in the 1890s, an English statistician named Karl Pearson developed an incredibly simple method for comparing maps or ranked lists.

To illustrate Pearson's method we can draw a horizontal line across the bottom of a piece of paper. We will let this line represent the map of percent urban. So, at the left end of this line we will write 32.1, which indicates the state with the lowest rate—Vermont. At the right end of the line we will write the number 92.6 to represent the state with the highest rate—California.

32.1 ———————————————— 92.6

Now we can draw a vertical line up the left side of the paper. Values for the motor vehicle theft rate will be plotted along this line. At the bottom of this line we write 120.9 to represent South Dakota, the lowest state. At the top we will write 1157.7 to represent Arizona, the state with the highest value.

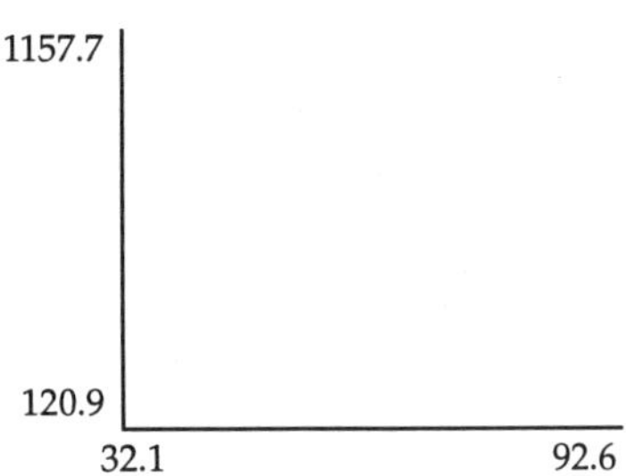

Now that we have a graph with an appropriate scale to represent each map, the next thing to do is refer to the distributions for each map to learn the value of each state. The state can then be located on the horizontal and vertical lines according to its scores. Let's start with California. Since it is the most urban state, we can easily find its place on the horizontal line above. Make a small mark at 92.6 to indicate the score on 31) %URBAN for California. Next find the motor vehicle rate for California. The rate is 887.9. Estimate where 887.9 is located on the vertical line and make a mark there. We can now locate California in the graph by drawing a vertical line up from its position on 31) %URBAN and drawing a horizontal line across from its position on 8) MV.THEFT. Where these two lines cross we can make a dot. The dot represents the location of California according to both variables—percent urban and rate of motor vehicle theft.

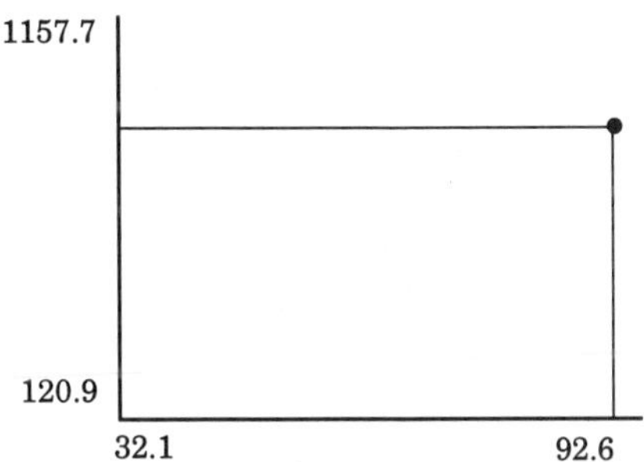

Next, let's locate another state, say, Vermont. Vermont has the lowest score on percent urban, 32.1, so make a mark on the horizontal line at that spot. Its motor vehicle theft rate is 135.7, so we can mark that point on the vertical line. Now we draw a line up from the mark on the horizontal line and draw one out from the mark on the vertical line. Where these two lines intersect we can make another dot, which represents the combined location for Vermont.

If we followed this procedure for each state, we would have 50 dots located within the space defined by the vertical and horizontal lines representing the two variables. This type of graph is called a **scatterplot**. Fortunately, you don't have to go to all this trouble. ExplorIt will do it for you.

To use ExplorIt's Scatterplot routine, you need to recall the distinction between **independent** and **dependent** variables, which was introduced briefly in the previous chapter. If we think that a variable might be the cause of something else, we say that the cause is the independent variable and the consequence (or the thing that is being caused) is the dependent variable. To help you remember the difference, think that the variables being caused are dependent on the causal variables, whereas causal variables are not dependent, but are independent. The scatterplot routine asks you to identify one variable as dependent and the other as independent. The guide that follows shows you how it's done.

Data File: **STATES**
➤ *Task:* **Scatterplot**
➤ *Dependent Variable:* **8) MV.THEFT**
➤ *Independent Variable:* **31) %URBAN**

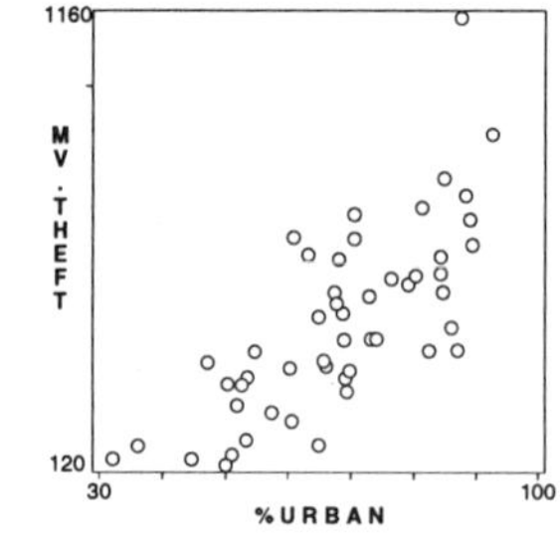

Your computer screen displays the scatterplot of the motor vehicle theft rate and the percent urban for all 50 states. Each dot represents a state. ExplorIt has special features that allow you to quickly obtain information for particular cases. For example, move your mouse to the dot at the uppermost point on the graph and click on it. A little box appears around the dot. To the left of the screen, the case is identified—in this example, the case is Arizona. The values for 31) %URBAN (the variable on the horizontal axis, or the "X" variable) and 8) MV.THEFT (the variable on the vertical axis, or the "Y" variable) are also listed.

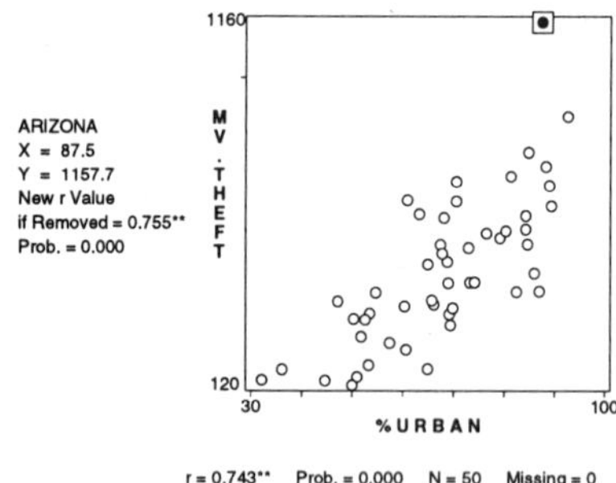

You can return to the original scatterplot by clicking anywhere outside the graph (in Student MicroCase for DOS, click the small "x" located at the top corner of the box). You can also request information for a particular state by name. Select the [Find Case] option, and when the pop-up window appears, check the box next to "Alabama," and then click [OK]. Now a box appears in the scatterplot around the dot representing Alabama. You can identify the location of any state on the graph using this procedure. To deselect Alabama, click [Find Case] again.

Once Pearson had created a scatterplot, his next step was to calculate what he called the regression line. To see this line click the [Reg. Line] option.

Data File: **STATES**
Task: **Scatterplot**
Dependent Variable: **8) MV.THEFT**
Independent Variable: **31) %URBAN**
➤ View: **Reg. Line**

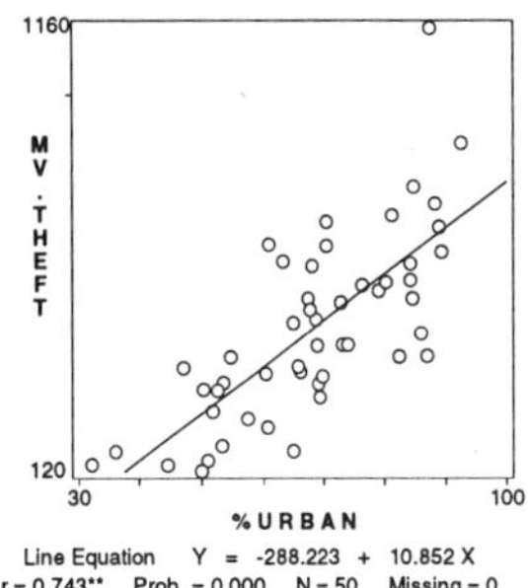

This line represents the best effort to draw a straight line to connect all of the dots. It is unnecessary for you to know how to calculate the location of the regression line—the program does it for you. But, if you would like to see how the regression line would look if all of the dots were along a straight line, all you need to do is examine the scatterplot for identical maps. So, if you create a scatterplot using the same variable as both independent and dependent, you will be comparing identical maps. For example, enter 8) MV.THEFT as both the dependent and independent variable.

Data File: **STATES**
Task: **Scatterplot**
Dependent Variable: **8) MV.THEFT**
➤ Independent Variable: **8) MV.THEFT**
➤ View: **Reg. Line**

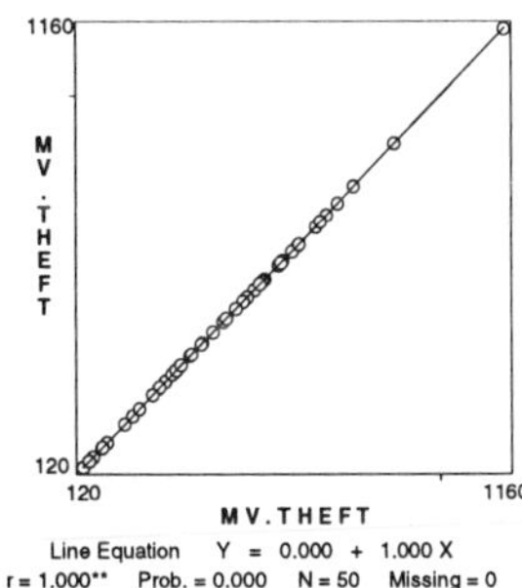

Notice that all of the dots representing states are on the regression line like a string of beads.

Now, let's return to the scatterplot for motor vehicle theft and percent urban.

Data File: **STATES**
Task: **Scatterplot**
Dependent Variable: **8) MV.THEFT**
➤ Independent Variable: **31) %URBAN**
➤ View: **Reg. Line**

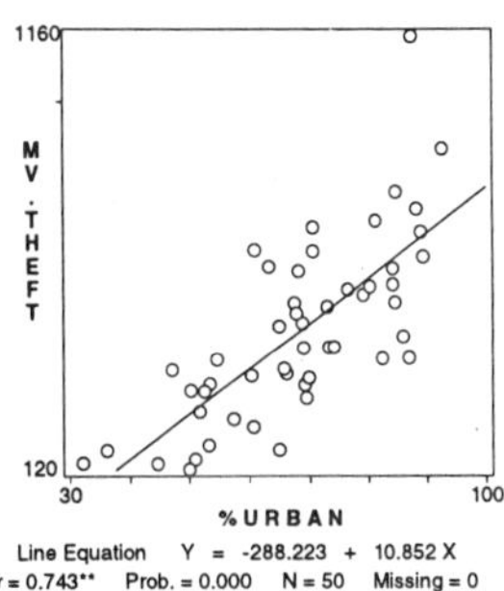

Recall that the maps for motor vehicle theft and for percent urban are only very similar, but not identical. Consequently, most of the dots are scattered near, but not on, the regression line. Pearson's method for calculating the degree of similarity of maps or lists is very easy, once the regression line has been drawn. What it amounts to is measuring the distance from the regression line to each dot. To see these distances, select the display option for "Residuals."

Data File: **STATES**
Task: **Scatterplot**
Dependent Variable: **8) MV.THEFT**
Independent Variable: **31) %URBAN**
➤ *View:* **Reg. Line/Residuals**

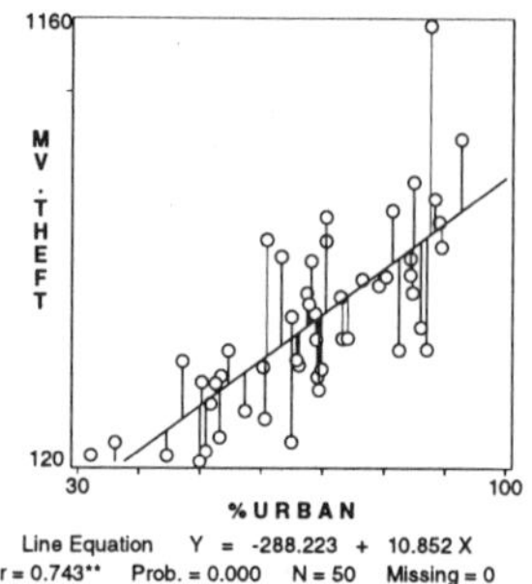

All these lines represent deviation from the regression line. If you added them together, you would have a sum of the deviation of the dots from the regression line. The smaller this sum, the more alike are two maps or ranked lists. For example, when the maps are identical, all the dots are on the regression line, so the sum of the deviations is 0.

To simplify the presentation of results, Pearson invented a procedure to convert the sums of deviations into a number that he called the **correlation coefficient**. Correlation coefficients may be either positive or negative. When maps are identical, the correlation coefficient will be +1.0. When maps are perfect opposites of one another, the correlation coefficient will be –1.0. When maps are completely unrelated, the correlation coefficient will be 0.0. Pearson used the letter **r** as the symbol for his correlation coefficient. Look at the left side of the bottom row of the screen and you will see r = 0.743**. This indicates that the maps are very similar. (Correlation coefficients are also reported in the MAPPING routine when two maps are compared.)

The positive sign of the coefficient reveals that high values on motor vehicle theft tend to be accompanied by high values on percent urban, and low values on motor vehicle theft tend to be accompanied by low values on percent urban. To the right of the correlation coefficient you will observe two asterisks. Asterisks indicate statistical significance—the odds that the observed pattern is a chance finding. (This is similar to chi-square tests and the V coefficient in the analysis of tables.) One asterisk indicates that the odds of a chance finding are 5 out of 100 or less (a significance level of .05), and two asterisks indicate that the odds of a chance finding are 1 out of 100 or less (a significance level of .01).

The point of calculating correlations is to discover connections between variables that might suggest causal relationships. Consider the following argument: inadequate police protection leads to high rates of motor vehicle theft. If we accept the premise that the relative number of police officers in a state is a reasonable indicator of police protection, we can derive the hypothesis that states with relatively few police officers will tend to exhibit high motor vehicle theft rates, while states with relatively large numbers of police officers will tend to exhibit low motor vehicle theft rates. To see if our hypothesis is supported, we can create a scatterplot of these two variables.

Data File: **STATES**
Task: **Scatterplot**
Dependent Variable: **8) MV.THEFT**
➤ Independent Variable: **13) COPS/10000**
➤ View: **Reg. Line**

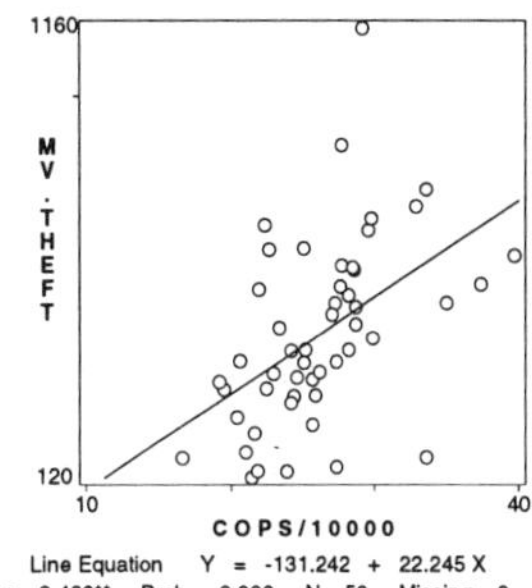

We find that the correlation coefficient is 0.486**. The two asterisks indicate that the correlation is statistically significant at the .01 level—the pattern is not likely to be due to chance. However, the pattern is contrary to our hypothesis. We predicted that low levels of police protection would accompany high rates of motor vehicle theft and that high levels of police protection would accompany low theft rates. In other words, our hypothesis predicted a negative (or inverse) relationship between the variables (the regression line should slope downward). The sign of the correlation coefficient (r), however, is positive, not negative, and the regression line slopes upward from left to right, not downward. The observed correlation is thus inconsistent with the claim that a lack of police protection causes higher rates of motor vehicle thefts.

Keep in mind, however, that correlation and causation are not the same thing. It is true that without correlation there can be no causation, although the correlation may be difficult to observe because of other factors. But correlations often occur between two variables without one being the cause of the other. For example, in any elementary school you would find a very high correlation between children's height and their reading ability. This correlation occurs because both height and reading ability reflect age—the taller kids are older and the older kids read better. The positive correlation between police officers per 10,000 population and rates of motor vehicle theft may be another example of a noncausal correlation. It seems rather far-fetched to argue that hiring more police officers will *cause* the motor vehicle theft rate to go up. A more plausible explanation is that high levels of both police employment and motor vehicle thefts reflect a common, underlying cause—that both are parts of contemporary urban life. That is, both police officers and motor vehicle thieves abound in major urban areas.

Another possibility is that the correlation between police officers per 10,000 and motor vehicle thefts does reflect a cause-and-effect relationship, but one that is in the reverse direction of our initial hypothesis. Rising motor vehicle theft rates might cause governments to hire more police. You can see that finding a correlation coefficient that is consistent with a causal hypothesis does not necessarily prove that the relationship is in fact a causal one. It is, however, suggestive that there may be such a relationship.

The correlations that we have looked at thus far have both been positive—where the motor vehicle theft is higher, the percent urban and the number of police officers per 10,000 tend to be higher too. To illustrate a very different pattern, we can examine the scatterplot between the motor vehicle theft rate and the circulation rate for *Field and Stream* magazine.

Data File: **STATES**
Task: **Scatterplot**
Dependent Variable: **8) MV.THEFT**
➤ *Independent Variable:* **84) F&STREAM**
➤ *View:* **Reg. Line**

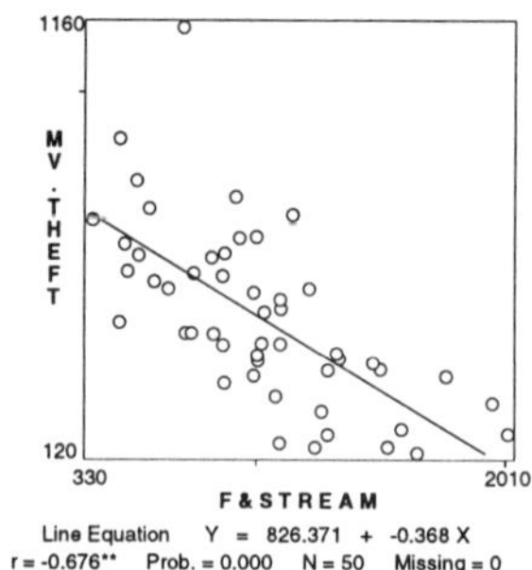

This scatterplot reveals an inverse or negative association between variables. Where the circulation rate for *Field & Stream* magazine is higher, motor vehicle theft rates are lower. Notice that the regression line slopes downward from left to right, rather than upward, which indicates a negative correlation. And notice that a minus sign now precedes the correlation coefficient: r = –0.676**. This finding is not really surprising given the previously observed association between percent urban and motor vehicle theft. Subscriptions to *Field & Stream* magazine are likely to be highest in areas of wide open country, that is, in rural areas.

Now let's consider a variable that does not seem to be a likely cause of motor vehicle theft rates: average elevation above sea level.

Data File: **STATES**
Task: **Scatterplot**
Dependent Variable: **8) MV.THEFT**
➤ *Independent Variable:* **17) ELEVATION**
➤ *View:* **Reg. Line**

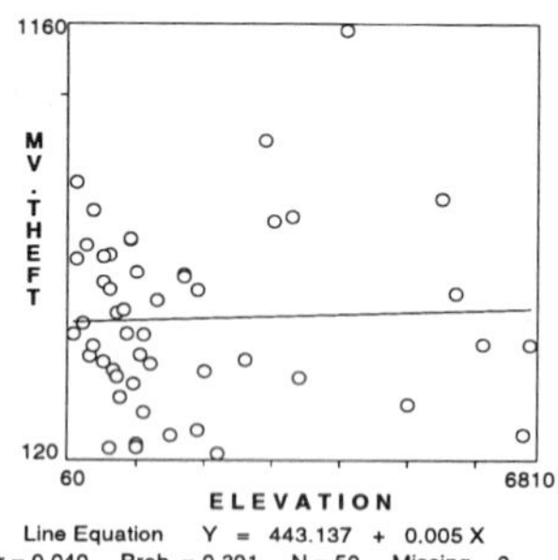

There seems to be no theoretical reason to expect rates of motor vehicle theft to vary along with elevation, and as the scatterplot reveals, there is no discernible pattern. The dots are scattered all over the screen, and you see that the line has virtually no slope; it simply crosses the screen from left to right. The trivial magnitude of the correlation coefficient (r = 0.040) indicates the lack of a correlation.

The scatterplot is a very useful device for representing relationships graphically, but it is not necessary for the computation of correlation coefficients. These coefficients can be calculated directly from mathematical formulas. ExplorIt contains another routine, in addition to "Scatterplot," called "Correlation," which can be used to obtain correlation coefficients. This is a particularly efficient way to report several correlations. The guide that follows shows you how to use the correlation task.

Data File: **STATES**
➤ *Task:* **Correlation**
➤ *Variables:* **8) MV.THEFT**
70) ABORTIONS
66) COKEUSER
83) HUNTING

Correlation Coefficients
PAIRWISE deletion (1-tailed test)   Significance Levels: ** =.01, * =.05

	MV.THEFT	ABORTIONS	COKEUSER	HUNTING
MV.THEFT	1.000 (50)	0.527 ** (50)	0.557 ** (50)	-0.485 ** (50)
ABORTIONS	0.527 ** (50)	1.000 (50)	0.526 ** (50)	-0.581 ** (50)
COKEUSER	0.557 ** (50)	0.526 ** (50)	1.000 (50)	-0.376 ** (50)
HUNTING	-0.485 ** (50)	-0.581 ** (50)	-0.376 ** (50)	1.000 (50)

The table on your screen reports the correlations between all pairs of variables (the technical term for this kind of table is a "correlation matrix"). You can discover the correlation between any two variables in either of two ways. You can locate one of the variables in the pair in the list across the top of the table and then look down the column to the row for the other variable in the pair. Thus you will see that the correlation between the abortion rate (second column) and the motor vehicle theft rate (first row) is 0.527**. Alternatively, you can locate one of the variables in the rows on the left and read across that row to the column containing the other variable in the pair. Remember that the correlation of a variable with itself is always perfect, that is, 1.000. All correlations that meet the .05 level of statistical significance are indicated by one asterisk, and all that meet the .01 level of significance are indicated by two asterisks. In this table, all of the correlations are statistically significant at the .01 level. Correlations involving hunting licenses are all negative (except, of course, the correlation of the variable with itself). All of the other correlations are positive. Some of the correlations probably are not causal but reflect various aspects of urban lifestyles. For example, it seems unlikely that abortion has a causal effect on motor vehicle thefts or that hunting licenses inhibit abortion. Other correlations, in contrast, might be causal. You will learn how to distinguish between noncausal correlations and causal relationships in Part III of the workbook.

Now, it's your turn to explore correlations.

WORKSHEET — CHAPTER 6

NAME:

COURSE:

DATE:

REVIEW QUESTIONS

Based on the first part of this chapter, answer True or False to the following items:

According to the National Crime Victimization Survey (NCVS), the vast majority of completed motor vehicle thefts are reported to the police. T F

The UCR statistics indicate that rates of motor vehicle theft reached a peak in the early 1960s and have declined steadily since that time. T F

The northern New England states tend to exhibit comparatively high rates of motor vehicle theft. T F

An "independent variable" is one that is a potential cause of other variables. T F

A correlation coefficient of "0" indicates a perfect correlation between two variables. T F

A significant correlation between two variables does not necessarily imply that the two variables are causally related. T F

EXPLORIT QUESTIONS: PART I

The questions in this section involve the interpretation of scatterplots. Use the .05 level of significance when determining whether a relationship is statistically significant.

1. Let's begin by examining the relationship between motor vehicle theft rates and an indicator of household density: the percentage of occupied housing units with approximately 2 or more persons per room.

➤ *Data File:* **STATES**
➤ *Task:* **Scatterplot**
➤ *Dependent Variable:* **8) MV.THEFT**
➤ *Independent Variable:* **58) TWO+/ROOM**
➤ *View:* **Reg. Line**

a. The states that are the highest on 58) TWO+/ROOM should appear as dots at the (circle one of the following)
   1. right of the scatterplot.
   2. left of the scatterplot.
   3. top of the scatterplot.
   4. bottom of the scatterplot.

b. The dots appearing at the bottom of the scatterplot represent the states that have the (circle one of the following)
   1. highest levels of household density.
   2. lowest levels of household density.
   3. highest rates of motor vehicle thefts.
   4. lowest rates of motor vehicle thefts.

c. What is the value of r for this scatterplot? r = __________

d. Which statement best describes the correlation between levels of household density and rates of motor vehicle theft? (circle one of the following)
   1. High levels of household density tend to accompany high rates of motor vehicle theft.
   2. Low levels of household density tend to accompany high rates of motor vehicle theft.
   3. There is no significant relationship between rates of motor vehicle theft and levels of household density.

e. Identify the case with the highest score on 58) TWO+/ROOM, and list the values for both X [58) TWO+/ROOM] and Y [8) MV.THEFT]. Case: __________

X = __________

Y = __________

2. Consider the relationship between motor vehicle theft rates and the prevalence of pick-up trucks.

Data File: **STATES**
Task: **Scatterplot**
Dependent Variable: **8) MV.THEFT**
➤ *Independent Variable:* **76) PICKUPS**
➤ *View:* **Reg. Line**

a. The states that are the highest on 8) MV.THEFT should appear as dots at the (circle one of the following)
   1. right of the scatterplot.
   2. left of the scatterplot.
   3. top of the scatterplot.
   4. bottom of the scatterplot.

b. The dots appearing at the right side of the scatterplot represent the states that have the (circle one of the following)
   1. highest rates of pickup trucks.
   2. lowest rates of pickup trucks.
   3. highest rates of motor vehicle thefts.
   4. lowest rates of motor vehicle thefts.

c. What is the value of r for this scatterplot? r = ___________

d. Which statement best describes the correlation between the number of pick-up trucks per 1,000 and rates of motor vehicle theft? (circle one of the following)
   1. High numbers of pick-up trucks tend to accompany high rates of motor vehicle theft.
   2. High numbers of pick-up trucks tend to accompany low rates of motor vehicle theft.
   3. There is no significant relationship between the number of pick-up trucks and rates of motor vehicle theft.

e. Identify the case with the lowest score on 76) PICKUPS, and list the values for both X [76) PICKUPS] and Y [8) MV.THEFT]. Case: ___________

X = ___________

Y = ___________

3. On the basis of the scatterplot between motor vehicle theft rates and the percentage of deaths caused by heart disease, answer True or False to the following statement.

Data File: **STATES**
Task: **Scatterplot**
Dependent Variable: **8) MV.THEFT**
➤ *Independent Variable:* **69) HEART DEAD**
➤ *View:* **Reg. Line**

The percentage of deaths caused by heart disease is not significantly related to the rate of motor vehicle theft. T F

4. Use a scatterplot to evaluate the following hypothesis: *States with a high percentage of teenage mothers (percentage of births to mothers under 20) tend to have high rates of motor vehicle theft.*

Data File: **STATES**
Task: **Scatterplot**
Dependent Variable: **8) MV.THEFT**
➤ *Independent Variable:* **36) MOMS <20**
➤ *View:* **Reg. Line**

a. Is the direction of the relationship consistent with the hypothesis? (That is, is the correlation coefficient positive if the relationship was predicted to be positive, or negative if the prediction was negative?) Yes No

b. Is the correlation statistically significant? Yes No

c. Is this hypothesis supported? Yes No

5. Use a scatterplot to evaluate the following hypothesis: *States with relatively large numbers of TV satellite dishes (satellite TV dishes per 10,000) tend to have high rates of motor vehicle theft.*

Data File: **STATES**
Task: **Scatterplot**
Dependent Variable: **8) MV.THEFT**
➤ *Independent Variable:* **82) TV DISHES**
➤ *View:* **Reg. Line**

a. Is the direction of the relationship consistent with the hypothesis? Yes No

b. Is the correlation statistically significant? Yes No

c. Is this hypothesis supported? Yes No

6. Use a scatterplot to evaluate the following hypothesis: *States with relatively large numbers of immigrants (new immigrants admitted per 10,000 population) tend to have high rates of motor vehicle theft.*

Data File: **STATES**
Task: **Scatterplot**
Dependent Variable: **8) MV.THEFT**
➤ *Independent Variable:* **29) IMMIGRANTS**
➤ *View:* **Reg. Line**

a. Is the direction of the relationship consistent with the hypothesis? Yes No

b. Is the correlation statistically significant? Yes No

c. Is this hypothesis supported? Yes No

EXPLORIT QUESTIONS: PART II

All questions in this section are based on the following correlation task. Use the .05 level of significance when determining whether a relationship is statistically significant.

Data File: **STATES**
➤ *Task:* **Correlation**
➤ *Variables:* **8) MV.THEFT**
2) HOMICIDE
32) %RURAL
52) NOT IN HS
68) AIDS

7. First, let's look at the correlation between rates of motor vehicle theft [MV.THEFT] and the percentage of those 16 to 19 who are not in high school and have not graduated [NOT IN HS].

   a. What is the correlation coefficient? r = ______

   b. Is this correlation statistically significant? Yes No

8. Next, consider the correlation between homicide rates [HOMICIDE] and percent rural [%RURAL].

   a. What is the correlation coefficient? r = ______

   b. Is this correlation statistically significant? Yes No

9. Which pair of variables exhibits the strongest positive correlation? (List the variable names.)

   ______ ______

10. Which pair of variables exhibits the strongest negative correlation? (List the variable names.)

    ______ ______

11. Which pair of variables exhibits the weakest correlation? (List the variable names.)

    ______ ______

12. Evaluate the following hypothesis: *States with high rates of motor vehicle thefts also tend to exhibit high homicide rates.*

    a. Is the direction of the relationship consistent with the hypothesis? Yes No

    b. Is the correlation statistically significant? Yes No

    c. Is this hypothesis supported? Yes No

<u>Essay Question</u>

13. List the variables that exhibit a significant relationship (positive or negative) with motor vehicle theft in the scatterplots examined in Part I of this chapter. Which of these relationships do you think are cause-and-effect relationships, and which do you think are not cause-and-effect relationships? Explain your answer. (Use the back side of this page to write your answer.)

Part II

APPLYING CRIMINOLOGICAL THEORIES

CHAPTER 7

SOCIAL PSYCHOLOGICAL PROCESSES: BONDS AND DEVIANT ASSOCIATIONS

In the end, control theory remains what it has always been: a theory in which deviation is not problematic. The question "Why do they do it?" is simply not the question to answer. The question is, "Why don't we do it?" There is much evidence that we would if we dared.

TRAVIS HIRSCHI, PAST PRESIDENT OF THE AMERICAN SOCIETY OF CRIMINOLOGY[1]

Defend me from my friends; I can defend myself from my enemies.

AN APHORISM ASSIGNED TO MARECHAL VILLARS, WHEN TAKING LEAVE OF LOUIS XIV[2]

Tasks: Cross-tabulation
Data Files: NYS, COLLEGE

In previous chapters, you have read about the kinds of data sources that criminologists use to measure crime and public opinion about crime. You have also learned some of the basic techniques that criminologists use to analyze crime data, and you know that a major purpose of criminological analysis is to explain variation. We want to find out, for example, why some people commit more or fewer crimes than do other people, and why some places have higher or lower levels of crime than do other places.

Most people have many ideas about the causes of crime. Indeed, when interpreting observed patterns in earlier chapters, you have undoubtedly drawn upon your taken-for-granted knowledge of the causes of crime. Criminologists also develop explanations of crime, but they try to come up with explanations that can account for a large number of instances in a logical and relatively concise manner. This task requires the construction of theories. A theory is a set of logically interrelated statements that imply relationships between variables. Much (but certainly not all) criminological research is devoted to testing hypotheses that have been deduced from the major theories of the causes of crime.

[1] Travis Hirschi, *Causes of Delinquency* (Berkeley, CA: University of California Press, 1969), p. 269.

[2] John Bartlett, *Familiar Quotations* [cited from http://www.columbia.edu/acis/bartleby/bartlett/334.html]

Criminology is interdisciplinary, and as a result, the field contains a wide variety of theories of the causes of crime. The criminological theorist Ronald Akers has proposed a useful distinction between two general types of theoretical approaches: processual and structural.[3] Processual theories attempt to explain why some individuals end up committing crimes rather than others. As the name implies, these theories emphasize processes, such as psychological processes and socialization processes. Structural theories, in contrast, are oriented to explaining variation in crime rates across groups (e.g., members of different social classes) or geographic territories (e.g., neighborhoods, cities, states, nations). And, as you can probably guess, these latter theories emphasize features of social structure in the explanation of crime.

One of the most influential social process theories over the past 30 years or so has been a theory proposed by Travis Hirschi. This theory is commonly referred to as *control theory* or *bonding theory*. Hirschi bases his theorizing on an assumption about human nature, which is hinted at in the quotation at the beginning of this chapter. Specifically, he assumes that everybody is tempted to violate the law. In his view, criminal behavior is actually very attractive to all of us. This is a simple fact of human nature. The interesting question, then, is not why some people go ahead and break the law. Rather, the interesting question is why everyone doesn't break the law all the time.

Hirschi's answer is that people are restrained from law-breaking as a result of the "bonds" that they have formed with conventional society. In his famous formulation, Hirschi differentiates between four major types of bonds. One is **attachment**, which refers to an emotional tie between the person and others. If we are emotionally attached to other people, we take their opinions seriously. We are thus inhibited from misbehaving because we worry that these others, whom we care about, might be disappointed in us and think less of us.

A second element of the social bond is **commitment**, which essentially refers to stakes in conformity. When people have invested time and effort in the creation of conventional, socially respected biographies, they can usually anticipate future rewards. Such people are reluctant to commit crimes because to do so would threaten their future rewards and jeopardize their investments.

A third type of bond is that of **involvement**, which refers simply to time spent in conventional activities. When we are busy with pro-social activities (e.g., Little League, community service, the PTA), there is little time to get into trouble.

The final element of the social bond according to Hirschi is **belief**, which refers to personal acceptance of societal values and norms, especially legal norms. People who accept and endorse the legitimacy of the conventional morality are unlikely to violate the law.

Hirschi's bonding theory has guided many research studies on crime and delinquency. To use the theory, criminologists have had to come up with measures that reflect the different elements of the bond. Consider the "belief" element. One way to measure acceptance of legal norms is simply to ask people how wrong they think it is to engage in specified, illegal acts. Such questions were in fact included in the seventh wave of the National Youth Survey, which was described in Chapter 3. For example, respondents were asked how wrong they think it is for someone to commit a minor theft, that is, to steal something worth less than $5. It seems reasonable to infer that people who claim that this act is clearly wrong accept the legitimacy of the conventional morality more than those who respond

---

[3] Ronald L. Akers, *Deviant Behavior: A Social Learning Approach*, 3rd ed. (Belmont, CA: Wadsworth, 1985).

that minor stealing is not very wrong. Given the logic of Hirschi's theory, then, we can deduce the hypothesis that those with a stronger belief in the "wrongfulness" of minor stealing should be less likely to commit crimes themselves.

Let's assess this hypothesis using the CROSS-TABULATION task.

➤ *Data File:* **NYS**
➤ *Task:* **Cross-tabulation**
➤ *Row Variable:* **16) ARRESTED**
➤ *Column Variable:* **46) WRONG$5**
➤ *View:* **Tables**
➤ *Display:* **Column %**

ARRESTED by WRONG$5
Cramer's V: 0.065 *

ARRESTED	WRONG$5 Not very	Wrong	Missing	TOTAL
No	123	1153	0	1276
	87.2%	92.9%		92.3%
Yes	18	88	1	106
	12.8%	7.1%		7.7%
TOTAL	141	1241	1	1382
	100.0%	100.0%		

You see that the cross-tabulation between belief about the "wrongfulness" of minor stealing and the likelihood of having been arrested is consistent with the hypothesis derived from bonding theory. Those who think such an act is clearly wrong are less likely to report being arrested than those who think it is not very wrong, 7.1 percent versus 12.8 percent. The difference is not very large, but remember that the experience of an arrest is relatively rare in the sample. The asterisk for the V coefficient indicates that the difference in percentages is statistically significant at the .05 level.

How might we measure the "attachment" element of the bond? When Hirschi introduced his theory, he proposed several different ways to measure attachment. One of these involved identification with others. Hirschi reasoned that wanting to be like some other person indicates that you identify with that person and have a strong emotional tie with him or her. His research focus was juvenile delinquency, so he was particularly interested in examining parental attachment. Parents are obviously very important figures in the lives of juveniles. Hirschi measured parental attachment by asking youths whether they wanted to be like the kind of persons their fathers or mothers were.

The data from the National Youth Survey that you are working with refer to young adults (age 21–29). Parents are probably not as central in the lives of these individuals as they are for juveniles. On the other hand, at these older ages many people have established close relationships with members of the opposite sex. The NYS asked such respondents about their emotional identification with their partners. Consistent with Hirschi's earlier measurement strategy, the specific question refers to the extent to which respondents want to be like their partners.

Bonding theory suggests that the item for "wanting to be like your partner" should be related to self-reports of injurious behavior toward the partner. Let's look at this relationship using an indicator of assault (having kicked, bit, or hit your partner within the past year).

Data File: **NYS**
Task: **Cross-tabulation**
➤ *Row Variable:* **32) HIT PRT2**
➤ *Column Variable:* **37) BLIKPART**
➤ *View:* **Tables**
➤ *Display:* **Column %**

HIT PRT2 by BLIKPART
Cramer's V: 0.085 *

HIT PRT2	BLIKPART Not much	A lot	Missing	TOTAL
No	168	482	8	650
	87.0%	92.5%		91.0%
Yes	25	39	1	64
	13.0%	7.5%		9.0%
Missing	2	0	658	660
TOTAL	193	521	667	714
	100.0%	100.0%		

The findings support the hypothesis derived from Hirschi's theory. Less than 8 percent of those who report that they want to be like their partner "a lot" admit to an assault, compared to 13 percent of those who give the "not much" response to wanting to be like their partner. Once again, while the difference is small, it is statistically significant and consistent with the prediction of bonding theory.

Let's turn to the sample of college students to examine the two other elements of the social bond. A common measure of "commitment" in research based on school populations is academic performance, or grades. Students who have attained high grades would surely seem to have a greater stake in conformity than those who have received low grades. They can expect greater rewards for conformity in the future, and they have more to lose by breaking the law. Is academic performance related to a fairly common offense among college students, namely, shoplifting?

➤ *Data File:* **COLLEGE**
➤ *Task:* **Cross-tabulation**
➤ *Row Variable:* **3) SHOPLIFT**
➤ *Column Variable:* **19) HI GRADES**
➤ *View:* **Tables**
➤ *Display:* **Column %**

SHOPLIFT by HI GRADES
Cramer's V: 0.105 **

SHOPLIFT	HI GRADES 3.0 +	< 3.0	Missing	TOTAL
Yes	222	75	12	297
	39.5%	52.4%		42.1%
No	340	68	23	408
	60.5%	47.6%		57.9%
Missing	2	0	19	21
TOTAL	562	143	54	705
	100.0%	100.0%		

The observed relationship is consistent with the "commitment" hypothesis. Over 52 percent of students with GPAs under 3.0 report having shoplifted, compared with just under 40 percent of those with a GPA of 3.0 or higher. The asterisks for the V coefficient indicate that the relationship is statistically significant.

The college students in the survey were also asked about how much studying they do in an average week. This information might be used to measure the notion of "involvement" in bonding theory. Students who are busy studying have less time to hang out and get into trouble than those who do not study much. Let's look at the cross-tabulation between studying and shoplifting.

Data File: **COLLEGE**
Task: **Cross-tabulation**
Row Variable: **3) SHOPLIFT**
➤ Column Variable: **17) HI STUDY**
➤ View: **Tables**
➤ Display: **Column %**

SHOPLIFT by HI STUDY
Cramer's V: 0.118 **

SHOPLIFT	HI STUDY 10+ hrs	Up to 10	Missing	TOTAL
Yes	99	179	31	278
	35.5%	47.2%		42.2%
No	180	200	51	380
	64.5%	52.8%		57.8%
Missing	1	0	20	21
TOTAL	279	379	102	658
	100.0%	100.0%		

You once again see support for bonding theory. About 47 percent of those who study only 10 or fewer hours a week report involvement in shoplifting, while less than 36 percent of the more studious respondents report such involvement, a difference that is highly significant.

A second influential criminological theory that is also commonly classified as a process theory is *social learning theory*. Proponents of this approach believe that the motivation for criminal behavior cannot be taken for granted as simply part of human nature. Rather, social learning theorists argue that motives for committing crime must be acquired, along with the specific techniques for committing crime. Moreover, these theorists maintain that learning to break the law entails the same kinds of processes that lead to the learning of conventional behavior.

A variety of social learning theories of crime have been proposed over the years, but one of the more famous is that of Ronald Akers.[4] Akers proposes that crime is learned through four basic processes. One is **differential association**. Persons who associate with criminals are more exposed to criminal behavior patterns and are more likely to learn them through such exposure. A second process involves the acquisition of **pro-criminal** attitudes or **definitions**. People who have attached positive meanings to crime in comparison with law-abiding behavior are more likely to become criminals than those who attach negative meanings to crime. A third process is **differential reinforcement**. This refers to rewards and punishments. If people are often rewarded and rarely punished when they violate the law, they learn that crime is an attractive pattern of behavior. The fourth process is **imitation**. People who observe criminal behavior may imitate this behavior themselves, especially if the "models" are important in the observer's personal life.

As you can probably guess, social learning theory emphasizes the critical role that friends play in the development of criminal behavior patterns. The theory implies that people who hang around with a "bad crowd" are likely to get into trouble themselves. You can begin to assess this hypothesis with data from the NYS. The survey asked respondents about whether or not their friends had committed various illegal acts within the past year, including having used marijuana. Let's look at the relationship between the respondents' use of marijuana and friends' use of marijuana.

[4] Ronald L. Akers, *Criminological Theories: Introduction and Evaluation* (Los Angeles: Roxbury, 1997).

➤ *Data File:* **NYS**
➤ *Task:* **Cross-tabulation**
➤ *Row Variable:* **13) USED MARIJ**
➤ *Column Variable:* **50) FRNDMJ**
➤ *View:* **Tables**
➤ *Display:* **Column %**

USED MARIJ by FRNDMJ
Cramer's V: 0.517 **

USED MARIJ	FRNDMJ No	Yes	Missing	TOTAL
No	472	391	10	863
	96.5%	44.5%		63.1%
Yes	17	488	5	505
	3.5%	55.5%		36.9%
TOTAL	489	879	15	1368
	100.0%	100.0%		

The data show that there is a very strong association between these variables. Very few respondents who did not have marijuana-using friends (3.5 percent) reported marijuana use themselves, compared with a clear majority (55.5 percent) of those who did have marijuana-using friends. Your findings are quite consistent with a large body of literature: association with criminal or delinquent peers is one of the strongest and most persistent correlates of crime and delinquency.

Your turn.

WORKSHEET

CHAPTER 7

NAME:

COURSE:

DATE:

REVIEW QUESTIONS

Based on the first part of this chapter, answer True or False to the following items:

Control or bonding theory is based on the assumption that the motivation for crime is part of human nature. T F

The "involvement" element of the social bond refers to the tendency for people involved in delinquent activities at a young age to become criminals in adulthood. T F

A central claim of bonding theory is that close emotional attachments to others inhibits people from committing crimes. T F

The evidence from the National Youth Survey indicates that there is no significant relationship between wanting to be like one's partner and assaultive behavior toward one's partner. T F

Social learning theory emphasizes the role of friends as a factor affecting the likelihood of criminal involvement. T F

EXPLORIT QUESTIONS: PART I

The following questions involve the application of bonding theory to examine the causes of self-reported drunk driving (having driven while drunk within the past year).

1. Consider the following question in the National Youth Survey: "How wrong is it for someone your age to exceed the speed limit by 10–20 mph?"

   a. Which element of the social bond does this question measure most directly? (Circle the appropriate answer.)

      1. attachment
      2. commitment
      3. involvement
      4. belief

b. Cross-tabulate this variable with self-reported drunk driving.

➤ *Data File:* **NYS**
➤ *Task:* **Cross-tabulation**
➤ *Row Variable:* **15) DWI**
➤ *Column Variable:* **48) WRONGSPD**
➤ *View:* **Tables**
➤ *Display:* **Column %**

	NOT VERY	**WRONG**
NO	________%	________%
YES	________%	________%

c. Is the relationship statistically significant? Yes No

d. Do the results support bonding theory? Yes No

2. Consider the following question in the National Youth Survey: "How loyal are you to your partner?"

a. Which element of the social bond does this question measure most directly? (Circle the appropriate answer.)

1. attachment
2. commitment
3. involvement
4. belief

b. Fill in the percentages for the cross-tabulation between self-reported drunk driving and the loyalty-to-partners question.

Data File: **NYS**
Task: **Cross-tabulation**
Row Variable: **15) DWI**
➤ *Column Variable:* **40) LOYLPART**
➤ *View:* **Tables**
➤ *Display:* **Column %**

	NOT MUCH	**A LOT**
NO	________%	________%
YES	________%	________%

c. Is the relationship statistically significant? Yes No

d. Do the results support bonding theory? Yes No

3. Consider the following question in the National Youth Survey: "How wrong is it for someone your age to cheat on their income taxes?"

   a. Which element of the social bond does this question measure most directly? (Circle the appropriate answer.)
      1. attachment
      2. commitment
      3. involvement
      4. belief

   b. Fill in the percentages for the cross-tabulation between 15) DWI and 44) WRONGTAX.

      Data File: **NYS**
      Task: **Cross-tabulation**
      Row Variable: **15) DWI**
      ➤ *Column Variable:* **44) WRONGTAX**
      ➤ *View:* **Tables**
      ➤ *Display:* **Column %**

	NOT VERY	WRONG
NO	________%	________%
YES	________%	________%

   c. Is the relationship statistically significant? Yes No

   d. Do the results support bonding theory? Yes No

4. Consider the following question in the National Youth Survey: "How much would you like to be the kind of person your closest friends are?"

   a. Which element of the social bond does this question measure most directly? (Circle the appropriate answer.)
      1. attachment
      2. commitment
      3. involvement
      4. belief

b. Fill in the percentages for the cross-tabulation between 15) DWI and 33) BLIKFRND.

Data File: **NYS**
Task: **Cross-tabulation**
Row Variable: **15) DWI**
➤ *Column Variable:* **33) BLIKFRND**
➤ *View:* **Tables**
➤ *Display:* **Column %**

	NOT MUCH	A LOT
NO	_______%	_______%
YES	_______%	_______%

c. Is the relationship statistically significant? Yes No

d. Do the results support bonding theory? Yes No

EXPLORIT QUESTIONS: PART II: Analyses of Arrests

The following questions involve the application of social learning theory to help explain criminal involvement.

5. The NYS asked respondents whether their friends engaged in the following three criminal activities in the past year:

stole something worth less than $5 (FRND$5)

stole something worth $50 or more (FRND$50)

cheated on their income taxes (FRNDTAX)

Examine the cross-tabulations between having been arrested and each of these three items. It will be helpful to print out the three cross-tabulations to answer the questions that follow.

Data File: **NYS**
Task: **Cross-tabulation**
➤ *Row Variable:* **16) ARRESTED**
➤ *Column Variable:* **51) FRND$5 [Repeat with 52) FRND$50; 49) FRNDTAX]**
➤ *View:* **Tables**
➤ *Display:* **Column %**

a. How many of the three cross-tabulations support the claim that people who have friends that steal and cheat are more likely to have been arrested themselves? (Circle the correct answer.) 1 2 3

b. How many of the relationships in the cross-tabulations are statistically significant? (Circle the correct answer.) 1 2 3

6. The NYS also asked respondents if their friends have suggested that they do something against the law.

Data File: **NYS**
Task: **Cross-tabulation**
➤ *Row Variable:* **15) DWI**
➤ *Column Variable:* **53) FRNDSUGG**
➤ *View:* **Tables**
➤ *Display:* **Column %**

a. Are respondents whose friends have suggested that they break the law more or less likely to have driven drunk during the past year? (Circle the correct answer.) More Less

b. Is this difference statistically significant? (Circle the correct answer.) Yes No

EXPLORIT QUESTIONS: PART III: Self-reported Deviance by College Students

Earlier in the exercise, you discovered that an indicator of the bond of commitment (grade point average) and an indicator of the bond of involvement (hours studying) were related to self-reported shoplifting in the sample of college students in your data file. See if these results are replicated for two other forms of deviance: marijuana use and cheating on exams.

7. Fill in the percentages for the cross-tabulation between 6) EV MARIJ and 19) HI GRADES (grade point average).

➤ *Data File:* **COLLEGE**
➤ *Task:* **Cross-tabulation**
➤ *Row Variable:* **6) EV MARIJ**
➤ *Column Variable:* **19) HI GRADES**
➤ *View:* **Tables**
➤ *Display:* **Column %**

	3.0+	**<3.0**
YES	________%	________%
NO	________%	________%

a. Is the relationship statistically significant? Yes No

b. Do the results support bonding theory? Yes No

8. Fill in the percentages for the cross-tabulation between 6) EV MARIJ and 17) HI STUDY (hours spent studying).

Data File: **COLLEGE**
Task: **Cross-tabulation**
Row Variable: **6) EV MARIJ**
➤ *Column Variable:* **17) HI STUDY**
➤ *View:* **Tables**
➤ *Display:* **Column %**

	10+ HRS	**UP TO 10**
YES	________%	________%
NO	________%	________%

a. Is the relationship statistically significant? Yes No

b. Do the results support bonding theory? Yes No

9. Fill in the percentages for the cross-tabulation between 10) OFT CHEAT and 19) HI GRADES (grade point average).

Data File: **COLLEGE**
Task: **Cross-tabulation**
➤ *Row Variable:* **10) OFT CHEAT**
➤ *Column Variable:* **19) HI GRADES**
➤ *View:* **Tables**
➤ *Display:* **Column %**

	3.0+	**<3.0**
OFTEN	________%	________%
RARE/NO	________%	________%

a. Is the relationship statistically significant? Yes No

b. Do the results support bonding theory? Yes No

10. Fill in the percentages for the cross-tabulation between cheating [10) OFT CHEAT] and hours of studying [17) HI STUDY].

Data File: **COLLEGE**
Task: **Cross-tabulation**
Row Variable: **10) OFT CHEAT**
➤ *Column Variable:* **17) HI STUDY**
➤ *View:* **Tables**
➤ *Display:* **Column %**

	10.0+ HRS	**UP TO 10**
OFTEN	________%	________%
RARE/NO	________%	________%

a. Is the relationship statistically significant? Yes No

b. Do the results support bonding theory? Yes No

ESSAY QUESTION

11. You probably expected to see some of the results observed in the worksheet section for this chapter, but other findings may have been surprising to you. Identify the two cross-tabulations that surprised you the most. Describe the relationship (or lack of a relationship) between variables observed in each of these cross-tabulations. Be sure to compare percentages and refer to statistical significance. Then, propose an explanation for the observed patterns. How could you account for these findings?

CHAPTER 8

SOCIAL DISORGANIZATION AND PROPERTY CRIME

Love thy neighbor as thyself.
THE OLD TESTAMENT[1]

Tasks: Mapping, Scatterplot, Correlation
Data Files: STATES

In the previous chapter, you examined patterns of self-reported crime using two influential social process theories. Recall that these theories focus on explaining why some individuals rather than others are involved in criminal acts. The various social process theories offer somewhat different explanations of the causes of crime, but they share a common concern with social psychological traits and individual socialization experiences. A second important theoretical approach in criminology is the *social structural* approach. Here, the focus is on the organization of social life and how differences in such organization can explain variation in levels or rates of crime across social groups. One of the most important structural approaches in criminology is **social disorganization theory**. This theory is sometimes referred to as the "Chicago School" because it was originally developed and popularized by scholars at the University of Chicago.

Social disorganization theory arose in response to the rapid growth of cities during the late 19th and early 20th centuries. As rural people and immigrants from abroad flocked to the booming industrial centers, these cities became populated by newcomers and strangers, especially in the urban core. The Chicago School theorists referred to these core areas of cities as transitional zones. The new migrants and immigrants were drawn to the **transitional zones** because real estate values were low and inexpensive housing could be found. At the same time, these areas were not very attractive places to live in, and thus people tried to move out to better neighborhoods as soon as they could. The transitional zones were thus characterized by a very diverse mix of people from different backgrounds who tended to move in and out of the community rapidly.

The Chicago School researchers discovered another striking feature of the transitional zones in cities: these areas were crime-infested and disorderly places. Why were crime rates so much higher in the transitional zones than in other parts of the city? The Chicago School theorists argued that the answer could be found in the nature of interpersonal relationships, that is, the social ties among the residents within a community. Strong, extensive ties among neighbors inhibit crime in two important ways. On the one hand, we obey rules or norms in part because we wish to protect our relationships with other people—to retain their good opinion of us. Concern over such relationships thereby serves as an internal control discouraging people from violating the law. At the same time, close ties among neighbors in a

---

[1] Leviticus 19:18.

community enhances the residents' capacity and willingness to monitor what is going on around them and to keep their eyes open for trouble. Strong attachments among neighbors, in other words, makes it more risky for potential offenders to engage in crime—it facilitates monitoring and thus external control. As cities grew rapidly, both of these restraints against crime (internal and external) eroded, especially in the transitional zones. Close human relationships with neighbors declined, and communities became socially disorganized. As a result, crime rates rose. This explanation for crime has become known over the years as *social disorganization theory*.

Social disorganization theory dominated the sociological study of crime in the early to middle decades of the 20th century. It inspired a number of famous studies of the social structural correlates of crime rates, not only in Chicago but in other U.S. cities as well. For a while, the approach waned in importance, but it has recently reemerged as a key theoretical perspective. In this chapter, we are going to see if social disorganization theory helps explain variation in two types of property crime—burglary and larceny—across the United States. We shall begin by testing the theory with data from the early 20th century, the approximate period during which the theory emerged on the criminological scene. Then, we shall see whether or not the theory can stand the test of time by examining data for later periods.

Let's begin by examining a map for a variable representing the number of persons sent to jail or prison for burglary per 100,000 population in 1923. This is not the same thing as the rate of burglaries known to the police—such UCR rates were not available at that time. However, in the absence of uniform police statistics, the rate of admissions to jails and prisons is a tolerable measure of the amount of crime occurring in various states.

➤ *Data File:* **STATES**
➤ *Task:* **Mapping**
➤ *Variable 1:* **97) BURGLARY23**
➤ *View:* **Map**

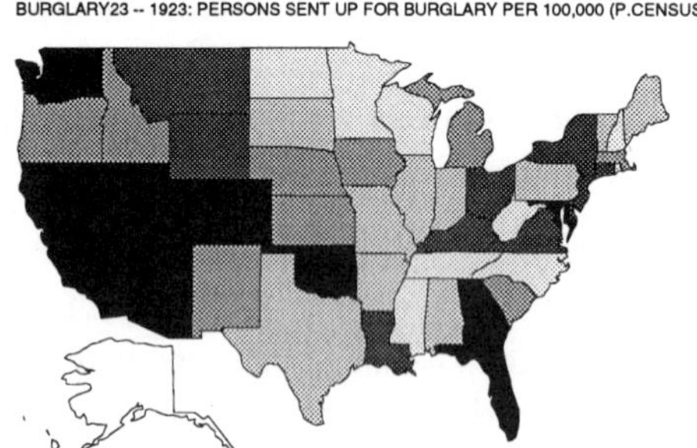

Notice that burglary tended to be highest in the West and, to a lesser extent, the South in 1923. Now look at the ranking of states.

Data File: **STATES**
Task: **Mapping**
Variable 1: **97) BURGLARY23**
➤ *View:* **List: Rank**

BURGLARY23: 1923: Persons sent up for burglary per 100,000

RANK	CASE NAME	VALUE
1	Nevada	13.00
2	Arizona	10.48
3	Oklahoma	9.76
4	Washington	8.62
5	California	7.56
6	Colorado	7.02
7	Maryland	6.41
8	Florida	6.20
9	Georgia	5.80
10	Utah	5.79

You see that Nevada was highest with a rate of 13 per 100,000 population. Arizona was second with a rate of 10.48. As you progress down the rankings, you will see that of the top 10 states, 6 were in the Pacific or mountain regions and 4 were in the South (Oklahoma, Maryland, Florida, and Georgia). New Hampshire was lowest. (Hawaii and Alaska lack crime rates because they were not states in 1923.)

Now, let's consider a variable for population change: the percentage growth (or decline) in a state's population during the 1910–1920 period, as recorded by the U.S. Census Bureau.

Data File: **STATES**
Task: **Mapping**
Variable 1: **97) BURGLARY23**
➤ *Variable 2:* **99) POP GO 20**
➤ *Views:* **Map**

BURGLARY23 -- 1923: PERSONS SENT UP FOR BURGLARY PER 100,000 (P.CENSUS)

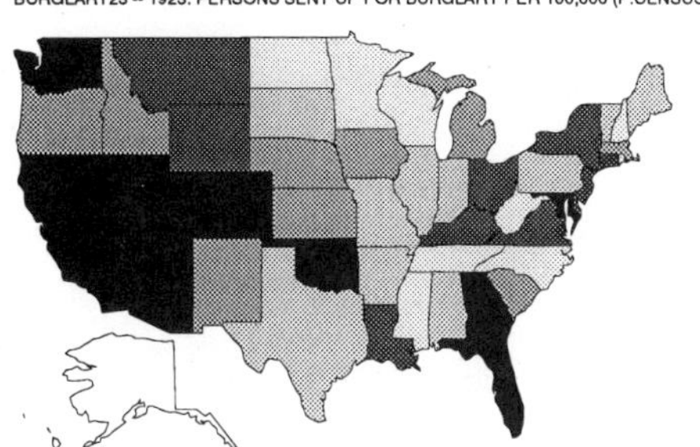

r = 0.334*

POP GO 20 -- PERCENT POPULATION GROWTH (OR -DECLINE), 1910-1920 (CENSUS)

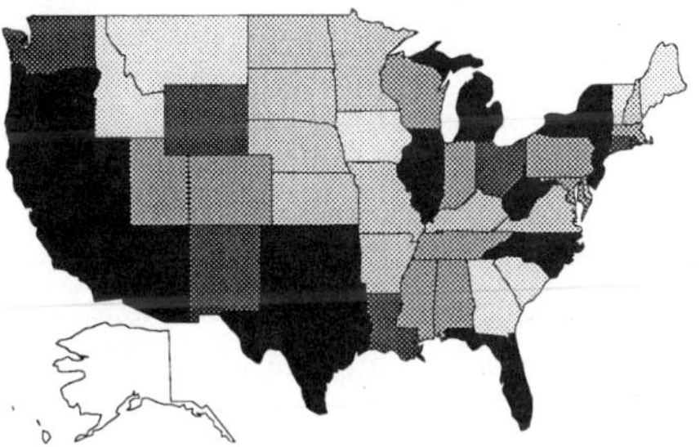

Social disorganization theory asserts that places where social relations have been disrupted by rapid population growth ought to have high rates of crime. We might expect, then, that the map for population change should be similar to that for burglary. A comparison of the two maps reveals a fair degree of resemblance. Population growth also tended to be a western and southwestern phenomenon in the early years of the 20th century. Let's look at the ranking of states.

Data File: **STATES**
Task: **Mapping**
Variable 1: **97) BURGLARY23**
Variable 2: **99) POP GO 20**
➤ *Views:* **List: Rank**

BURGLARY23: 1923: Persons sent up for burglary per 100,000

RANK	CASE NAME	VALUE
1	Nevada	13.00
2	Arizona	10.48
3	Oklahoma	9.76
4	Washington	8.62
5	California	7.56

POP GO 20: Percent population growth (or decline), 1910–1920

RANK	CASE NAME	VALUE
1	California	66
2	Florida	52
3	Michigan	32
4	Arizona	31
5	New Jersey	28

California was the state with the highest growth rate over the 1910–20 decade—66 percent. Florida was second with a growth rate of 52 percent. You no doubt observed in the comparison of maps that although the two are somewhat alike, they are far from identical. In cases where maps are only somewhat alike it is also helpful to examine the relationship between variables with a scatterplot.

Data File: **STATES**
➤ *Task:* **Scatterplot**
➤ *Dependent Variable:* **97) BURGLARY23**
➤ *Independent Variable:* **99) POP GO 20**
➤ *View:* **Reg. Line**

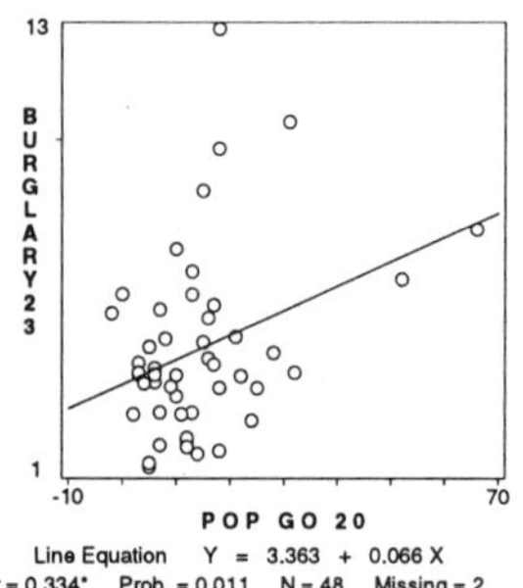

The pattern shows a positive linear association between population growth and the burglary rate: states experiencing growing populations tend to have high burglary rates. The correlation coefficient is 0.334*, which is statistically significant. These results support our hypothesis derived from social disorganization theory.

Let's compare the map for the burglary rate in 1923 with another map, that for the percentage of the population in each state in 1920 who were born in that state.

Data File: **STATES**
➤ *Task:* **Mapping**
➤ *Variable 1:* **97) BURGLARY23**
➤ *Variable 2:* **96) %LOCALS 20**
➤ *Views:* **Map**

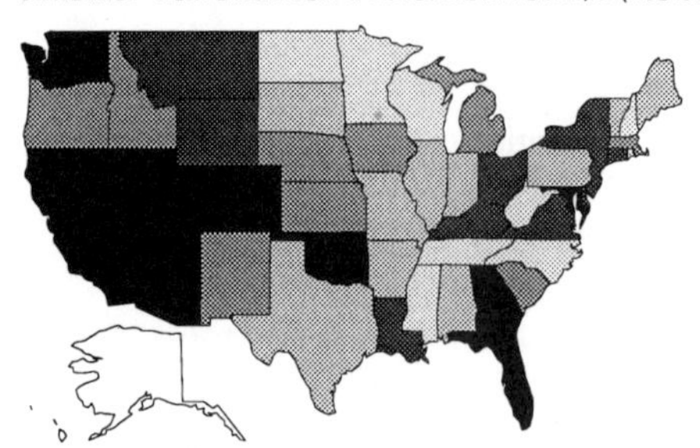

r = –0.484**

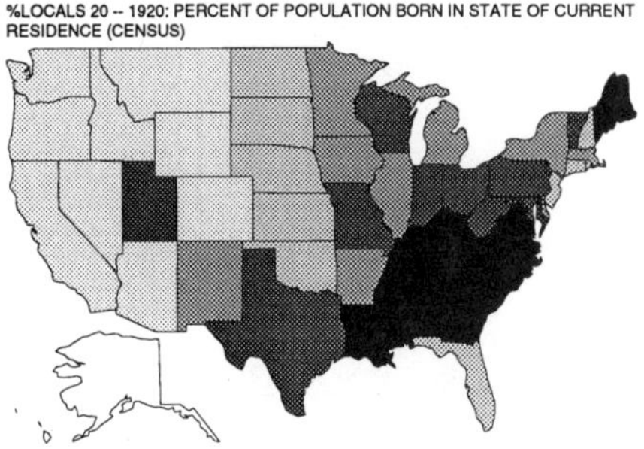

There are some striking differences between the two maps. Note in particular that western states tend to be comparatively low on %LOCALS 20. This really should not be very surprising to you. The variable for the percentage who were born in the state is in some sense the reverse of the previously examined variable for population growth. Only states without much migration into the state will have high rates of their population who are native born. The variable for percentage born in that state is essentially a reflection of **stability** in the population rather than change. From the standpoint of social disorganization theory, we would expect an inverse relationship between stable populations and burglary rate. Consider the scatterplot.

Data File: **STATES**
➤ *Task:* **Scatterplot**
➤ *Dependent Variable:* **97) BURGLARY23**
➤ *Independent Variable:* **96) %LOCALS 20**
➤ *View:* **Reg. Line**

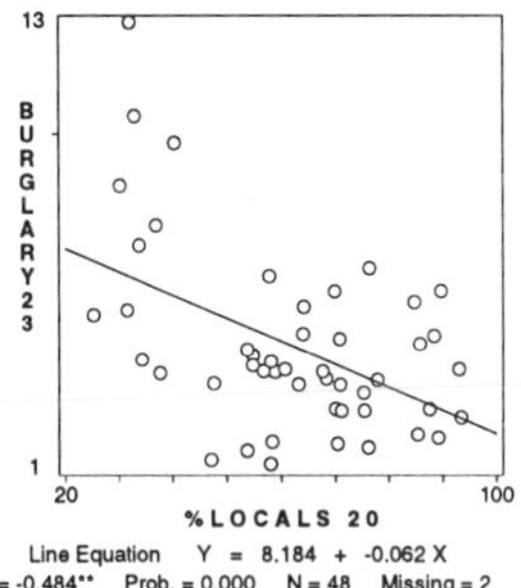

The scatterplot for these two variables is once again consistent with our hypothesis. States with large numbers of residents born in the state tend to have low burglary rates. This is reflected in the significantly negative correlation coefficient: r = –0.484**.

Let's see if social disorganization theory also helps explain interstate variation for another criminal offense in the 1920s—the number of persons sent to jail or prison in 1923 for larceny/theft. This offense is similar to burglary in that it also involves the illegal acquisition of property. We might expect, then, that the social structural causes of the two crimes might be similar. To see if this is the case, let's look at correlations.

Data File: **STATES**
➤ *Task:* **Correlation**
➤ *Variables:* **97) BURGLARY23**
98) LARCENY23
99) POP GO 20
96) %LOCALS 20

Correlation Coefficients
PAIRWISE deletion (1-tailed test) Significance Levels: ** =.01, * =.05

	BURGLARY23	LARCENY23	POP GO 20	%LOCALS 20
BURGLARY23	1.000 (48)	0.665 ** (48)	0.334 * (48)	-0.484 ** (48)
LARCENY23	0.665 ** (48)	1.000 (48)	0.429 ** (48)	-0.441 ** (48)
POP GO 20	0.334 * (48)	0.429 ** (48)	1.000 (50)	-0.235 (48)
%LOCALS 20	-0.484 ** (48)	-0.441 ** (48)	-0.235 (48)	1.000 (48)

Notice first that there is a fairly strong positive correlation between burglary and larceny rates: r = 0.665**. Not surprisingly, states exhibiting high rates of one of these types of property crime tend to exhibit high rates of the other as well. Turning to the measure of population change, the correlation for larceny is in fact similar to that observed for burglary. States with more rapid population growth have higher larceny rates. This significant positive correlation (r = 0.429**) is consistent with social disorganization theory. Finally, the significant negative correlation between larceny rates and the percentage of the population who are native born (r = –0.441**) also supports social disorganization theory. States with relatively large numbers of native residents (a stable population) have lower larceny rates.

Although the analyses thus far have confirmed hypotheses based on social disorganization theory, criminologists are reluctant to trust research findings until they have turned up repeatedly. Instead, confidence in findings increases to the extent that hypotheses have been tested again and again with different data and similar results have been obtained. The process of re-testing a hypothesis is known as **replication** (it comes from the word *replica*, meaning a copy or a reproduction).

In the remainder of this chapter, you will have the chance to see if these findings for the 1920s can be replicated in other eras using UCR data on burglary and larceny rates.

WORKSHEET	CHAPTER
NAME:	8
COURSE:	
DATE:	

REVIEW QUESTIONS

Based on the first part of this chapter, answer True or False to the following items:

Social disorganization theory is classified as a structural approach to the explanation of crime.	T	F
According to social disorganization theory, transitional zones are areas of the city in which crime rates are beginning to fall.	T	F
Social disorganization theory implies that areas characterized by rapid growth ("boomtowns") will tend to have high rates of crime.	T	F
Rates of burglary and larceny tend to vary inversely across states.	T	F
Data for the 1920s indicate that states with relatively large percentages of residents who were born within the state tended to exhibit relatively low larceny rates.	T	F

EXPLORIT QUESTIONS: PART I

The questions in this section ask you to compare correlations reported for the 1920s, which supported social disorganization theory, with correlations for later years. You examined correlations for the 1920s in the introduction to this chapter. To make it easier to answer the questions that follow, repeat the correlation task for larceny, burglary, and population growth for the 1920s and print out the resulting table.

➤ *Data File:* **STATES**
➤ *Task:* **Correlation**
➤ *Variables:* **99) POP GO 20**
97) BURGLARY23
98) LARCENY23

1. Fill in the correlation matrix below (be sure to indicate statistical significance):

Data File: **STATES**
Task: **Correlation**
➤ *Variables:* **102) POP GO 40**
100) BURGLARY40
101) LARCENY 40

	POP GO 40	BURGLARY40	LARCENY 40
POP GO 40	1.000	________	________
BURGLARY40	________	1.000	________
LARCENY 40	________	________	1.000

a. What is the correlation between burglary (BURGLARY40) and population growth (POP GO 40) for the 1940s? ________

b. Is the correlation statistically significant? Yes No

c. Is this correlation between burglary and population growth for the 1940s stronger or weaker than the correlation for the 1920s? Stronger than 1920s

Weaker than 1920s

d. What is the correlation between larceny (LARCENY40) and population growth (POP GO 40) for the 1940s? ________

e. Is the correlation statistically significant? Yes No

f. Is this correlation between larceny and population growth for the 1940s stronger or weaker than the correlation for the 1920s? Stronger than 1920s

Weaker than 1920s

2. Fill in the correlation matrix below (be sure to indicate statistical significance):

Data File: **STATES**
Task: **Correlation**
➤ *Variables:* **107) POP GO 60**
104) BURGLARY60
105) LARCENY 60

	POP GO 60	BURGLARY60	LARCENY 60
POP GO 60	1.00	________	________
BURGLARY60	________	1.00	________
LARCENY 60	________	________	1.00

a. What is the correlation between burglary (BURGLARY60) and population growth (POP GO 60) for the 1960s? ________

b. Is the correlation statistically significant? Yes No

c. Is this correlation between burglary and population growth for the 1960s stronger or weaker than the correlation for the 1920s? Stronger than 1920s

Weaker than 1920s

d. What is the correlation between larceny and population growth for the 1960s? ________

e. Is the correlation statistically significant? Yes No

f. Is this correlation between larceny and population growth for the 1960s stronger or weaker than the correlation for the 1920s? Stronger than 1920s

Weaker than 1920s

3. Fill in the correlation matrix below (be sure to indicate statistical significance):

Data File: **STATES**
Task: **Correlation**
➤ *Variables:* **108) POP GO 80**
112) BURGLARY82
113) LARCENY 82

	POP GO 80	BURGLARY82	LARCENY 82
POP GO 80	1.00	________	________
BURGLARY82	________	1.00	________
LARCENY 82	________	________	1.00

a. What is the correlation between burglary (BURGLARY82) and population growth (POP GO 80) for the 1980s? ________

b. Is the correlation statistically significant? Yes No

c. Is this correlation between burglary and population growth for the 1980s stronger or weaker than the correlation for the 1920s? Stronger than 1920s

Weaker than 1920s

d. What is the correlation between larceny (LARCENY 82) and population growth (POP GO 80) for the 1980s? ________

e. Is the correlation statistically significant? Yes No

f. Is this correlation between larceny and population growth for the 1980s stronger or weaker than the correlation for the 1920s? Stronger than 1920s

Weaker than 1920s

4. Now consider the data in your file for the most recent period—the 1990s. Fill in the correlation matrix below (be sure to indicate statistical significance):

Data File: **STATES**
Task: **Correlation**
➤ *Variables:* **33) POP GROWTH**
6) BURGLARY
7) LARCENY

	POP GROWTH	BURGLARY	LARCENY
POP GROWTH	1.00	________	________
BURGLARY	________	1.00	________
LARCENY	________	________	1.00

Answer True or False to the following items:

a. The correlation between burglary and population growth for the 1990s is significantly positive. T F

b. The correlation between larceny and population growth for the 1990s is not significant. T F

c. The correlation between burglary and population growth for the 1990s is stronger than the correlation for the 1920s. T F

d. The correlation between larceny and population growth for the 1990s is stronger than the correlation for the 1920s. T F

5. On the basis of the above correlations between property crime rates and population growth in the 1940s, 1950s, 1980s, and 1990s, indicate below which results support social disorganization theory (circle the appropriate response).
   a. only the correlation for burglary
   b. only the correlation for larceny
   c. neither correlation
   d. correlations for both crimes

EXPLORIT QUESTIONS: PART II

The following hypothesis is based on social disorganization theory: *States with a high percentage of the population that has not moved in the past 5 years will tend to have low rates of property crime.* Let's first examine historical data.

Data File: **STATES**
Task: **Correlation**
➤ *Variables:* **103) NOT MOVE40**
100) BURGLARY40
101) LARCENY 40
106) NO MOVE 60
104) BURGLARY60
105) LARCENY 60

6. On the basis of the correlations between NOT MOVE40 and property crime rates for the 1940s, indicate below which results support social disorganization theory (circle the appropriate response).
   a. only the correlation for burglary
   b. only the correlation for larceny
   c. neither correlation
   d. correlations for both crimes

7. On the basis of the correlations between NO MOVE60 and property crime rates for the 1960s, indicate below which results support social disorganization theory (circle the appropriate response).
   a. only the correlation for burglary
   b. only the correlation for larceny
   c. neither correlation
   d. correlations for both crimes

Let's test the same hypothesis (*States with a high percentage of the population born in that state will tend to have low rates of property crime)* using data from the 1990s.

Data File: **STATES**
Task: **Correlation**
➤ *Variables:* **30) %NO MOVE**
6) BURGLARY
7) LARCENY

8. On the basis of the correlations between %NO MOVE and property crime rates for the 1990s, indicate below which results support social disorganization theory (circle the appropriate response).
   a. only the correlation for burglary
   b. only the correlation for larceny
   c. neither correlation
   d. correlations for both crimes

ESSAY QUESTION

9. Social disorganization theorists argue that weak social control and high rates of crime are likely in communities with diverse populations. This is because people with different backgrounds have a difficult time joining together for collective purposes, such as fighting crime. In view of this argument, explain what kind of relationship you expect to see between the percentage of a state's population speaking a language other than English at home and property crime rates. Test this hypothesis by examining the correlations between (a) the percentage of a state's population speaking a language other than English [28) %NON-ENG] and the burglary rate [6) BURGLARY]; and (b) the percentage of a state's population speaking a language other than English [28) %NON-ENG] and the larceny rate [7) LARCENY].

   a. What is your hypothesis?

   b. Summarize your results in a brief paragraph.

   c. What are the implications of the results for social disorganization theory?

CHAPTER 9

ANOMIE, ROUTINE ACTIVITIES, AND ROBBERY RATES

Honesty is the best policy—when there is money in it.
MARK TWAIN[1]

Opportunity makes the thief.
TRADITIONAL APHORISM[2]

Tasks: Mapping, Scatterplot, Correlation
Data Files: STATES

The previous chapter introduced you to social disorganization theory, an influential structural explanation for crime that was originally developed at the University of Chicago during the early years of the 20th century. The Chicago School theorists focused on differences in the strength of social relationships across urban neighborhoods and the implications of these differences for rates of crime and other forms of social deviance. In the late 1930s, the sociologist Robert K. Merton published an article that inspired a somewhat different social structural approach to the study of crime: anomie theory.[3]

Merton was concerned with ways in which the basic features of American society—its culture and social structure—contribute to crime. Our culture places a very strong emphasis on the goal of monetary success. People are strongly encouraged to accumulate money and to acquire the "good things in life." Our culture also restricts the "means" through which people are supposed to pursue their goals. Some means are regarded as legitimate (e.g., working hard and saving your money), whereas other means are culturally disapproved of (e.g., forging checks to be able to take a nice vacation). However, the peculiar feature of American culture, according to Merton, is the differential emphasis on goals and means. Reaching the goals is what really matters, and how you get there is not nearly as important. As Vince Lombardi, the famous football coach of the Green Bay Packers once said, "winning isn't everything; it's the only thing." Merton referred to this cultural situation wherein the "means" of striving for goals have become relatively unimportant as a situation of **anomie**.

Why is American culture prone to anomie? Merton theorized that there is a basic contradiction between the distribution of opportunities in society and the culture. Everyone is exhorted to strive for

[1] Quoted from http://www.starlingtech.com/quotes/qsearch.cgi.

[2] Marcus Felson, *Crime and Everyday Life: Insight and Implications for Society* (Thousand Oaks, CA: Pine Forge Press, 1994), p. 17.

[3] Robert K. Merton, "Social Structure and Anomie," *American Sociological Review* 3: (1938) 672–682.

the goal of monetary success—the cultural goal is in this sense **universalistic**. At the same time, access to the legitimate means for success is unequal. Some people, because of their location in the social structure (especially those at the bottom of the social hierarchy), find it very difficult to succeed legitimately. Such persons may adapt to this dilemma by criminal innovation, that is, by substituting technically effective but illegal ways to achieve their goals. In short, according to Merton's formulation of anomie theory, the structural source of crime in American society is **blocked access** to the legitimate means of success.

In the 1970s, Lawrence Cohen and Marcus Felson proposed a very different social structural theory of crime: routine activities theory.[4] Cohen and Felson argued that there are three essential requisites for a successful crime. For a crime to occur, a **motivated offender** (someone who is potentially willing to violate the law) must come into contact with a **suitable target** (a person or piece of property attractive to the potential offender), in the **absence of a capable guardian** (someone who could intervene to thwart the criminal act). This claim about the requisites for a crime probably does not surprise you. Indeed, it seems like little more than common sense. However, Cohen and Felson went on to argue that the probability that these three requisites of crime will come together in the same place at the same time depends on normal, **routine activities**—the ways in which people go about earning their living and spending their leisure time. It follows, then, that the nature of routine activities will affect levels of crime and that changes in routine activities will produce changes in levels of crime.

Cohen and Felson illustrated their theoretical arguments with data on changing crime rates during the post–World War II period (1947–74) in the United States. This was a period of generally increasing crime rates. Paradoxically, it was also a time of relative economic prosperity. Many criminological theories (including anomie theory) would imply decreases, rather than increases, in crime over this period. In contrast with these theories, Cohen and Felson pointed to fundamental changes in routine activities that might have promoted higher levels of crime. For example, women entered the labor force in great numbers. This resulted in less guardianship at home—households were more likely to be unoccupied for extended periods of the day. In addition, the risk of coming into contact with motivated offenders increased for women as they left the relative security of the home and spent greater amounts of time in public places, places which are potentially dangerous. In addition, technological changes altered the attractiveness of property for theft. Advancements in the electronics industry, for example, led to very valuable, lightweight products (televisions, stereos) that could be easily transported by thieves. In other words, according to Cohen and Felson, the increased crime rates during the post–World War II period might have been the result of changes in routine activities that expanded the **opportunities** for crime. This rise in the level of crime could have occurred even in the absence of any change in the number of motivated offenders in the nation's population.

Let's use these criminological theories to help us explain interstate variation in robbery. **Robbery** is defined in the UCR as the taking away of anything of value by force or threat of force, or by putting the victim in fear. Robbery is a special type of offense in that in entails a threat both to property and to the person. Because of this latter component, robbery is regarded as a very serious offense, and it is classified by the FBI as a crime of violence. Take a look at the map for robbery rates.

---

[4] Lawrence E. Cohen and Marcus Felson, "Social Change and Crime Rate Trends: A Routine Activities Approach," *American Sociological Review* 44 (1979): 588–608.

➤ *Data File:* **STATES**
➤ *Task:* **Mapping**
➤ *Variable 1:* **4) ROBBERY**
➤ *View:* **Map**

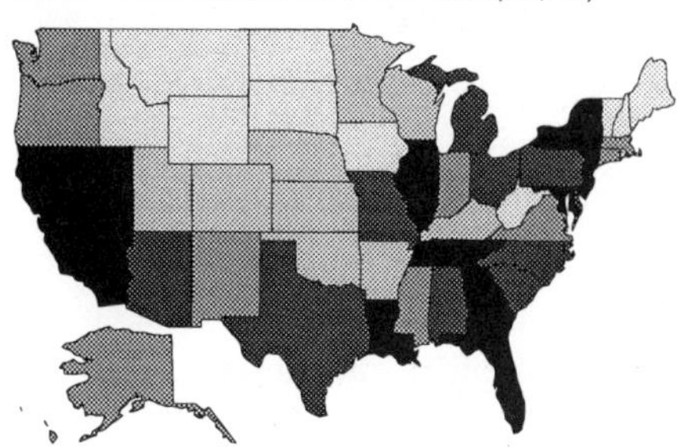

The map reveals a definite regional pattern. Relatively high rates are observed in the south and in the west (especially California), while comparatively low rates appear in the northern plains and in northern New England. What else might be distinctive about the regions with high and low robbery rates? Perhaps the most obvious factor to come to mind is climate. Southern regions (and California) are obviously warmer than the northern plains and New England.

To illustrate the regional differences in climate, select for comparison a variable indicating a warm winter: the average low temperature during the month of January.

Data File: **STATES**
Task: **Mapping**
Variable 1: **4) ROBBERY**
➤ *Variable 2:* **16) WARM WINTR**
➤ *Views:* **Map**

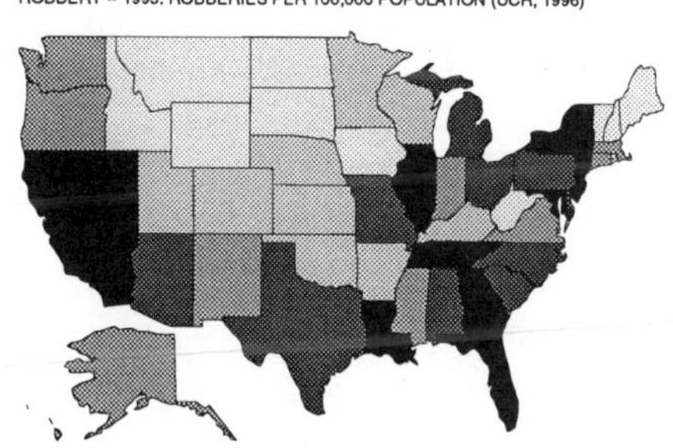

r = 0.488**

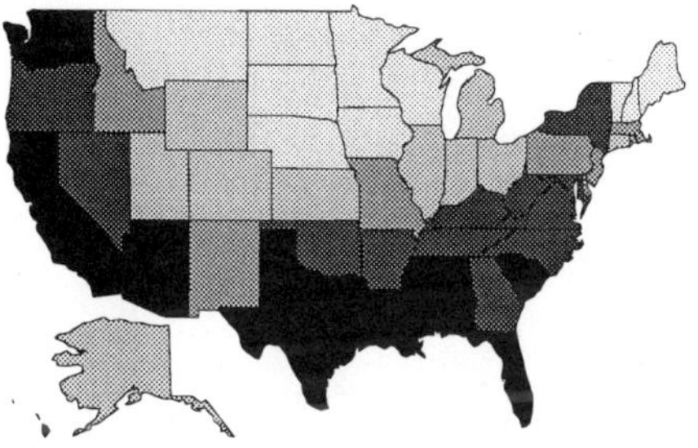

The two maps are fairly similar. Note also that the correlation coefficient is positive and statistically significant (r = 0.488**), indicating that states with warm winters tend to have higher robbery rates than those with colder winters. Routine activities theory offers a plausible explanation for this relationship. In areas with a mild climate, people are likely to spend more time in public places where contact with strangers is frequent and where the risk of victimization is greater. Persons in cold climates, on the other hand, limit their activities to a greater extent to relatively safe places, especially during the winter.

Consider another factor that might influence routine activities in a state: household composition. Persons who are unmarried are more likely than married persons to be out late at night alone, spending time in comparatively risky places, such as bars and nightclubs. On the other hand, married persons, especially those with children in the household, are more likely to confine their leisure activities to the comparatively safe home. The logic of routine activities theories thus implies a relationship between a state's household composition and its robbery rate.

You can look for such a relationship by examining the scatterplot between the robbery rate and the percentage of households comprised of married couples with their own children.

Data File: **STATES**
➤ *Task:* **Scatterplot**
➤ *Dependent Variable:* **4) ROBBERY**
➤ *Independent Variable:* **41) COU.CHILD**
➤ *View:* **Reg. Line**

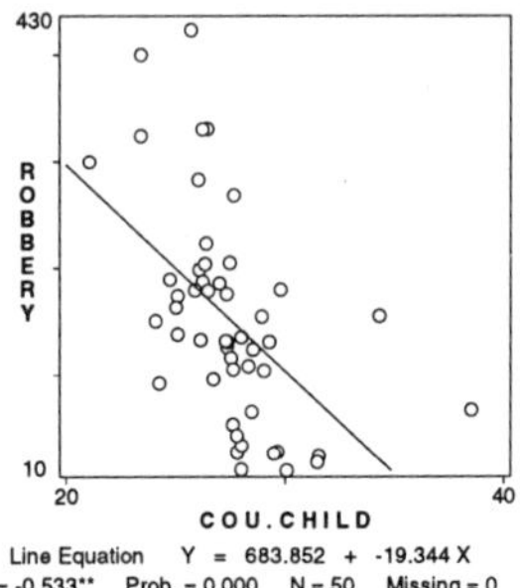

The scatterplot reveals a clear, inverse pattern: states with relatively large numbers of married couples with children tend to have relatively low robbery rates (r = –0.533**). This is exactly what we would expect to see on the basis of routine activities theory.

Now, let's identify some potential predictors of robbery rates using anomie theory. For most people in the United States, the principal legitimate "means" for attaining material success is a job. Anomie theory therefore suggests that failure to attain employment should be a potential motivating factor for robbery. It follows that unemployment rates for states should be positively related to robbery rates. We can test this hypothesis by examining another scatterplot.

Data File: **STATES**
Task: **Scatterplot**
Dependent Variable: **4) ROBBERY**
➤ *Independent Variable:* **48) UNEMPLMNT**
➤ *View:* **Reg. Line**

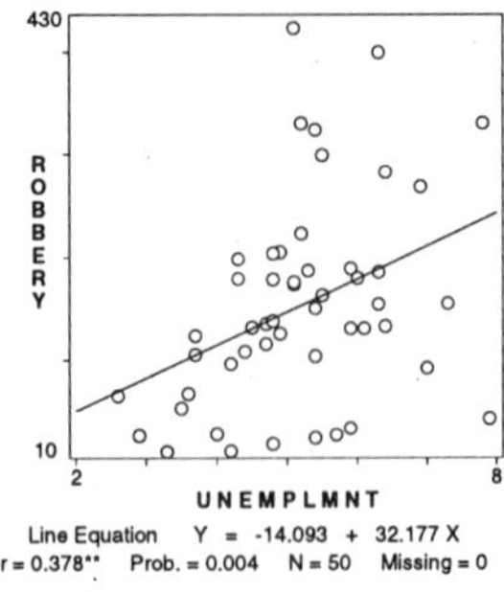

The data offer support for this hypothesis. The scatterplot reveals a positive relationship: states with high unemployment rates tend to have high robbery rates. The correlation coefficient (r = 0.378**) indicates a moderate, statistically significant association.

Finally, consider the variable of home ownership. Let's assume that owning a home is an important status symbol for many people in our society. Let's further assume that the frequency of home ownership is a rough indicator of the extent to which people have been able to meet the cultural goal of monetary success. Given these assumptions, we can once again use anomie theory to derive a prediction about robbery rates. States with high levels of home ownership should exhibit relatively low robbery rates.

Data File: **STATES**
Task: **Scatterplot**
Dependent Variable: **4) ROBBERY**
➤ *Independent Variable:* **57) OWN HOME**
➤ *View:* **Reg. Line**

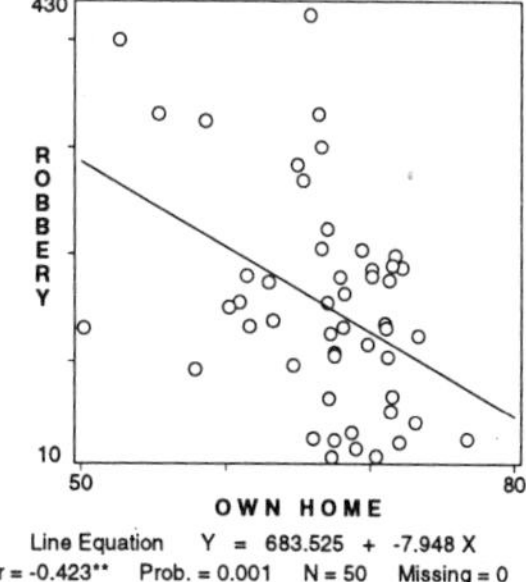

The scatterplot supports our hypothesis. As expected, the relationship between robbery rates and home ownership is inverse and moderately strong (r = –0.423**).

Much criminological research proceeds in the manner illustrated in this chapter and the previous two chapters. Researchers consider the logic of various theories, they derive hypotheses, and they evaluate these hypotheses with available evidence. The process might appear to be very simple and straightforward. However, it turns out that the results of hypothesis testing are not always clear-cut. Consider the example of home ownership and robbery rates. If we assume that home ownership reflects the realization of cultural success goals, then the observed inverse association between home ownership and robbery rates supports anomie theory. But home ownership might be interpreted differently. Perhaps widespread home ownership actually indicates a high degree of commitment to local communities and the existence of strong social ties among residents. If this is so, the observed inverse association between home ownership and robbery rates bears more directly on social disorganization theory than anomie theory.

Criminologists recognize that the process of hypothesis testing inevitably entails ambiguities. In part, this is the result of limitations in measurement. In addition, we must be careful when we interpret the relationship between any single independent variable and a dependent variable, because other variables might also be operating in ways that affect what we see (you will learn more about this in the section on multiple causes of crime that follows). Nevertheless, as we are able to confirm more and more hypotheses derived from a theory, we grow ever more confident about the credibility of that theory.

Now, it's your turn to derive and test some hypotheses using anomie theory and routine activities theory.

WORKSHEET	CHAPTER
NAME:	9
COURSE:	
DATE:	

REVIEW QUESTIONS

Based on the first part of this chapter, answer True or False to the following items:

According to Merton's formulation of anomie theory, anomie characterizes a culture where there is an exaggerated emphasis on cultural goals and a weak emphasis on the appropriate means to achieve these goals. T F

Anomie theory implies that crime rates will be high where there are structural obstacles to the legitimate means for success. T F

According to routine activities theory, the three essential requisites for a crime are weak ego controls, poor socialization, and lax enforcement of the laws. T F

In their application of routine activities theory, Lawrence Cohen and Marcus Felson propose that increases in crime rates during the post–World War II period in the United States were largely the result of the growth of a deprived underclass in the inner cities. T F

The offense of robbery is classified by the FBI as a violent rather than a property crime. T F

EXPLORIT QUESTIONS

1. Research indicates that single males are particularly likely to go out alone at night and to frequent bars and taverns.

   a. What is the most plausible relationship to expect between the percentage of single males in a state and that state's robbery rate, given the logic of routine activities theory? Positive Negative

Create the following scatterplot:

➤ *Data File:* **STATES**
➤ *Task:* **Scatterplot**
➤ *Dependent Variable:* **4) ROBBERY**
➤ *Independent Variable:* **40) %SNG.MEN**
➤ *View:* **Reg. Line**

b. What kind of relationship do you observe between the percentage of single males and the robbery rate? (circle one of the following)

1. positive
2. negative
3. none (not significant)

c. Does this finding support routine activities theory? Yes No

2. Assume that a high percentage employed in entertainment and recreation services in a state indicates a high volume of leisure activity occurring outside of the household.

a. What is the most plausible relationship to expect between the percentage employed in entertainment and recreation services in a state and that state's robbery rate, given the logic of routine activities theory? Positive Negative

Create the following scatterplot:

Data File: **STATES**
Task: **Scatterplot**
Dependent Variable: **4) ROBBERY**
➤ *Independent Variable:* **51) %ENTER.EST**
➤ *View:* **Reg. Line**

b. What kind of relationship do you observe between percentage employed in entertainment and recreation services and the robbery rate? (circle one of the following). [Note: Nevada is an outlier in the scatterplot. You might want to "find" this case by clicking it on the graph, remove it, and then look at the significance of the correlation to see if the results are similar.]

1. positive
2. negative
3. none (not significant)

c. Does this finding support routine activities theory? Yes No

3. Assume that a high percentage of females in the labor force indicates a high likelihood of interaction with strangers for women.

a. What is the most plausible relationship to expect between the percentage of females in the labor force in a state and that state's robbery rate, given the logic of routine activities theory? Positive Negative

Create the following scatterplot:

Data File: **STATES**
Task: **Scatterplot**
Dependent Variable: **4) ROBBERY**
➤ *Independent Variable:* **49) %FEM.LABOR**
➤ *View:* **Reg. Line**

b. What kind of relationship do you observe between the percentage of females in the labor force and the robbery rate? (circle one of the following)

1. positive
2. negative
3. none (not significant)

c. Does this finding support routine activities theory? Yes No

4. Assume that the frequent use of public transportation indicates a high likelihood of interaction with strangers.

a. What is the most plausible relationship to expect between the percentage who use public transportation in a state and that state's robbery rate, given the logic of routine activities theory? Positive Negative

Create the following scatterplot:

Data File: **STATES**
Task: **Scatterplot**
Dependent Variable: **4) ROBBERY**
➤ *Independent Variable:* **78) PUB.TRANS**
➤ *View:* **Reg. Line**

b. What kind of relationship do you observe between the use of public transportation and the robbery rate? (circle one of the following)

1. positive
2. negative
3. none (not significant)

c. Does this finding support routine activities theory? Yes No

5. Apply anomie theory to derive hypotheses about the likely relationship between robbery rates and each of the following socioeconomic characteristics of states:

a. States that have a high percentage of the population below the poverty line will have ________ (high/low) robbery rates. High Low

b. States that have a high number of vehicles available per household will have ________ (high/low) robbery rates. High Low

c. States that have a high percentage of families receiving aid to families with dependent children will have ________ (high/low) robbery rates. High Low

d. States that have a high percentage of people living in emergency shelters for the homeless will have ________ (high/low) robbery rates. High Low

e. States that have a high percentage of people 25 or over who have completed college degrees will have ________ (high/low) robbery rates. High Low

6. For each socioeconomic characteristic referred to in Question 5, record the observed correlation with robbery, and indicate whether the corresponding hypothesis derived from anomie theory is supported.

Data File: **STATES**
➤ *Task:* **Correlation**
➤ *Variables:* **4) ROBBERY**
44) %POOR
77) CARS/HOUSE
47) % AFDC
63) %HOMELESS
53) COL.DEGREE

a. Percentage below the poverty line (%POOR) r = ________

Hypothesis supported? Yes No

b. Cars per household (CARS/HOUSE) r = ________

Hypothesis supported? Yes No

c. Percentage of families receiving aid to families with dependent children (% AFDC) r = ________

Hypothesis supported? Yes No

d. Percentage living in emergency shelters for the homeless (%HOMELESS) r = ________

Hypothesis supported? Yes No

e. Percentage of those 25 or over who have completed a college degree (COL.DEGREE) r = ________

Hypothesis supported? Yes No

NAME

CHAPTER 9

ESSAY QUESTION

7. Consider two possible interpretations of the measure of per capita income of a state. (1) The measure indicates the extent to which the goal of monetary success has been realized. High values indicate widespread success; low values indicate limited success. (2) The measure indicates the attractiveness of potential victims of theft. High values indicate many lucrative targets; low values indicate few lucrative targets.

   a. Assume that the measure of per capita income indicates the extent to which the goal of monetary success has been realized. Indicate what kind of relationship you would predict between per capita income and robbery rates, applying anomie theory. Explain the rationale for your prediction.

   b. Assume that the measure of per capita income indicates the attractiveness of potential victims of theft. Now what kind of relationship would you predict between per capita income and robbery rates, applying routine activities theory? Explain the rationale for your prediction.

   c. Examine the scatterplot between robbery rates and per capita income. Report the observed correlation, and indicate which hypothesis—the one derived from anomie theory or the one derived from routine activities theory—is supported by this finding.

Data File: **STATES**
➤ *Task:* **Scatterplot**
➤ *Dependent Variable:* **4) ROBBERY**
➤ *Independent Variable:* **45) PER CAP$**
➤ *Display:* **Reg. Line**

Part III

MULTIPLE CAUSES OF CRIME AND DETECTING SPURIOUSNESS

CHAPTER 10

SUBSTANCE ABUSE AND CRIME

Straight, I don't have the guts to rape. I could fight a man but not that.

COMMENTS BY A SELF-CONFESSED RAPIST, ATTRIBUTING HIS CRIME TO THE CONSUMPTION OF EIGHT BEERS AND FOUR HITS OF ACID[1]

Tasks: Cross-tabulation
Data Files: NYS, COLLEGE

Substance abuse is a widely recognized social problem in the contemporary United States. Although the numbers vary in different surveys, appreciable percentages of respondents in public opinion polls typically cite substance abuse (especially drug use) as among the most important problems facing the nation.[2] Criminologists are interested in substance abuse for several reasons. The law prohibits the possession and sale of certain substances, thereby creating a special kind of criminal offense—substance violations. There were, in fact, 1,476,100 arrests for "drug abuse violations" in the United States in 1995. In addition, laws regulate the sale and use of certain substances that are not entirely prohibited, such as alcohol. Well over a million persons were arrested for "driving under the influence" in 1995; another half million were arrested for liquor law violations; and over 700,000 were arrested for drunkenness.[3] These figures refer to arrests and thus undoubtedly underestimate the actual volume of these behaviors. For example, most people who sometimes drink and drive do not get caught, and no one is arrested for drunkenness unless he or she goes out in public while drunk. Similarly, only a small fraction of those who use illegal drugs get arrested for it.

Perhaps the most important reason why criminologists study substance abuse is to explore its relationship with other crimes. Numerous theories have been put forth to explain why the use of drugs (includ-

---

[1] Quoted in Diana Scully and Joseph Marolla, "Convicted Rapists' Vocabulary of Motive: Excuses and Justifications," *Social Problems* 31 (1984): 530–544.

[2] Kathleen Maguire and Ann L. Pastore (eds.), *Sourcebook of Criminal Justice Statistics 1995*, U.S. Department of Justice, Bureau of Justice Statistics (Washington, DC: U.S. Government Printing Office, 1995), p.128.

[3] Kathleen Maguire and Ann L. Pastore (eds.), *Sourcebook of Criminal Justice Statistics 1996*, U.S. Department of Justice, Bureau of Justice Statistics (Washington, DC: U.S. Government Printing Office, 1997), p.368.

ing alcohol) might lead people to commit crimes.[4] Some theories point to a **disinhibition effect.** In other words, ingesting drugs might somehow break down the normal inhibitions that control behavior. Such disinhibition could be due to biological factors—the impact of drugs on brain functioning—or it could be due to widely shared expectations about how people act when "under the influence"—the common view that drugs and booze "loosen people up." Another explanation emphasizes economic factors. Drug users might have to commit crimes to get the money necessary to support their drug habits. Yet another explanation maintains that drug markets, which supply people with drugs, often stimulate violent conflicts aimed at "protecting turf." If so, we'd expect high rates of violent crime to go hand in hand with high levels of drug use.

A good deal of evidence has been reported indicating an association between drug use and criminal activity. Surveys reveal that a history of drug use is very common among prison inmates, and studies done in several cities report that a large proportion of arrestees test positive for drug use at the time of arrest.[5] However, criminologists disagree over the extent to which drug use actually *causes* crime. Part of the difficulty here is making sure that there isn't another factor which is related to both drug use and crime, thereby producing a statistical association between the two which is not a cause-and-effect relationship. Let's explore the nature of the drug-crime connection and techniques that researchers use to take into account other factors.

We might suspect that people who use one kind of drug, such as alcohol, are more likely to use other drugs than are those who abstain from drinking. Indeed, alcohol is sometimes viewed as a precursor to more serious drug use. The data file based on the National Youth Survey allows us to look at the relationship between having been drunk in public in the past year and having used marijuana in the past year.

➤ *Data File:* **NYS**
➤ *Task:* **Cross-tabulation**
➤ *Row Variable:* **13) USED MARIJ**
➤ *Column Variable:* **11) PUB DRUNK**
➤ *View:* **Tables**
➤ *Display:* **Column %**

USED MARIJ by PUB DRUNK
Cramer's V: 0.347 **

USED MARIJ	PUB DRUNK No	PUB DRUNK Yes	TOTAL
No	604	269	873
	77.9%	44.2%	63.1%
Yes	171	339	510
	22.1%	55.8%	36.9%
TOTAL	775	608	1383
	100.0%	100.0%	

The results indicate that these two forms of substance use are in fact related: More than half of those reporting having been drunk in public also report having used marijuana—55.8 percent, while less than a quarter of those reporting that they have not been drunk in public report marijuana use—22.1 percent. The asterisks for the V coefficient indicate that the relationship is statistically significant.

Thus far, you have been using Cramer's V simply to assess statistical significance. Now let's consider the interpretation of the coefficient itself. Cramer's V is a statistic used to describe the strength of the relationship in a cross-tabulation like this. The larger the value of V, the stronger is the relationship between variables in a table. A value of zero would indicate no relationship at all. V is conceptually

[4] See Howard B. Kaplan and Kelly R. Damphouse, "Self-Attitudes and Antisocial Personality as Moderators of the Drug Use–Violence Relationship," in *Drugs, Crime and Other Deviant Adaptations: Longitudinal Studies*, edited by Howard B. Kaplan (New York: Plenum Press, 1995), pp. 187–210.

[5] Larry J. Siegel, *Criminology* (Minneapolis/St. Paul: West, 1995), p. 422.

similar to "r," the correlation coefficient invented by Pearson which you have worked with in previous chapters. For a variety of technical reasons which need not concern you, correlations based on aggregate data (like the U.S. states) tend to be larger than those based on survey data. Thus, a V of this size (0.347) is regarded as large, indicating a very strong relationship. Of course, you also have significance to help you decide whether a hypothesis is supported or rejected by the data. Remember that one asterisk indicates that the relationship is statistically significant at the .05 level; two asterisks indicate that the relationship is statistically significant at the .01 level. As explained earlier, for most purposes in sociological analysis the .05 level of significance is considered to be sufficient. Thus, you should consider a V with *either* one or two asterisks as a significant coefficient. If V is followed by no asterisks, then you should conclude that the relationship is not significant.

Does marijuana use increase the likelihood that someone has been arrested? We might expect such a relationship for two reasons. Somebody might get arrested simply for using marijuana, although such arrests are rather rare nowadays. Additionally, marijuana users might be prone to commit other offenses for the reasons discussed earlier in this chapter.

Data File: **NYS**
Task: **Cross-tabulation**
➤ *Row Variable:* **16) ARRESTED**
➤ *Column Variable:* **13) USED MARIJ**
➤ *View:* **Tables**
➤ *Display:* **Column %**

ARRESTED by USED MARIJ
Cramer's V: 0.177 **

ARRESTED		USED MARIJ: No	Yes	TOTAL
No		837	439	1276
		95.9%	86.1%	92.3%
Yes		36	71	107
		4.1%	13.9%	7.7%
TOTAL		873	510	1383
		100.0%	100.0%	

The data from the NYS reveal that there is in fact an association between marijuana use and arrest: 13.9 percent of users report an arrest compared with 4.1 percent of non-users. The V statistic is 0.177 and is accompanied by two asterisks. Thus, the relationship is statistically significant.

Of course, people who get arrested are likely to differ from those who don't with respect to a wide range of characteristics, and not simply the use of marijuana. The sex of a person, for example, is a well-documented correlate of criminal offending. For many offenses, males exhibit higher levels of involvement than do females. Let's look at the relationship between sex and having been arrested.

Data File: **NYS**
Task: **Cross-tabulation**
Row Variable: **16) ARRESTED**
➤ *Column Variable:* **1) SEX**
➤ *View:* **Tables**
➤ *Display:* **Column %**

ARRESTED by SEX
Cramer's V: 0.156 **

ARRESTED		SEX: Male	Female	TOTAL
No		617	659	1276
		88.1%	96.5%	92.3%
Yes		83	24	107
		11.9%	3.5%	7.7%
TOTAL		700	683	1383
		100.0%	100.0%	

As you can see, the NYS data on arrests are consistent with the general pattern. Almost 12 percent of the male respondents report an arrest compared with 3.5 percent of females. Once again, V (0.156**) is highly significant.

What about the relationship between sex and marijuana use?

Data File: **NYS**
Task: **Cross-tabulation**
➤ Row Variable: **13) USED MARIJ**
➤ Column Variable: **1) SEX**
➤ View: **Tables**
➤ Display: **Column %**

USED MARIJ by SEX
Cramer's V: 0.114 **

USED MARIJ	SEX: Male	Female	TOTAL
No	404	469	873
	57.7%	68.7%	63.1%
Yes	296	214	510
	42.3%	31.3%	36.9%
TOTAL	700	683	1383
	100.0%	100.0%	

In the National Youth Survey, slightly over 42 percent of the males report marijuana use within the past year, while about 31 percent of females report marijuana use (V = 0.114**). This relationship is also significant.

Now, think about the implications of the tables we've just examined. We've discovered that males are more likely than females to use marijuana, and males are more likely than females to get arrested. This raises an important question about the observed relationship between marijuana use and arrests. Maybe the only reason that users are more likely than non-users to have been arrested is because users tend to be males, and males tend to get arrested. The relationship between marijuana use and getting arrested might therefore not be a cause-and-effect relationship at all. It may simply reflect the influence of sex. Social scientists refer to this kind of non-causal relationship between two variables as a **spurious relationship**. In other words, a spurious relationship is a non-causal statistical association that is due to the influence of some other factor.

Before proceeding any further with the analyses, let's reflect further on the notion of spuriousness. A common example of spuriousness used by instructors in research methods classes points to a relationship between ice cream sales and drownings: when ice cream sales are high so are the number of drownings. It would be silly to suggest that the eating of ice cream is causing people to drown. Instead, there is a third variable—temperature—that is causally related to both ice cream sales and drownings. Warm weather induces people to consume more ice cream and to go swimming, thereby increasing the risk of drowning.

How can we test to see if a relationship between two variables is a spurious one rather than a cause-and-effect relationship? Let's return to the example of marijuana use and arrest. We can confront the issue of spuriousness by rearranging our data so that sex is **statistically controlled**. What this means in practice is that we look at tables for males and females separately. Whatever relationship we see inside each of these tables cannot be due to sex differences, because the people in the respective tables do not vary on sex—one table is made up of all males, and the other is made up of all females. The fancy name for this procedure is **multivariate cross-tabulation**.

To conduct this kind of analysis with the ExplorIt CROSS-TABULATION task, you not only identify a row variable and a column variable, you also enter a control variable. In this instance select SEX as the control variable.

Data File:	**NYS**
Task:	**Cross-tabulation**
➤ *Row Variable:*	**16) ARRESTED**
➤ *Column Variable:*	**13) USED MARIJ**
➤ *Control Variable:*	**1) SEX**
➤ *View:*	**Tables: Males**
➤ *Display:*	**Column %**

ARRESTED by USED MARIJ
Controls: SEX: Male
Cramer's V: 0.178 **

ARRESTED		USED MARIJ No	Yes	TOTAL
	No	376	241	617
		93.1%	81.4%	88.1%
	Yes	28	55	83
		6.9%	18.6%	11.9%
	TOTAL	404	296	700
		100.0%	100.0%	

The option for selecting a control variable is located on the same screen you use to select other variables. For this example, select 1) SEX as a control variable and then click [OK] to continue as usual. Separate tables for males and females will now be shown for the 16) ARRESTED and 13) USED MARIJ cross-tabulation.

Your screen displays a table with the categories for ARRESTED in the rows and those for USED MARIJ in the columns. At first glance this table looks just like previous tables. However, near the top of the screen you will see this line: Controls: SEX: Male. This reminds you that SEX is the control variable and the table being displayed contains only males. You analyze this table just as you have previous ones, but remember that you are looking only at males. The results show that even when we examine males alone, marijuana users are still more likely to have been arrested than non-users—18.6 percent versus 6.9 percent. The V coefficient is 0.178 and is accompanied by two asterisks. Thus, the relationship between marijuana use and arrest is statistically significant for males.

Now look at the results for females.

Data File:	**NYS**
Task:	**Cross-tabulation**
Row Variable:	**16) ARRESTED**
Column Variable:	**13) USED MARIJ**
Control Variable:	**1) SEX**
➤ *View:*	**Tables: Females**
➤ *Display:*	**Column %**

ARRESTED by USED MARIJ
Controls: SEX: Female
Cramer's V: 0.145 **

ARRESTED		USED MARIJ No	Yes	TOTAL
	No	461	198	659
		98.3%	92.5%	96.5%
	Yes	8	16	24
		1.7%	7.5%	3.5%
	TOTAL	469	214	683
		100.0%	100.0%	

Click the appropriate button at the bottom of the task bar to look at the second (or "next") partial table for 1) SEX. [After you switch views, you can go back to the table for males by clicking the button at the bottom of the task bar for the prior screen.]

Similar to the pattern for males, female marijuana users are more likely to have been arrested than female non-users (7.5 percent vs. 1.7 percent), a difference which is statistically significant (check the V coefficient).

What we see is that even when we statistically control for sex by examining males and females separately, marijuana users are still more likely to have been arrested than non-users. These findings lead us to conclude that the relationship between marijuana use and getting arrested is not entirely due to sex. In other words, it does not appear to be spurious due to sex. As a practical rule of thumb, you can reject the hypothesis that a relationship is spurious if you still see a significant V coefficient when you look at tables separately for a control variable (such as in the "all male" and "all female" tables in this example).

Of course, there may be other factors that we have not yet taken into account that could give rise to a spurious relationship between marijuana use and getting arrested. Criminological researchers try to anticipate such factors and control them statistically in their analyses. As you can now appreciate, determining whether drug use is a cause of crime is no easy task!

Now, it's your turn to explore some relationships between drug use and crime.

WORKSHEET	CHAPTER
NAME:	10
COURSE:	
DATE:	

REVIEW QUESTIONS

Based on the first part of this chapter, answer True or False to the following items:

Surveys have revealed that a history of drug use is common among prison inmates.	T	F
Data from the National Youth Survey (NYS) indicate that there is no significant relationship between having been drunk in public and the use of marijuana.	T	F
The larger the value of the "V" coefficient (Cramer's V), the stronger the relationship between two variables.	T	F
A spurious relationship is a noncausal statistical association between two variables that is due to the influence of some other factor.	T	F
It is impossible to control statistically for an inborn characteristic such as a person's sex.	T	F

EXPLORIT QUESTIONS

In the introductory section of this chapter, you examined the seventh wave of the National Youth Survey, which is based on a nationally representative sample of young adults age 21–29. The following questions are based on the sample of first-year college students from a state university.

1. Fill in the appropriate percentages indicating the relationship between drinking and marijuana use.

➤ *Data File:* **COLLEGE**
➤ *Task:* **Cross-tabulation**
➤ *Row Variable:* **6) EV MARIJ**
➤ *Column Variable:* **4) DRINK**
➤ *View:* **Tables**
➤ *Display:* **Column %**

	DRINK NOW	ABSTAIN
YES	________%	________%
NO	________%	________%

a. Are drinkers or abstainers more likely to use marijuana? Drinkers Abstainers

b. Record the value of Cramer's V for this table. V = __________

c. Is the relationship between drinking and marijuana use statistically significant? Yes No

2. Let's look at the relationship between being picked up by the police and drinking.

Data File: **COLLEGE**
Task: **Cross-tabulation**
➤ *Row Variable:* **2) PICKED UP**
➤ *Column Variable:* **4) DRINK**
➤ *View:* **Tables**
➤ *Display:* **Column %**

Which statement is best supported by this cross-tabulation? (Circle the appropriate answer.)

a. Drinkers are significantly more likely to report having been picked up by the police than abstainers.

b. Abstainers are significantly more likely to report having been picked up by the police than drinkers.

c. There is no significant relationship between drinking and having been picked up by the police.

3. Now look at the relationship between being picked up by the police and smoking.

Data File: **COLLEGE**
Task: **Cross-tabulation**
Row Variable: **2) PICKED UP**
➤ *Column Variable:* **12) SMOKE**
➤ *View:* **Tables**
➤ *Display:* **Column %**

Which statement is best supported by this cross-tabulation? (Circle the appropriate answer.)

a. Smokers are significantly more likely to report having been picked up by the police than non-smokers.

b. Non-smokers are significantly more likely to report having been picked up by the police than smokers.

c. There is no significant relationship between smoking and having been picked up by the police.

4. What about the relationship between being picked up by the police and having a personal computer?

Data File: **COLLEGE**
Task: **Cross-tabulation**
Row Variable: **2) PICKED UP**
➤ *Column Variable:* **15) PC**
➤ *View:* **Tables**
➤ *Display:* **Column %**

Which statement is best supported by this cross-tabulation? (Circle the appropriate answer.)

a. PC possessors (hackers?) are significantly more likely to report having been picked up by the police than non-owners.

b. Non-owners of PCs are significantly more likely to report having been picked up by the police than PC possessors.

c. There is no significant relationship between having a PC and having been picked up by the police.

5. Consider the following hypothesis: *Males are more likely to be drinkers than are females.*

Data File: **COLLEGE**
Task: **Cross-tabulation**
➤ *Row Variable:* **4) DRINK**
➤ *Column Variable:* **26) GENDER**
➤ *View:* **Tables**
➤ *Display:* **Column %**

a. Is the pattern of percentages consistent with the hypothesis (i.e., are the high and low categories the ones that are predicted)? Yes No

b. Is the difference in percentages statistically significant? Yes No

c. Is the hypothesis supported? Yes No

6. Consider the following hypothesis: *Males are more likely to be marijuana users than are females.*

Data File: **COLLEGE**
Task: **Cross-tabulation**
➤ *Row Variable:* **6) EV MARIJ**
➤ *Column Variable:* **26) GENDER**
➤ *View:* **Tables**
➤ *Display:* **Column %**

a. Is the pattern of percentages consistent with the hypothesis (i.e., are the high and low categories the ones that are predicted)? Yes No

b. Is the difference in percentages statistically significant? Yes No

c. Is the hypothesis supported? Yes No

7. Consider the following hypothesis: *Males are more likely to have been picked up by police than are females.*

Data File: **COLLEGE**
Task: **Cross-tabulation**
➤ *Row Variable:* **2) PICKED UP**
➤ *Column Variable:* **26) GENDER**
➤ *View:* **Tables**
➤ *Display:* **Column %**

a. Is the pattern of percentages consistent with the hypothesis (i.e., are the high and low categories the ones that are predicted)? Yes No

b. Is the difference in percentages statistically significant? Yes No

c. Is the hypothesis supported? Yes No

NOTE: The following questions require you to examine the cross-tabulation between marijuana use and having been picked up by the police, controlling for gender.

Data File: **COLLEGE**
Task: **Cross-tabulation**
Row Variable: **2) PICKED UP**
➤ *Column Variable:* **6) EV MARIJ**
➤ *Control Variable:* **26) GENDER**
➤ *View:* **Tables**
➤ *Display:* **Column %**

The option for selecting a control variable is located on the same screen you use to select other variables. For this example, select 26) GENDER as a control variable and then click [OK] to continue as usual. Separate tables for males and females will now be shown for the 2) PICKED UP and 6) EV MARIJ cross-tabulation.

8. Consider the following hypothesis: *When females are examined separately, there is no significant relationship between marijuana use and having been picked up by the police.*

a. Report the percentage of female marijuana users picked up by the police. ________

b. Report the percentage of female marijuana non-users picked up by the police. ________

c. Is the difference in percentages statistically significant? Yes No

d. Is the hypothesis supported? Yes No

9. Click the appropriate button at the bottom of the task bar to look at the second (or "next") control table for males. Consider the following hypothesis: *When males are examined separately, there is no significant relationship between marijuana use and having been picked up by the police.*

   a. Report the percentage of male marijuana users picked up by the police. ______

   b. Report the percentage of male marijuana non-users picked up by the police. ______

   c. Is the difference in percentages statistically significant? Yes No

   d. Is the hypothesis supported? Yes No

10. On the basis of your answers to Questions 8 and 9, answer True or False to the following item:

    The relationship between marijuana use and having been picked up by the police is spurious due to the influence of gender. T F

ESSAY QUESTION

11. Use multivariate cross-tabulation with the COLLEGE sample to determine whether the relationship between marijuana use [6) EV MARIJ] and drinking [4) DRINK] is spurious due to the effect of gender (you examined the simple relationship between marijuana use and drinking in Question 1). Explain the basis of your conclusion with statistical evidence.

CHAPTER 11

VIOLENCE AND THE OLD WEST: AN INTRODUCTION TO REGRESSION

This is as good a day to die as any.

A REMARK MADE BY THE GUNSLINGER CHEROKEE BILL, CONDEMNED TO BE HANGED, AS HE STEPPED INTO THE COURTYARD AT FORT SMITH AND SAW THE GALLOWS, MARCH 17, 1896[1]

Tasks: Mapping, Correlation, Regression
Data Files: STATES

In the previous chapter, you examined cross-tabulations with control variables. That kind of procedure is a form of multivariate analysis—any analysis involving more than two variables at a time. In this chapter, you will learn another procedure for multivariate analysis called multiple regression. Multiple regression allows us to examine the joint or combined effects of several independent variables on a dependent variable. It also shows us the unique or net effects of independent variables, controlling for other factors. We will use regression techniques to explore the question: Was the Old West really violent?

Those of us who have seen a lot of western movies may find the answer to the question to be obvious—of course it was violent. After all, the western frontier offered unique opportunities for crime. As the criminological historian Werner Einstadter has observed, the vast expanse of the frontier provided "a geography conducive to flight." Wily offenders could ride away into the sunset one step ahead of the sheriff and posse. In addition, the settlers on the frontier had a "reverence for weapons."[2] Firearms were readily available, and people knew how to use them. This meant that the everyday conflicts of social life could easily lead to lethal outcomes.

However, in recent years some social historians have suggested that the "Wild West" was a myth created by dime novelists and sustained by Hollywood.[3] Indeed, such revisionism has found its way into the popular press. For example, the *New York Times* reported a while ago that the scale of homi-

---

1 Quoted from http://www.gunslinger.com/goldsby.html.

2 Werner J. Einstadter, "Robbery-Outlawry on the U.S. Frontier, 1860–1890," in *Violent Crime: Historical and Contemporary Issues*, edited by James A. Inciardi and Anne E. Pottieger (Beverly Hills, CA: Sage, 1978), pp. 23, 25.

3 For a discussion of the emergence of the Wild West in folklore, see James Inciardi, Alan A. Block, and Lyle A. Hallowell, *Historical Approaches to Crime: Research Strategies and Issues* (Beverly Hills, CA: Sage, 1977).

cides in modern America dwarfs that of the Old West: "In its busiest year, the Boot Hill cemetery in rough-and-tumble Dodge City, Kansas, welcomed only 20 gunfighters. In contrast, 2,245 persons were murdered in New York City in 1990."

Chapter 1 should have alerted you to the dangers of using raw numbers to make comparisons. Hence, before agreeing with the *Times'* editorialist that 20 dead gunfighters is a very small number, we would want to calculate a rate. Since Dodge City never had a population larger than 3,000, 25 dead gunfighters in one year would by themselves have constituted a homicide rate of 667 per 100,000, which is over 25 times higher than the rate for New York City in 1990 (26.9 per 100,000), and over 41 times higher than its rate in 1995 (16.1 per 100,000). Moreover, presumably some gunfighters who were shot down in Dodge City that year left funds insufficient to afford entombment in Boot Hill and thus were omitted from this count. Nor does this total include any ordinary, non-gunfighting citizens who may have been murdered that year. All-in-all, it's hard to imagine a contemporary place with a homicide rate as high as it must have been in Dodge City, if the figures on the burial of gunslingers is correct. In comparison, modern American cities seem relatively peaceful, as these 1995 homicide rates per 100,000 suggest:

New Orleans	74.5
Washington, DC	65.0
Detroit	47.6
Atlanta	45.5
Miami	29.1
Los Angeles	24.5
Phoenix	19.7
Houston	18.2
New York	16.1
San Francisco	13.4
San Diego	7.9

Now that you have been alerted to the need to use rates, not raw numbers, for comparisons, let us return to our question: Just how violent was the western frontier in the 19th century? To get started, the first thing we have to do is to find a way of identifying, or locating, the frontier.

➤ *Data File:* **STATES**
➤ *Task:* **Mapping**
➤ *Variable 1:* **90) OLD WEST18**
➤ *View:* **Map**

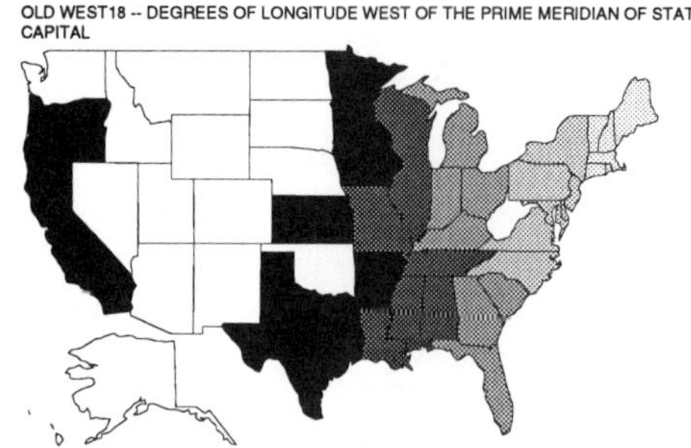

The map on your screen identifies the frontier areas in 1860 simply as a function of how far west they are (the location of the entire state is set at the position of the state's capital). A number of states are blank because they were not yet states in 1860. West Virginia is blank because it was not created as a state separate from Virginia until after the Civil War.

Another way of thinking about the frontier is in terms of the opening up of new territories for settlement. The variable 91) NEWNESS 18 is based on the year a state was admitted to the Union, minus 1787—the year the first states entered the Union. Let's look at the map for this variable.

Data File: **STATES**
Task: **Mapping**
➤ *Variable 1:* **91) NEWNESS 18**
➤ *View:* **Map**

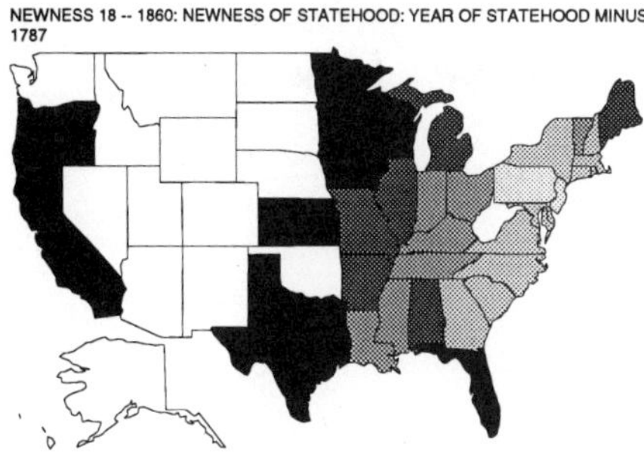

You see a pattern fairly similar to that in the previous map. Now consider the rankings on NEWNESS 18.

Data File: **STATES**
Task: **Mapping**
Variable 1: **91) NEWNESS 18**
➤ *View:* **List: Rank**

NEWNESS 18: 1860: Newness of statehood: year of state hood minus 1787

RANK	CASE NAME	VALUE
1	Kansas	74
2	Oregon	72
3	Minnesota	71
4	California	63
5	Wisconsin	61
6	Iowa	59
7	Florida	58
7	Texas	58
9	Michigan	50
10	Arkansas	49

Kansas scores 74 as the newest state. If you scroll down to the bottom, you see that Pennsylvania and New Jersey score zero on newness, being among the oldest states.

Frontiers are also typically boom areas where rapid population growth is taking place.

Data File: **STATES**
Task: **Mapping**
➤ *Variable 1:* **89) POP GO1860**
➤ *View:* **Map**

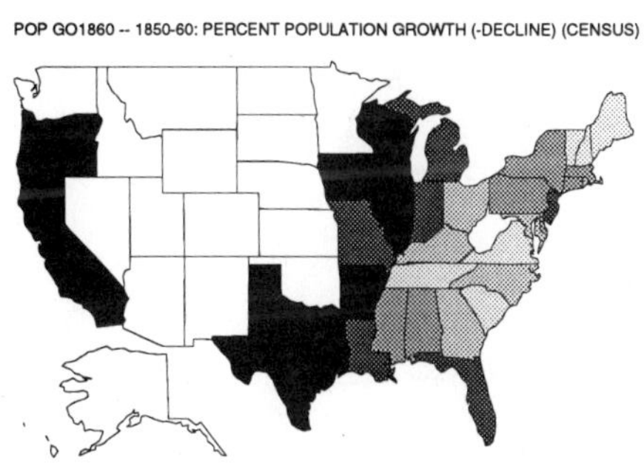

Not surprisingly, then, the map for a measure of percent population growth over the previous decade (1850–1860) resembles the other two maps. The fastest growing states were western. Consider the rankings of states.

Data File: **STATES**
Task: **Mapping**
Variable 1: **89) POP GO1860**
➤ *View:* **List: Rank**

POP GO1860: 1850–60: Percent population growth (-decline)

RANK	CASE NAME	VALUE
1	California	310.4
2	Oregon	294.7
3	Iowa	251.1
4	Texas	184.2
5	Wisconsin	154.1
6	Arkansas	107.5
7	Illinois	101.2
8	Michigan	88.4
9	Missouri	73.3
10	Florida	60.6

California ranks at the top, with an increase in population of 310.4 percent. Oregon is close behind. Vermont hardly grew at all—0.3 percent—and New Hampshire wasn't growing much faster (2.5 percent).

Now that we have found the frontier in 1860, let's see how violent it was. Where were homicide rates highest?

Data File: **STATES**
Task: **Mapping**
➤ *Variable 1:* **86) HOMICIDE18**
➤ *View:* **Map**

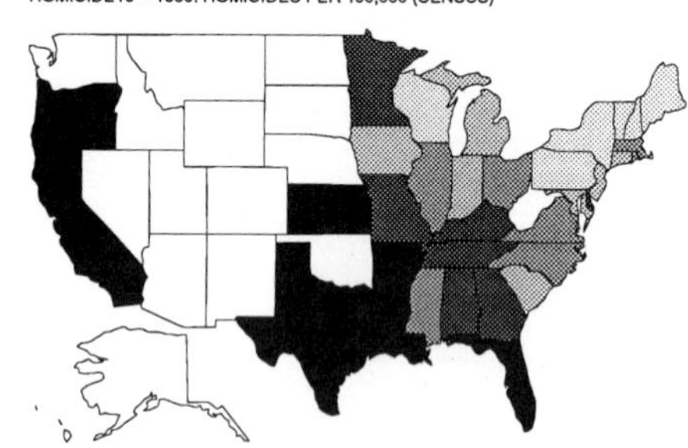

The map for homicide shows the expected spatial patterning. Again, let's look at specific state rankings.

Data File: **STATES**
Task: **Mapping**
Variable 1: **86) HOMICIDE18**
➤ *View:* **List: Rank**

HOMICIDE18: 1860: Homicides per 100,000

RANK	CASE NAME	VALUE
1	Texas	20.03
2	California	19.74
3	Kansas	14.92
4	Oregon	13.34
5	Louisiana	6.92
6	Arkansas	6.43
7	Florida	6.41
8	Kentucky	4.67
9	Missouri	4.06
10	Georgia	3.69

Texas ranks highest, with a homicide rate of 20.03 per 100,000 population. California is second with a rate of 19.74. In contrast, in 1860 many states had homicide rates less than 2 per 100,000. It is clear that in terms of homicide rates, the frontier areas were far more violent than the rest of the nation.

How do the rates in 1860 compare with those for recent years? Before making such a comparison, it's important to know how these earlier figures were collected. At the time, the federal government did not receive crime statistics from local law enforcement agencies (there were no Uniform Crime Reports), nor did it receive data on causes of death from local coroners' reports. Beginning in 1850, the census-takers asked at each household whether anyone in that household had died in the past year, and if so, what was the cause of death. Eventually it was demonstrated that mortality statistics gained in this way greatly underreported the number of deaths and were subject to errors as to cause because survivors were sometimes mistaken. Moreover, many survivors didn't truly know what had been the cause of death—often the attending physician, when there was one, didn't know either.

Of course, such problems are minimized for violent deaths. Nevertheless, state rates of deaths due to homicide based on census interviews are no doubt far lower than the true rates, if for no other reason than victims who left no surviving household had no one to report their deaths to the census-takers. Presumably, homicide victims would have been overselected from among the ranks of single, male drifters who populate the saloon scenes in cowboy movies. Therefore, the underreporting of homicides would have been greatest on the frontiers, where men like this tended to congregate.

Keeping in mind that the 1860 data undoubtedly underestimate homicide rates, let's compare selected results with those for 1995.

Data File: **STATES**
Task: **Mapping**
➤ *Variable 1:* **2) HOMICIDE**
➤ *View:* **List: Rank**

HOMICIDE: 1995: Criminal homicides per 100,000 population

RANK	CASE NAME	VALUE
1	Louisiana	17.0
2	Mississippi	12.9
3	Oklahoma	12.2
4	Maryland	11.8
5	Alabama	11.2
5	California	11.2
7	Nevada	10.7
8	Tennessee	10.6
9	Arizona	10.4
9	Arkansas	10.4

Louisiana ranked highest with a rate of 17.0, followed by Mississippi, with a rate of 12.9. As was true in 1860, the northern New England states had relatively low rates. When we compare the rates for 1860 and 1995, we find that the states with the highest homicide rates in 1860 had higher rates than the highest states in 1995, but the differences are rather small. Does that mean that the Old West wasn't so wild after all? Not necessarily. For one thing, the modern rates are far more complete—very few homicides today go unreported to the police and their reports to the FBI are checked carefully. A second factor has to do with what people in the Wild West were willing to call murder.

In addition to collecting information about deaths caused by homicide, the census-takers recorded the number of deaths from "accidental" gunshot wounds. If the data adequately reflect underlying social reality, the two ought to be very highly correlated on the grounds that where there are lots of guns, lots of people get murdered and lots of others get shot accidentally—in fact, along the frontiers some people probably got shot accidentally on purpose! You can compare maps to check for similar spatial patterns for these two variables.

Data File: **STATES**
Task: **Mapping**
➤ *Variable 1:* **86) HOMICIDE18**
➤ *Variable 2:* **87) GUN KILL18**
➤ *Views:* **Map**

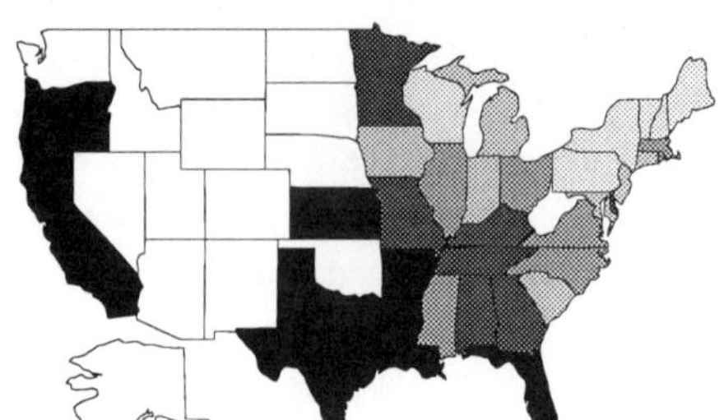

r = 0.858**

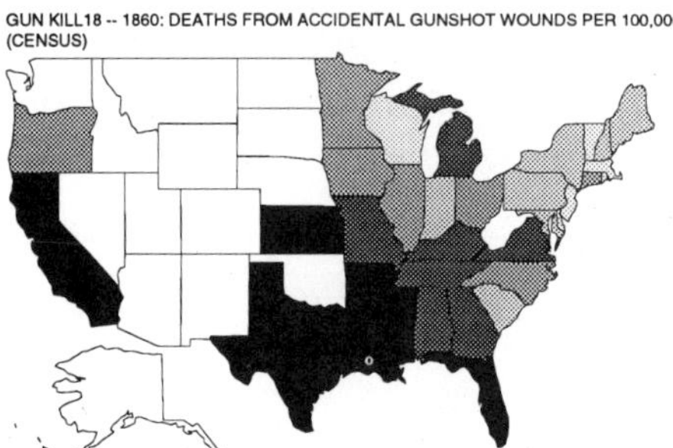

The maps for homicide rates and deaths from accidental gunshot wounds are in fact very similar, and the correlation between these two variables is strongly positive: r = 0.858**.

Data File: **STATES**
Task: **Mapping**
Variable 1: **86) HOMICIDE18**
Variable 2: **87) GUN KILL18**
➤ *Views:* **List: Rank**

HOMICIDE18: 1860: Homicides per 100,000

RANK	CASE NAME	VALUE
1	Texas	20.03
2	California	19.74
3	Kansas	14.92
4	Oregon	13.34
5	Louisiana	6.92

GUN KILL18: 1860: Deaths from accidental gunshot wounds per 100,000

RANK	CASE NAME	VALUE
1	California	11.32
2	Texas	8.44
3	Kansas	8.40
4	Louisiana	6.64
5	Florida	5.70

Looking at the ranking for accidental gunshot wounds, you see that California is highest—11.32 per 100,000. Texas is next highest with 8.44. Kansas is third and Louisiana is fourth. In contrast, the rankings are very low in the Northeast. If we assume that most of these deaths were not really accidents, and if we add these deaths to the deaths reported as homicides, then the homicide rates for the Old West would be very high indeed: California's rate would be 31.1 and Texas' rate would be 28.5—more than double their rates for 1995.

Now, let's use the CORRELATION task to test the following hypothesis: In 1860, homicide rates were highest on the western frontier.

Data File: **STATES**

➤ *Task:* **Correlation**

➤ *Variables:* **86) HOMICIDE18**
90) OLD WEST18
91) NEWNESS 18
89) POP GO1860

Correlation Coefficients
PAIRWISE deletion (1-tailed test) Significance Levels: ** =.01, * =.05

	HOMICIDE18	OLD WEST18	NEWNESS 18	POP GO1860
HOMICIDE18	1.000 (34)	0.769 ** (34)	0.599 ** (34)	0.694 ** (32)
OLD WEST18	0.769 ** (34)	1.000 (34)	0.757 ** (34)	0.861 ** (32)
NEWNESS 18	0.599 ** (34)	0.757 ** (34)	1.000 (34)	0.821 ** (32)
POP GO1860	0.694 ** (32)	0.861 ** (32)	0.821 ** (32)	1.000 (32)

The correlations between homicide rates and the three indicators of frontier are all strongly positive, supporting the hypothesis.

Recall, however, that correlation does not necessarily demonstrate causation—variables may be correlated without one being the cause of the other. It would be illogical to suggest, for example, that the correlation between POP GO1860 and NEWNESS 18 reflects cause-and-effect. States aren't newer because their populations are growing faster.

However, the hypothesis we just tested does imply causation (as have most of the hypotheses we have tested thus far in this book). That is, we aren't interested in "accidental" correlations between measures of the Old West and homicide. Instead, we think that social and cultural conditions typical of the Old West *caused* high homicide rates. The finding of the predicted correlations between the indicators of frontier and homicide does not prove a cause-and-effect relationship. But, had we failed to find these correlations, we would have become very skeptical about any causal connection.

Thus far we have used correlations to tell us the degree to which two variables are related to one another. For example, we can see that population growth is highly correlated with the homicide rate—where the population grew more rapidly, the homicide rates were higher. But what if we wanted to see the effect of two independent variables on a third variable, say, the **combined effects** of population growth and westernness on homicide? We know that each of these variables is highly correlated with homicide and with one another. To sort out these correlations, social scientists use a technique called **multiple regression**.

Multiple regression is a technique for modeling a dependent variable using two or more independent variables. As in other analyses in this workbook, the dependent variable is the variable we wish to explain, the one we think of as being caused by other things. In this case the dependent variable is the homicide rate. The independent variables are those factors that we regard as potentially causing the dependent variable. In this example, the independent variables are population growth (POP GO1860) and westernness (OLD WEST18). Here is the ExplorIt guide for this example of regression:

Data File: **STATES**
➤ *Task:* **Regression**
➤ *Dependent Variable:* **86) HOMICIDE18**
➤ *Independent Variables:* **89) POP GO1860**
90) OLD WEST18
➤ *View:* **Graph**

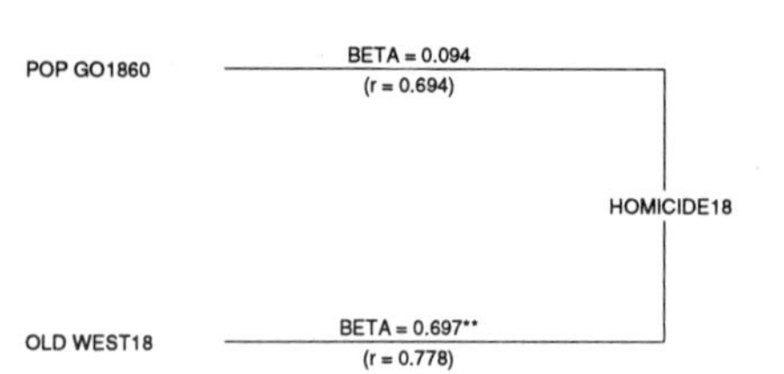

You see on your screen a graph of the regression results. In the upper right-hand corner, the screen reads: **Multiple R-Squared** = 0.608**. Multiple R-Squared is a coefficient which measures the **combined effects** of the two independent variables on the dependent variable. This coefficient is often interpreted as a percentage, that is, as the percentage of variance explained. In plain English this means that the two independent variables together account for about 61 percent of the variation in homicide rates across states in 1860. Put another way, if all states had grown by the same percentage from 1850 and 1860, and if all of them had been equally western, there would have been 61 percent less variation in their homicide rates.

That's not all that we can see in the graph. Beneath each of the horizontal lines is the value of r, which is Pearson's correlation coefficient. You are already familiar with this statistic from the scatterplot and correlation procedures. Above each line is the word **beta**, followed by a numerical value. This number indicates the **independent effect** of each independent variable on the dependent variable, adjusting for the other independent variable. Just as with correlation coefficients, the statistical significance of the beta is indicated by asterisks. One asterisk indicates significance at the .05 level; two asterisks, significance at the .01 level.

Because both independent variables in this analysis are highly correlated, they overlap to a considerable extent and measure the same thing—in this case the location of the frontier. What regression does is to sort out the independent contributions of these two variables. And what we discover is that population growth influences homicide rates *only* because it is highly correlated with geography—growth tended to be high in the West. But, with the effects of the West removed, growth is not correlated with variations in homicide. We know this because the beta for population growth is tiny (0.094) and not statistically significant (no asterisks follow the value for beta). On the other hand, the beta for Old West is a huge 0.697**. Two asterisks follow this beta, indicating that it is statistically significant at the .01 level.

Let's try another one. Once again, select homicide rates as the dependent variable, but select the newness of the state and westernness as the independent variables.

Data File:	**STATES**
Task:	**Regression**
Dependent Variable:	**86) HOMICIDE18**
➤ *Independent Variables:*	**91) NEWNESS 18**
	90) OLD WEST18
➤ *View:*	**Graph**

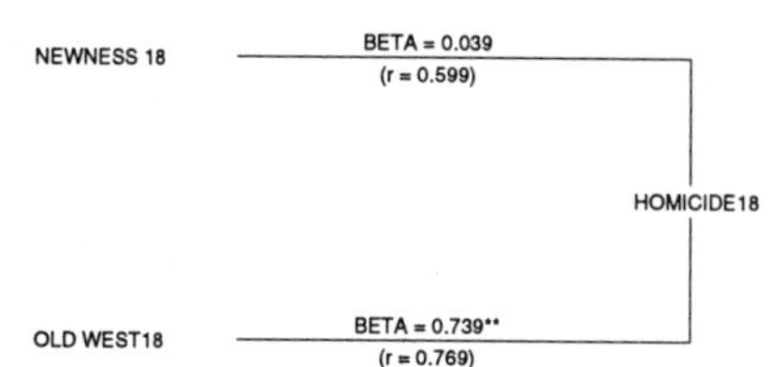

We find once again that the whole effect on homicide is caused by the westernness variable. It has a beta of 0.739** and is significant at the .01 level. The newness variable has no appreciable independent effect. The beta is very small (0.039) and is not significant.

Now, let's see what happens if we use all three of these independent variables at one time.

Data File:	**STATES**
Task:	**Regression**
Dependent Variable:	**86) HOMICIDE18**
➤ *Independent Variables:*	**89) POP GO1860**
	91) NEWNESS 18
	90) OLD WEST18
➤ *View:*	**Graph**

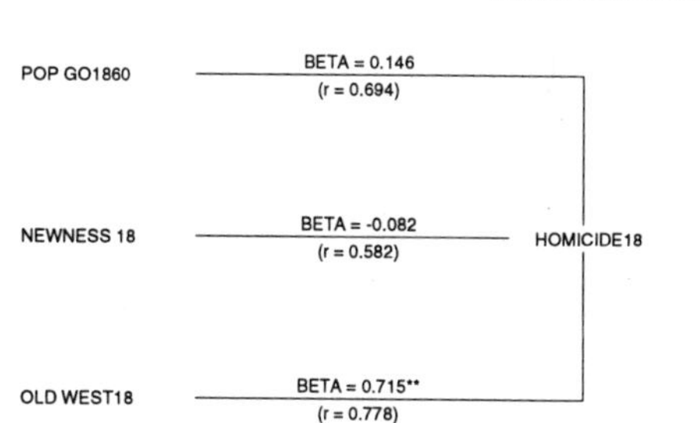

These results confirm what was found in the previous analyses. Westernness accounts for all of the effect on homicide rates. It yields the only significant beta, indicating that this variable is the only one with an appreciable independent effect.

So, now you know that homicide rates were strongly related to geography in 1860: social and cultural conditions associated with western location were conducive to lethal violence. And you know how to use regression analysis to discover the joint, or combined, effects of several independent variables (look at the Multiple R-Squared), as well as their individual or net effects (check the beta coefficient). In the following worksheets, you can begin to explore why the West was so violent.

WORKSHEET	CHAPTER
NAME:	11
COURSE:	
DATE:	

REVIEW QUESTIONS

Based on the first part of this chapter, answer True or False to the following items:

According to the data on states for 1860, death rates from accidental gunshot wounds are highly correlated with homicide rates. T F

As a result of immigration from Europe, eastern states exhibited the highest levels of population growth in 1860. T F

The homicide rates of the highest ranked states in 1860, as recorded by census-takers, are slightly higher than the homicide rates for the highest ranked states in 1995 as recorded in the FBI's Uniform Crime Reports. T F

Multiple R-squared is a measure of the combined (or joint) effect of independent variables on a dependent variable in a regression analysis. T F

A large beta coefficient in a regression analysis indicates that a variable has no independent effect on a dependent variable. T F

EXPLORIT QUESTIONS: PART I

The following ExplorIt questions involve testing hypotheses with correlation and regression analysis. Be sure to look at both the signs of relationships (positive and negative) and their significance when determining whether or not hypotheses have been supported (use the .05 level of statistical significance).

I. Use the CORRELATION task with the following variables to answer the next four questions about states in 1860.

➤ *Data File:* **STATES**
➤ *Task:* **Correlation**
➤ *Variables:* **86) HOMICIDE18**
88) ALC.DIE 18
92) CHURCHED18
90) OLD WEST18

1. The hypothesis is: *States with high rates of alcohol deaths will have high rates of homicide.*

   a. Record the correlation between alcohol deaths (ALC.DIE18) and homicide (HOMICIDE18). r = ________

   b. Is the correlation statistically significant? Yes No

   c. Is the hypothesis supported? Yes No

2. The hypothesis is: *States with high rates of religious adherents will have low rates of homicide.*

   a. Record the correlation between religious adherents (CHURCHED18) and homicide (HOMICIDE18). r = ________

   b. Is the correlation statistically significant? Yes No

   c. Is the hypothesis supported? Yes No

3. The hypothesis is: *States with high rates of alcohol deaths will tend to be located in western territories.*

   a. Record the correlation between alcohol deaths (ALC.DIE18) and westernness (OLD WEST18). r = ________

   b. Is the correlation statistically significant? Yes No

   c. Is the hypothesis supported? Yes No

4. The hypothesis is: *States with low rates of religious adherents will tend to be located in western territories.*

   a. Record the correlation between religious adherents (CHURCHED18) and western location (OLD WEST18). r = ________

   b. Is the correlation statistically significant? Yes No

   c. Is the hypothesis supported? Yes No

II. Use the REGRESSION task with the following variables to answer the next three questions about states in 1860.

Data File: **STATES**
➤ *Task:* **Regression**
➤ *Dependent Variable:* **86) HOMICIDE18**
➤ *Independent Variables:* **88) ALC.DIE18**
92) CHURCHED18
90) OLD WEST18
➤ *View* **Graph**

5. The hypothesis is: *When included in a regression with religious adherents and westernness, deaths due to alcohol will have an independent, positive effect on homicide.*

   a. Record the beta for alcohol deaths (ALC.DIE18) beta = ________

   b. Is the beta statistically significant? Yes No

   c. Is the hypothesis supported? Yes No

6. The hypothesis is: *When included in a regression with alcohol deaths and westernness, religious adherents will have an independent, negative effect on homicide.*

   a. Record the beta for religious adherents (CHURCHED18). beta = ________

   b. Is the beta statistically significant? Yes No

   c. Is the hypothesis supported? Yes No

7. The hypothesis is: *When included in a regression with alcohol deaths and religious adherents, westernness will have an independent, positive effect on homicide.*

   a. Record the beta for westernness (OLD WEST18). beta = ________

   b. Is the beta statistically significant? Yes No

   c. Is the hypothesis supported? Yes No

EXPLORIT QUESTIONS: PART II

States of the Old West were characterized by a distinctive economy based on herding and ranching. Some scholars have suggested that this type of economy is conducive to violent cultural values and lifestyles.[4] In the exercise below, you can assess whether an indicator of a herding and ranching economy (livestock per capita), along with a measure of the sex composition of the population, helps account for the relationship between western location and criminal violence in the 1860s.

I. Use the CORRELATION task with the following variables to answer the next four questions about states in 1860.

Data File: **STATES**
➤ *Task:* **Correlation**
➤ *Variables:* **86) HOMICIDE18**
93) S.RATIO 18
94) HERDS PC18
90) OLD WEST18

8. The hypothesis is: *States with an excess of men will have high rates of homicide.*

   a. Record the correlation between an excess of men (S.RATIO 18) and homicide (HOMICIDE18). r = __________

   b. Is the correlation statistically significant? Yes No

   c. Is the hypothesis supported? Yes No

9. The hypothesis is: *States with lots of livestock will have high rates of homicide.*

   a. Record the correlation between amount of livestock (HERDS PC18) and homicide (HOMICIDE18). r = __________

   b. Is the correlation statistically significant? Yes No

   c. Is the hypothesis supported? Yes No

10. The hypothesis is: *States with an excess of men will tend to be located in the western territories.*

   a. Record the correlation between an excess of men (S.RATIO 18) and westerness (OLD WEST18). r = __________

   b. Is the correlation statistically significant? Yes No

   c. Is the hypothesis supported? Yes No

[4] Richard E. Nisbett and Dov Cohen, *The Culture of Honor: The Psychology of Violence in the South* (Boulder, CO: Westview Press, 1996).

NAME ______________________ **CHAPTER 11**

11. The hypothesis is: *States with lots of livestock will tend to be located in western territories.*

   a. Record the correlation between the amount of livestock (HERDS PC18) and western location (OLD WEST18). beta = ________

   b. Is the correlation statistically significant? Yes No

   c. Is the hypothesis supported? Yes No

II. Use the REGRESSION task to answer the next three questions.

Data File:	**STATES**
➤ *Task:*	**Regression**
➤ *Dependent Variable:*	**86) HOMICIDE18**
➤ *Independent Variables:*	**93) S.RATIO 18**
	94) HERDS PC18
	90) OLD WEST18
➤ *View*	**Graph**

12. The hypothesis is: *When included in a regression with the amount of livestock and westernness, the measure of an excess of men will have an independent, positive effect on homicide.*

   a. Record the beta for an excess of men (S.RATIO 18). beta = ________

   b. Is the beta statistically significant? Yes No

   c. Is the hypothesis supported? Yes No

13. The hypothesis is: *When included in a regression with the measure of an excess of men and westernness, the amount of livestock will have an independent, positive effect on homicide.*

   a. Record the beta for amount of livestock (HERDS PC18). beta = ________

   b. Is the beta statistically significant? Yes No

   c. Is the hypothesis supported? Yes No

14. The hypothesis is: *When included in a regression with the measure of an excess of men and amount of livestock, westernness will no longer have an independent effect on homicide.*

   a. Record the beta for westernness (OLD WEST18). beta = ________

   b. Is the beta statistically significant? Yes No

   c. Is the hypothesis supported? Yes No

ESSAY QUESTION

15. The results of your research reveal certain factors that do not appear to explain why the Old West was violent, and certain factors that do help explain why the Old West was violent. Identify both kinds of factors, and explain how you know that a given factor helps or does not help explain levels of violence. In what ways are the movies about why the Old West was violent correct or incorrect? Be sure to include statistical evidence throughout your essay to support your conclusions.

CHAPTER 12

"MASS MEDIA" CRIMINOLOGY: DETECTING SPURIOUSNESS USING REGRESSION

Tasks: Mapping, Scatterplot, Correlation, Regression
Data Files: STATES

In recent years, the news media have begun to report a lot of social science research. Some of the stories are accurate, and some of the research is well done. But, it often seems that the more questionable the quality of the research, or the more silly the conclusions drawn from it, the more likely it is to be selected for press coverage. Take a look at the following hypothetical news story:

Hunting Reduces Homicide

Combined Wired Services. Contrary to the popular belief that hunting makes people indifferent to bloodshed, a new study has found that hunting seems to make people less likely to commit criminal homicides.

States where a larger percentage of the population goes hunting have lower homicide rates.

The author of the study, Dr. Preema Ture, claims that his findings are consistent with the principle of "displacement" popularized in Sigmund Freud's psychoanalytic theory. According to Freud, aggression is sometimes redirected away from its original source to an alternative target. Dr. Ture draws on psychoanalytic theory to explain the relationship between hunting and homicides. "Apparently, hunting lets people vent their rage on animals, thus saving the lives of human beings," Dr. Ture writes in his report.

In this last chapter, you will apply the technique of multiple regression to guard against foolish research findings. Recall from the previous chapter that multiple regression enables the researcher to identify the net effect of an independent variable on a dependent variable, taking into account the influence of other independent variables. This proves to be extremely valuable for detecting **spuriousness**. As explained in Chapter 10, a spurious relationship is one where two variables are associated but not because one causes the other. Instead, the association comes about because a third variable affects both of these variables. The results of multiple regression can help us distinguish between spurious associations and genuine causal relationships.

Let's begin our inquiry by considering the relationship between homicide rates and the popularity of hunting, a relationship referred to in the fake newspaper story printed above.

➤ *Data File:* **STATES**
➤ *Task:* **Scatterplot**
➤ *Dependent Variable:* **2) HOMICIDE**
➤ *Independent Variable:* **83) HUNTING**
➤ *View:* **Reg. Line**

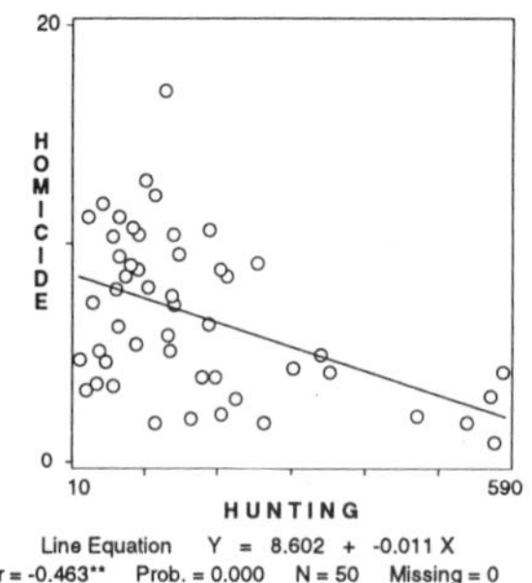

As you can see in the scatterplot between homicide rates and a measure of participation in hunting, there is indeed an inverse association (r = –0.463**), which is consistent with the findings reported by Dr. Ture. States with relatively large numbers of residents who purchase hunting licenses tend to exhibit low homicide rates. The question, however, is whether hunting actually makes people less likely to commit homicides. To address this question, we need to think about other characteristics of states that might also be related to homicide and that might be related to the popularity of hunting as well.

A useful place to start is by examining the maps for the variables HOMICIDE and HUNTING.

Data File: **STATES**
➤ *Task:* **Mapping**
➤ *Variable 1:* **2) HOMICIDE**
➤ *Variable 2:* **83) HUNTING**
➤ *Views:* **Map**

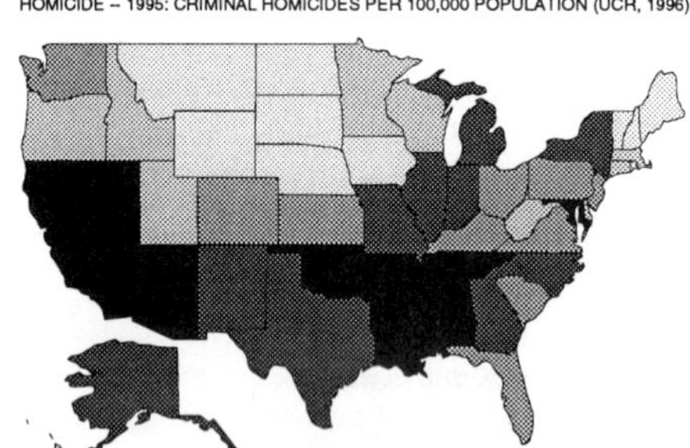

r = –0.463**

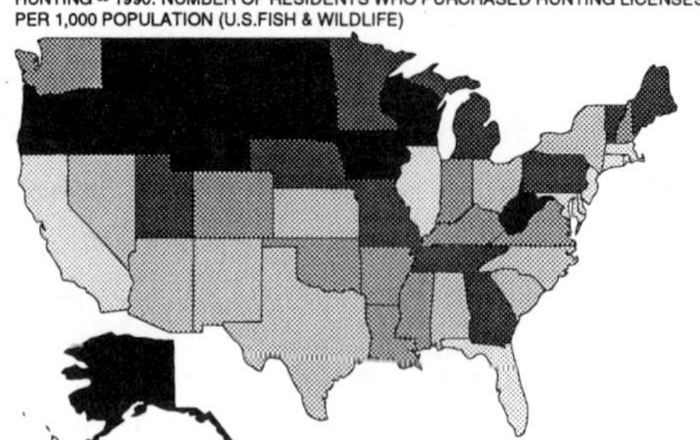

Notice that homicide is heavily concentrated in the Sun Belt states. On the other hand, hunting is concentrated in the states of the northern Great Plains and in the Rocky Mountains. In Idaho, the Dakotas, and Montana, more than half the population buys a hunting license.

Now look at the map for WARM WINTR. This is the average low temperature in January; the higher the score on this variable, the warmer the winter in the state.

Data File: **STATES**
Task: **Mapping**
Variable 1: **2) HOMICIDE**
➤ *Variable 2:* **16) WARM WINTR**
➤ *Views:* **Map**

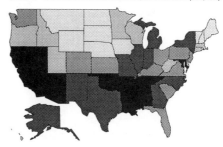

HOMICIDE – 1995: CRIMINAL HOMICIDES PER 100,000 POPULATION (UCR, 1996)

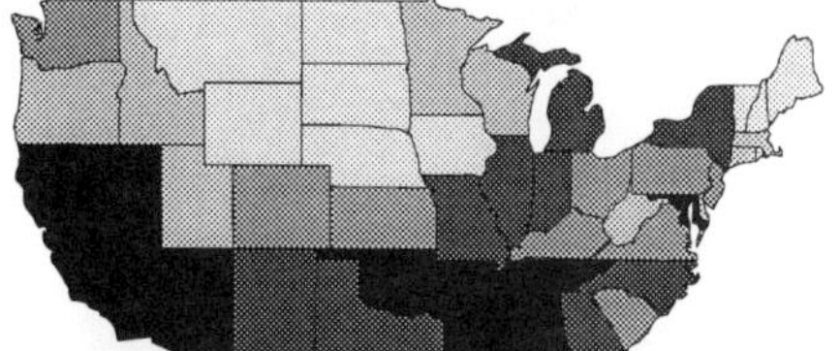

r = 0.567**

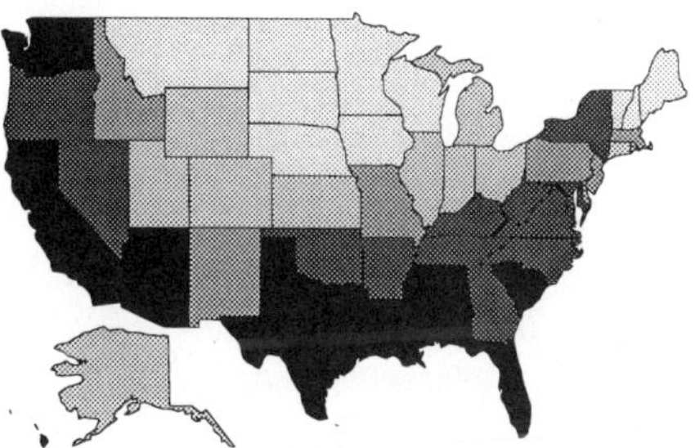

Not surprisingly the Sun Belt states are warmest and the northern Great Plains are coldest. Notice, too, how much this map looks like the homicide map. The warmest states tend to have the highest homicide rates, and the coldest states tend to have the lowest rates. This relationship is reflected in the significant, positive correlation between the two variables (r = 0.567**).

The fact is that, nationally, homicide fluctuates over the course of different months. The highest rates are always in July and August, while the lowest rates are in January and February. The reason for this pattern is that homicide is typically a social interaction crime, unlike, say, burglary—burglars do their best to avoid contact with their victims. Factors that facilitate interaction increase homicides, whereas factors that inhibit interaction reduce homicides. Cold weather reduces interaction and thus reduces homicides. This conclusion is supported by two additional facts. First, homicide does not vary as much by months in states with very warm winters. Second, nationally, homicide rates always show a second, sudden peak in December. This is a time for many holiday gatherings and increased social interaction. Note that the high numbers of homicides in December indicate that homicide is not strictly "seasonal," since December is a winter month.[1]

Let's make one additional comparison of maps, those for HUNTING and WARM WINTR.

---

[1] For a detailed discussion of homicide and season, see Derral Cheatwood, "Is There a Season for Homicide?" *Criminology* 26 (1988): 287–306.

Data File: **STATES**
Task: **Mapping**
➤ *Variable 1:* **83) HUNTING**
➤ *Variable 2:* **16) WARM WINTR**
➤ *Views:* **Map**

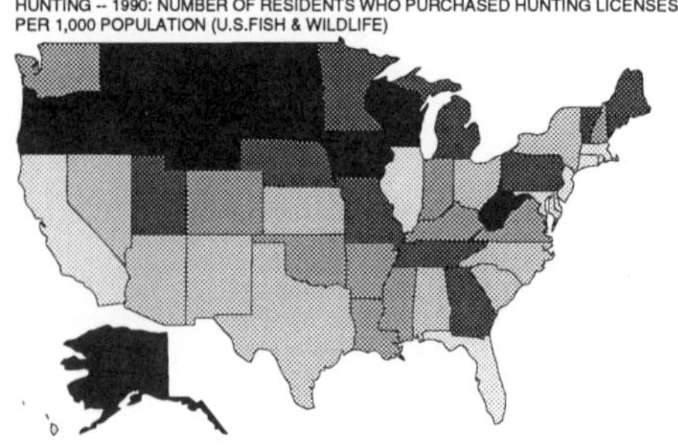

r = –0.522**

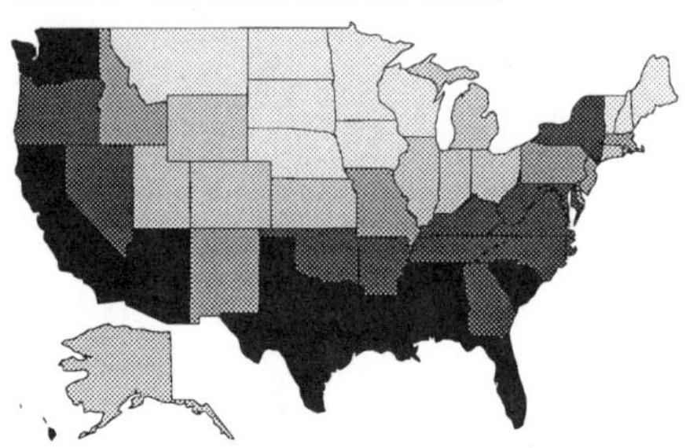

The two maps are largely the opposites of one another (r = –0.522**). Evidently, hunting is most popular in the coldest states.

Now we can use multiple regression to see if controlling for the climate of a state eliminates the correlation between hunting and homicide.

Data File: **STATES**
➤ *Task:* **Regression**
➤ *Dependent Variable:* **2) HOMICIDE**
➤ *Independent Variables:* **83) HUNTING**
16) WARM WINTR
➤ *View:* **Graph**

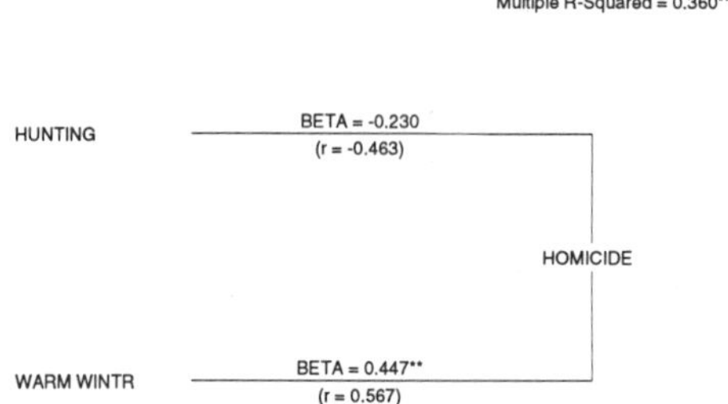

Recall that the beta coefficient represents the net effect of an independent variable on the dependent variable, controlling for the other predictors in the model. The beta for hunting has fallen to nonsignificance (note the absence of any asterisks). This implies that Professor Ture's observed correlation is not a causal one. Rather, it represents a spurious correlation. With weather controlled, states with high rates of hunting do not have significantly lower homicide rates.

The effect of warm winters on homicide, on the other hand, remains significant in the regression analysis: beta = 0.447**. Also, both variables combined explain 36 percent of the variation in state homicide rates (Multiple R-Squared = 0.360**).

In the case of hunting and homicides, the warmth of the winters produces a spurious, inverse correlation (recall that the sign of the correlation between hunting and homicides is negative). To see how this comes about, examine the [Correlation] view.

Data File: **STATES**
Task: **Regression**
Dependent Variable: **2) HOMICIDE**
Independent Variables: **83) HUNTING**
16) WARM WINTR
➤ *View:* **Correlation**

Correlation Coefficients
N: 50 Missing: 0
Cronbach's alpha: Not calculated--negative correlations
LISTWISE deletion (1-tailed test) Significance Levels: ** =.01, * =.05

	HUNTING	WARM WINTR	HOMICIDE
HUNTING	1.000	-0.522 **	-0.463 **
WARM WINTR	-0.522 **	1.000	0.567 **
HOMICIDE	-0.463 **	0.567 **	1.000

Your screen now displays all correlations between the variables in the regression exercise. The results reveal that warmth of winters is positively correlated with homicides (r = .567**) and negatively correlated with hunting (r = –.522**).

What might happen if another variable is positively correlated with both the independent and dependent variable? Let's explore this possibility by looking at correlations between the number of psychiatrists per 100,000 population and robbery rates.

Data File: **STATES**
➤ *Task:* **Correlation**
➤ *Variables:* **4) ROBBERY**
71) SHRINKS
31) %URBAN

Correlation Coefficients
PAIRWISE deletion (1-tailed test) Significance Levels: ** =.01, * =.05

	ROBBERY	SHRINKS	%URBAN
ROBBERY	1.000 (50)	0.370 ** (50)	0.603 ** (50)
SHRINKS	0.370 ** (50)	1.000 (50)	0.368 ** (50)
%URBAN	0.603 ** (50)	0.368 ** (50)	1.000 (50)

The correlation between these two variables is significantly positive (r = 0.370**). States with relatively large numbers of psychiatrists tend to have high rates of robbery. Perhaps psychiatrists moonlight as robbers, or perhaps they encourage their patients to steal to pay their bills. These speculations are obviously silly. A more likely interpretation is that the relationship is spurious.

As you examine the correlation matrix further, you also see a significant, positive correlation between the number of psychiatrists and the percent of the population living in urban areas (r = 0.368**). The more urbanized states tend to attract psychiatrists. Perhaps psychiatrists prefer urban lifestyles, or perhaps the market for psychiatric services is greater in cities. Notice also that the more urbanized states have higher robbery rates (r = 0.603**). Robbery is often thought of as a "big city" crime, and robbery rates are in fact highest in metropolitan areas. Now, the crucial question is whether the number of psychiatrists is related to robbery rates once the degree of urban development of states is statistically controlled.

Regression analysis allows us to answer this question.

Data File: **STATES**
➤ *Task:* **Regression**
➤ *Dependent Variable:* **4) ROBBERY**
➤ *Independent Variables:* **71) SHRINKS**
31) %URBAN
➤ *View:* **Graph**

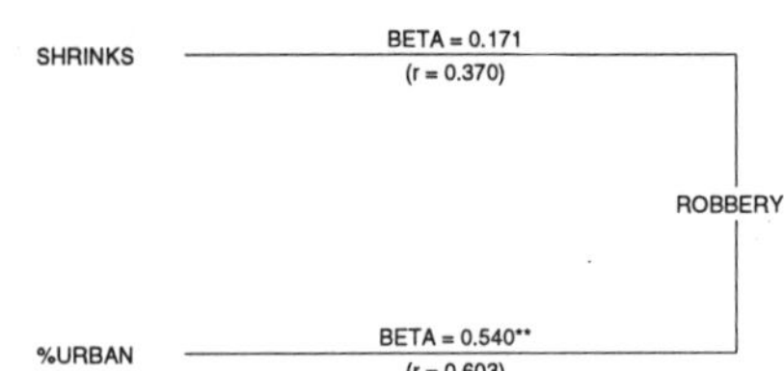

The beta coefficient for the number of psychiatrists is no longer statistically significant. Once again, the bivariate relationship (which is printed under the line for SHRINKS) appears to be a spurious one rather than a causal one. States with many psychiatrists do indeed have high robbery rates, but this is because such states tend to be highly urbanized, and urbanized areas have high robbery rates.

In other words, both inverse (negative) and positive correlations may be spurious due to the influence of other variables. In either situation, the **principle for detecting a spurious relationship** is the same: when other relevant factors are controlled, a spurious relationship disappears.

Your turn.

WORKSHEET — CHAPTER 12

NAME:

COURSE:

DATE:

REVIEW QUESTIONS

Based on the first part of this chapter, answer True or False to the following items:

A spurious relationship comes about because another variable affects both a dependent and an independent variable. T F

Homicides are most common at times and in places with intense social interaction. T F

States where hunting is very common tend to exhibit comparatively high rates of homicide. T F

When features of climate are statistically controlled, the association between hunting and homicide becomes much stronger. T F

Both positive and negative correlations can be spurious. T F

EXPLORIT QUESTIONS: PART I

The ExplorIt questions that follow require you to assess the plausibility of causal arguments put forth in the hypothetical news stories below.

STORY I.

Pickup Trucks Deter Motor Vehicle Thefts

A recent study reveals that states with large numbers of pickup trucks have relatively low rates of motor vehicle thefts. The author of the study, Dr. Tim Wheeler, speculates that the explanation may lie in the slow acceleration of pickups in comparison with most cars. "The unfortunate thief who breaks into a pickup truck discovers that his get-away is impeded by the slow response of the vehicle, enabling the police to apprehend the offender," writes Dr. Wheeler. Potential offenders are likely to regard pickups as unattractive vehicles to steal, thereby reducing the rates of motor vehicle thefts in states where pickup trucks are particularly popular.

1. Use the CORRELATION task below to answer the following questions.

➤ *Data File:* **STATES**
➤ *Task:* **Correlation**
➤ *Variables:* **8) MV. THEFT**
76) PICKUPS
31) %URBAN

a. Record the correlation between the number of pickup trucks per 1,000 population (PICKUPS) and the rate of motor vehicle thefts (MV. THEFT). r = ________

b. Is the correlation statistically significant? Yes No

c. Record the correlation between the percent of the population living in urban areas (%URBAN) and the number of pickup trucks (PICKUPS). r = ________

d. Is the correlation statistically significant? Yes No

e. Record the correlation between the percent of the population living in urban areas (%URBAN) and the rate of motor vehicle thefts (MV. THEFT). r = ________

f. Is the correlation statistically significant? Yes No

2. Use the REGRESSION task to answer the following questions.

Data File: **STATES**
➤ *Task:* **Regression**
➤ *Dependent Variables* **8) MV. THEFT**
➤ *Independent Variable* **76) PICKUPS**
31) %URBAN

a. What is the combined variance explained by these two independent variables on rates of motor vehicle theft? (Remember to convert your value to a percentage.) ________%

b. What is the independent or net effect of the number of pickup trucks on rates of motor vehicle theft? ________

c. Is the effect statistically significant? Yes No

d. What is the independent or net effect of %URBAN on rates of motor vehicle theft? ________

e. Is the effect statistically significant? Yes No

f. Does the regression analysis support the causal argument in the news report? Supports

Does not support

STORY II.

Family Breakdown Linked with Violence

Recent research indicates that states with large numbers of female-headed households have relatively high rates of homicide. Dr. Amy Smart, spokesperson for the National Criminological Society, reports that this recent finding is consistent with several prior studies which have examined cities. Criminologists hypothesize that violence is likely to be high in areas with large numbers of female-headed families because children grow up in unsupervised environments. Dr. Smart further notes that family structure influences state homicide levels regardless of racial composition.

3. Use the CORRELATION task below to answer the following questions.

Data File: **STATES**
➤ *Task:* **Correlation**
➤ *Variables:* **2) HOMICIDE**
42) FEM.HEAD
25) %BLACK

a. Record the correlation between the percentage of households that are female-headed (FEM.HEAD) and the homicide rate (HOMICIDE). r = ______

b. Is the correlation statistically significant? Yes No

c. Record the correlation between the percentage of the population that is African American (%BLACK) and the percentage of female-headed households (FEM.HEAD). r = ______

d. Is the correlation statistically significant? Yes No

e. Record the correlation between the percentage of the population that is African American (%BLACK) and the homicide rate (HOMICIDE). r = ______

f. Is the correlation statistically significant? Yes No

4. Use the REGRESSION task to answer the following questions.

Data File: **STATES**
➤ *Task:* **Regression**
➤ *Dependent Variables* **2) HOMICIDE**
➤ *Independent Variable* **42) FEM.HEAD**
25) %BLACK

a. What is the combined variance explained by these two independent variables on homicide rates? (Remember to convert your value to a percentage.) ______%

b. What is the independent or net effect of female-headed households on homicide rates? ______

c. Is the effect statistically significant? Yes No

d. What is the independent or net effect of %BLACK on homicide rates? ______

e. Is the effect statistically significant? Yes No

f. Does the regression analysis support the causal argument in the news report? Supports

Does not support

STORY III.

Tornadoes Leave More Than Property Damage in Their Wake

Newly released data from the Federal Emergency Assistance Authority (FEAA) reveal that states with high average numbers of tornadoes tend to have high assault rates. FEAA officials speculate that this association reflects the lingering psychological impact of tornadoes on victims. According to experts at FEAA, people who witness the severe devastation of tornadoes begin to feel that events cannot be controlled, which weakens their inhibitions against harming others.

5. Use the CORRELATION task below to answer the following questions.

Data File: **STATES**
➤ *Task:* **Correlation**
➤ *Variables:* **5) ASSAULT**
18) TORNADO RT
15) SOUTHNESS

a. Record the correlation between the average number of tornadoes per year per 1,000 square miles (TORNADO RT) and the assault rate (ASSAULT). r = ______

b. Is the correlation statistically significant? Yes No

c. Record the correlation between the southern location of a state (SOUTHNESS) and the frequency of tornadoes (TORNADO RT). r = ______

d. Is the correlation statistically significant? Yes No

e. Record the correlation between the southern location of a state (SOUTHNESS) and the assault rate (ASSAULT). r = ______

f. Is the correlation statistically significant? Yes No

6. Use the REGRESSION task to answer the following questions.

   Data File: **STATES**
   ➤ *Task:* **Regression**
   ➤ *Dependent Variables* **5) ASSAULT**
   ➤ *Independent Variable* **18) TORNADO RT**
   15) SOUTHNESS

   a. What is the combined variance explained by these two independent variables on assault rates? ________%

   b. What is the independent or net effect of the frequency of tornadoes on the assault rate? ________

   c. Is the effect statistically significant? Yes No

   d. What is the independent or net effect of southern location on the assault rate? ________

   e. Is the effect statistically significant? Yes No

   f. Does the regression analysis support the causal argument in the news report? Supports

   Does not support

STORY IV.

Church-Going No Cure for Crime

A controversial editorial just published in *Criminology Today* has challenged the widely held view that religion acts as a deterrent to crime. The author of the editorial, Dr. Wyman Guy, argues that previously reported data on church membership and larceny rates have been misinterpreted. Past studies have reported that states with large numbers of church members exhibit relatively low levels of larceny. Dr. Guy maintains that this association occurs because states with older populations have both more church members and lower larceny rates. According to Dr. Guy, once the average age of residents in a state is taken into account, states with large numbers of church members do not have unusually low larceny rates.

7. Use the CORRELATION task that follows to answer the following questions.

   Data File: **STATES**
   ➤ *Task:* **Correlation**
   ➤ *Variables:* **7) LARCENY**
   65) CHURCH.MEM
   21) AVE. AGE

   a. Record the correlation between the percentage of the population belonging to a local church (CHURCH.MEM) and the larceny rate (LARCENY). r = ________

   b. Is the correlation statistically significant? Yes No

c. Record the correlation between the average age of a state's population (AVE. AGE) and church membership (CHURCH.MEM). r = ________

d. Is the correlation statistically significant? Yes No

e. Record the correlation between the average age of a state's population (AVE. AGE) and the larceny rate (LARCENY). r = ________

f. Is the correlation statistically significant? Yes No

8. Use the REGRESSION task to answer the following questions.

Data File:	**STATES**
➤ *Task:*	**Regression**
➤ *Dependent Variables*	**7) LARCENY**
➤ *Independent Variable*	**65) CHURCH.MEM**
	21) AVE. AGE

a. What is the combined variance explained by these two independent variables on larceny rates? ________%

b. What is the independent or net effect of the church membership on the larceny rate? ________

c. Is the effect statistically significant? Yes No

d. What is the independent or net effect of the average age of a state's population on the larceny rate? ________

e. Is the effect statistically significant? Yes No

f. Does the analysis support the causal argument in Dr. Guy's editorial referred to in the news report? Supports

Does not support

ESSAY QUESTION

9. Identify the news stories presented in these worksheets that are misleading because the researcher confuses a spurious correlation with a causal relationship. For each of these stories, explain how this spurious correlation comes about and how you know that this correlation is spurious. (Attach additional pages as necessary.)

APPENDIX A: INDEPENDENT PROJECTS

There are many variables in your data sets that have been little used, or not used at all, in this book. These variables could provide the basis for an independent research project, either for your present course or for some other course. If you have completed the workbook, you are now familiar with both simple and more advanced techniques for data analysis, so you can address a wide range of important research questions. Here are a few suggestions for further research using your ExplorIt data files.

PROJECT 1

You have explored features of robbery incidents reported in the National Crime Victimization Survey (NCVS) using the UNIVARIATE task. Now, consider some possible bivariate relationships. How might the victimization of females differ from that of males? Specifically, victims of which sex do you think are more likely to be robbed by multiple offenders, by strangers, and by offenders with a weapon? Victims of which sex do you think are more likely to take protective action, report the incident to the police, and receive help from social service agencies after the crime? Begin by formulating hypotheses about the sex differences that you expect to see for each of these characteristics of robberies. Then, use cross-tabulations to test your hypotheses with the NCVS data file. The following should be the row variables for the various cross-tabulations: 6) MULTOFF; 7) STRANGER; 9) WEAPON; 11) PROTECT; 14) REPORTED; 18) AGEN.HELP. Treat: 1) VICSEX as the column variable in all of these analyses.

PROJECT 2

Data from the General Social Survey reveal that about three-quarters of the adult population in the United States favor capital punishment for persons convicted of murder. What kind of people do you think are more likely to be in favor, and what kind of people less likely to be in favor? Specifically, consider the following sociodemographic characteristics of respondents: sex, race, political party, marital status, religious preference, region, age, education, and income. Pose hypotheses about the relationships that you expect to see between each of these nine variables and support for capital punishment: 2) CAPPUN. Then, examine the actual cross-tabulations using the AUTO-ANALYZER task with the GSS data file (CAPPUN should be identified as the analyzer variable). Finally, assess your hypotheses.

PROJECT 3

In the introduction to Chapter 7, you examined two cross-tabulations based on the college sample to assess hypotheses derived from Hirschi's social bonding theory:

a. 3) SHOPLIFT [row variable] and 19) HI GRADES [column variable].

b. 3) SHOPLIFT [row variable] and 17) HI STUDY [column variable].

The results showed that, consistent with bonding theory, college students who have high grades and who spend a lot of time studying are less likely to report having shoplifted. Do you think these relationships are the same for males and females? Does academic performance (grades) provide more of an inhibition against shoplifting for males or for females? Does studying discourage shoplifting more for one sex or for the other? Provide tentative answers to these questions. Then, with the COLLEGE data file, repeat the two cross-tabulations cited above, this time introducing 26) GENDER as a control variable. Were your answers correct? How would you explain the observed results?

PROJECT 4

In Chapter 1, you examined maps to identify the regional patterning of homicide rates, looking to see if there is evidence of a southern culture of violence. Revisit the issue of southern violence with the STATES data file. Examine the scatterplot between 2) HOMICIDE (dependent variable) and an indicator of southern location: 15) SOUTHNESS (independent variable). Now, assess the effect of southernness on homicide rates controlling for another variable using the REGRESSION task. Treat 2) HOMICIDE as the dependent variable and 15) SOUTHNESS and 44) %POOR as independent variables. What happens to the southernness effect when you control for poverty? Perform the REGRESSION task again, replacing 44) %POOR with 42) FEM.HEAD. What happens when you control for the prevalence of female-headed households? Finally, search for other characteristics of states that might make the beta for southernness nonsignificant in a regression analysis. Discuss how that "new" variable helps explain the observation of high rates of homicide in the South.

PROJECT 5

In the preliminary discussion of Chapter 9, you examined scatterplots between robbery rates for U.S. states and a feature of climate (the warmth of the winters) and family structure (percent of households with married couple with their own children). The results were consistent with routine activities theory. Robbery rates tend to be high in states with warm winters and relatively small numbers of married couples with children. With the STATES data file, use the REGRESSION task to see if these two independent variables—16) WARM WINTR and 41) COU.CHILD—still exhibit a statistically significant association with robbery rates when both of them are taken into account. Treat 4) ROBBERY as the dependent variable. Look at the Multiple R-Squared statistic to see how much of the variation in robbery rates is explained by these two independent variables. Next, see if you can find another variable that you can add to the regression, along with WARM WINTR and COU.CHILD, that will make the Multiple R-Squared statistic larger. Finally, interpret the beta coefficients for this model with three independent variables. Are the effects of climate and family structure still significant? Can the effect of the "new" independent variable be interpreted with reference to a criminological theory?

APPENDIX B: STUDENT ExplorIt REFERENCE SECTION

This appendix provides additional information on using Student ExplorIt. If you have not already done so, read the instructions in *Getting Started* at the beginning of this book.

The first part of this appendix provides information on *Student ExplorIt for Windows*. Little information is provided here because most of it is available via the on-line help. The second part of this appendix provides information on *Student ExplorIt for DOS*. This section is substantially longer because on-line help is not provided in the DOS version of the program.

STUDENT EXPLORIT FOR WINDOWS

INSTALLATION

The instructions for installing *Student ExplorIt for Windows* have been provided in the *Getting Started* section of this workbook. If you have problems installing Student ExplorIt, first check to see that your computer has the minimum system requirements. (Note: *Student ExplorIt for Windows* does not work on computers running Windows 3.0 or 3.1. You should instead use *Student ExplorIt for DOS*.)

During the installation, you are asked whether you want the data files (e.g., GSS, STATES, etc.) installed on your hard drive. If you choose *not* to install the data files on your hard drive, you must insert the 3.5" diskette (which contains the data files) every time you run Student ExplorIt. If you later change your mind about the data file option you want to use, you will need to reinstall the program.

ON-LINE HELP AND SOFTWARE QUESTIONS

Student ExplorIt for Windows offers extensive on-line help. You can obtain task-specific help by pressing **[F1]** at any point in the program. For example, if you are performing a scatterplot analysis, you can press **[F1]** to see the help for the SCATTERPLOT task.

If you prefer to browse through a list of the available help topics, select **Help** from the pull-down menu at the top of the screen and select the **Help Topics** option. At this point, you will be provided with a list of topic areas. Each topic area is represented by a closed-book icon. To see what information is available in a given topic area, double-click on a book to "open" it. (For this version of the software, use only the "Student ExplorIt" section of help; do not use the "Student MicroCase" section.) When you double-click on a book icon, a list of help topics is shown. A help topic is represented by a piece of paper with a question mark on it. Double-click on a help topic to view it.

If you have questions about *Student ExplorIt for Windows*, the first step is to try the on-line help described above. If you are not very familiar with software or computers, a second option is to ask a classmate or your instructor for assistance. If you are still unable to get an answer to your question or to resolve a problem, go to the Technical Support section of MicroCase's web site at http://www.microcase.com/student/support.html.

STUDENT ExplorIt FOR DOS

If you have not already done so, read the instructions in *Getting Started* at the beginning of this book. This appendix provides additional information on using *Student ExplorIt for DOS*. (If you are using *Student ExplorIt for Windows 95/98*, refer to the previous page.)

GETTING YOUR MOUSE WORKING

If you are using *Student ExplorIt for DOS* on a Windows 3.0/3.1 computer and the mouse arrow fails to appear on your screen, follow these instructions for loading the mouse driver:

1. Exit Windows. (You can exit by using <Alt> <F4> to close each window.)
2. At the DOS prompt (C:\>), type **MOUSE** and press <Enter>.
3. If you get an error message (e.g., "Bad command or file name," "Invalid directory"), try typing either **C:\MOUSE\MOUSE** and pressing <Enter> or **C:\LMOUSE\MOUSE** and pressing <Enter>.
4. If you get a message that tells you the mouse driver has been loaded, type **A:EXPLORIT** and press <ENTER> to start the program. If the mouse works now, you will need to follow the same procedure for loading the mouse driver each time you want to run the ExplorIt program.
5. If you still cannot see the mouse on the screen, contact the manufacturer of your computer to obtain a DOS mouse driver.
6. To return to Windows, type **WIN** and press <ENTER>.

HELP AND SOFTWARE QUESTIONS

If you encounter problems with *Student ExplorIt for DOS*, the first step is to review relevant sections in this workbook that might address your problem, such as this appendix. Next, you should try the help instructions provided at the bottoms of most screens. If you are not very familiar with software or computers, a third option is to ask a classmate or your instructor for assistance. If you are still unable to get an answer to your question or to resolve a problem, go to the Technical Support section of MicroCase's web site at http://www.microcase.com/student/support.html.

STANDARD OPERATIONS

These operations appear on the top row of onscreen buttons in *Student ExplorIt for DOS* (not all buttons appear on all screens):

EXIT

When you are within a task, clicking the [Exit] button will return you to the variable selection screen for the task. If you are at the variable selection screen within a particular task, this button will return you to the main menu. If you are at the main menu, you can exit the program by clicking the [Exit] button.

PRINT

To print the information shown on the screen, click the [Print] button. A window will open giving the current settings for the printer. If the settings are correct, click [OK] to send the results to the printer. If you change your mind about printing something, click [Cancel]. If the printer settings are incorrect, click [Settings] and follow the instructions in the next paragraph. If you want to save results to a disk file and print it later, use the [Disk File] option. In this case, type in the directory and file name you want to use (using standard DOS conventions) and click [OK]. This option will save text screens, but *not* graphics screens, to the named file. Also use the [Disk File] option if your printer is not supported by *Student ExplorIt for DOS*. Such files can be opened and printed using any word processor program.

Changing Printer Settings

To change the printer settings, click [Print] and then choose [Settings]. To select a new printer from the list, click its name and then click [OK]. If your printer doesn't appear on the list, try each printer and use the one that works best. The [Text (ASCII)] option will not allow you to print graphics.

You are also given the option of directing the printer to a particular port (the physical connector from your computer to your printer). Use LPT1: unless you have been instructed otherwise. (If you are printing over a network and are unable to print, check with your instructor or network administrator for additional information.)

VARIABLES

The [Variables] button will let you look at the list of variables for the data file that is currently open. The description of the highlighted variable is shown in a box at the lower right of the window. You can move this highlight through the list of variables by clicking on the scroll buttons to the right of the list box, by using the up and down cursor keys (as well as the <PgUp>, <PgDn>, <Home>, and <End> keys), or by clicking a variable once with the mouse.

You can also search the variable names and descriptions for a word, a partial word, or a phrase. Perhaps, for example, you want to find a variable about income. Click the [Search] button. Type **income** and press <Enter> (or click [OK]). The variable list window now contains only the variables that have the word *income* in either the variable name or the variable description. To return to the full list of variables, click [Full List].

SELECTING A SUBSET

Most statistical analysis tasks in Student ExplorIt allow you to analyze a subset of cases. For example, if you wanted to look only at females in the GSS, you would need to select a subset.

To limit your analysis to a subset of cases, select the primary variables for analysis as usual. But before you click [OK] to see the final results, click the [Subset Variables] button. A subset selection screen will appear and you may select up to four subset variables. You should select a subset variable as you would a regular variable. But upon choosing a variable, you will immediately be prompted to provide information on the *categories* to be used in selecting cases for the subset. Since there are two different types of variables, there are two different ways to select subset categories.

Selecting Subsets with Categorical Variables

A variable is a "categorical variable" when each of its categories has a discrete name or label (e.g., "Male" or "Female" for the variable SEX). After you select a subset variable, the screen will ask you to select a category for a subset. Click it once to move the highlight to it and then click a second time to select the category. An "x" will appear in the box to the left of the name. You may select as many or as few categories as you wish.

After you have selected the categories, you must indicate whether cases in the indicated categories are to be *included* or *excluded* in the analysis. For example, if you select SEX as the subset variable and "Male" as the category, you may choose to "include" only males in the analysis, or you may choose to "exclude" them and look only at females ("non-male"). Just click the option you want. Then click [OK] to return to the variable selection screen.

Selecting Subsets with Noncategorical Variables

If a variable uses a range of numbers for its values (e.g., 1.2–13.3) and these values do not fall into discrete categories (such as "male" or "female"), a different method of selecting cases is used. After you select the subset variable, the screen will ask for the low and the high value to be used in selecting the cases. For example, if you type 1.2 as the low value and 6.7 as the high value, cases with values between 1.2 and 6.7 on the subset variable will be included in the analysis. Then click [OK] to return to the variable selection screen.

MULTIPLE SUBSET VARIABLES

If you want to base the subset on more than one variable, select a second variable and define another subset. For example, if you wanted to include *only* white females, you would define your subset using two subset variables: RACE (include category white) and SEX (include category female).

DELETING SUBSETS

All variable selections, including selections of subset variables, are saved by Student ExplorIt after you exit from a results screen. If you are going to conduct another analysis using the same task, it is important to delete or clear subset variables when you are finished with them. There are three ways to accomplish this. First, you can click the [Clear All] button on the variable selection screen, which will clear all selected variables. Second, you can click the [Subset Variables] button and then click [Delete] to eliminate each subset variable individually. Or, third, you can return to the main menu, which will automatically deletes all variable selections.

AUTO-ANALYZER

SELECTING VARIABLES

Select an analyzer variable according to the variable selection instructions in *Getting Started*, at the beginning of this book. Click [OK] to continue.

Views

Univariate: Auto-Analyzer first shows the overall distribution of the selected variable. In addition, a brief description of this distribution is shown below the table.

Demographic Views: Nine demographic views are available from Auto-Analyzer: Sex, Race, Political Party, Marital, Religion, Region, Age, Education, and Income. Each option shows the table linking the selected variable and the demographic variable, with proper percentages. In addition, a textual description of the table is provided. If the description contains a scroll bar, use the mouse or cursor keys to see the additional information.

Summary: This option includes the textual summaries for each of the nine demographic variables and the distribution for the primary variable.

Univariate Statistics

Selecting Variables

Select a primary variable according to the variable selection instructions in *Getting Started* at the beginning of this book. If you want a subset of cases, see the *Selecting Subsets* section toward the beginning of this appendix. (If you need to erase all existing variable information for this task, click the [Clear All] button.)

Once your variables have been selected, click [OK] to obtain the results of your analysis.

Views

These options are located on the top row of buttons on the results screen:

Pie: This shows the distribution of the variable and displays it in the form of a pie chart.

Bar [Frequency]: This displays the distribution of cases in the form of a bar graph. Information on the first category of the variable is shown below the bar graph. To see information on other categories, click the bar of your choice.

Bar [Cumulative]: This displays the cumulative percentage of cases for the category displayed.

Statistics: This button produces the frequency, percent, cumulative percent, and z-score for each category of the variable. Summary statistics are shown at the top of the screen.

Cross-Tabulation

Selecting Variables

Select a row variable and a column variable according to the variable selection instructions in *Getting Started* at the beginning of this book. If you want a subset of cases, see the instructions on selecting subsets at the beginning of this appendix. (If you wish to erase all existing variable information for this task, click the [Clear All] option.)

Control Variables (optional)

The [Control Variables] option can be selected from the variable selection screen in the CROSS-TABULATION task. A window for selecting control variables will open. At this point you may select up to three control variables using the usual method of selecting variables. When you have selected the control variables for your analysis, click [OK] to return to the variable selection. When the final results are displayed, a "partial table" is shown for each level of the control variable(s).

Once your variables have been selected, click [OK] to obtain the results of your analysis.

VIEWS

Table: This shows the cross-tabulation results for the selected row and column variables. If one or more control variables have been selected, the categories of the cases contained in this subtable are shown at the top of the screen. If the entire table will not fit on the screen, use the cursor keys or click the scroll bars at the bottom and/or right of the table to scroll through additional rows and columns.

Display (these options are located in the menu at the right):

Column %: This option provides the column percentages for the table. Missing data are ignored.

Row %: This option provides the row percentages for the table. Missing data are ignored.

Total %: This option provides the total percentages for the table. Missing data are ignored.

Freq.: This option returns the table to the original frequencies.

Previous (Optional): If a control variable has been selected, this option will let you return to previously viewed subtables.

Next (Optional): If a control variable has been selected, this option will take you to the next subtable.

Stats: This view shows the summary statistics for the table.

Bar: This shows a stacked bar chart representing the table.

Collapse: The [Collapse] button appears whenever a cross-tabulation table is showing. This option allows you to combine categories of a table or to drop categories entirely. (No changes using the [Collapse] option permanently modify the variable—the changes disappear as soon as you leave the results screen.) To select the categories to be combined or dropped, click the category labels (this causes the entire row or column to be highlighted). Then click the [Collapse] button. Here you are given the choice of creating a new collapsed category or turning the highlighted categories into missing data. To create a new collapsed category, type in a category name and click [OK]. If you want to drop the highlighted categories, click the [Drop] button. The table will then be updated according to your selections. The [Collapse] option will work with both the row and column variables in a cross-tabulation table, although only one variable at a time can be modified.

MAPPING

SELECTING VARIABLES

Select a variable according to the variable selection instructions in *Getting Started*, at the beginning of this book. If you want to use a subset of cases, see the instructions on selecting subsets at the beginning of this appendix. If you wish to erase all existing variable information for this task, click the [Clear All] option.

Once you select your variables, click [OK] to obtain the map.

VIEWS

These options are located on the top row of buttons.

Map: The selected variable is mapped into five different levels from light (lowest) to dark (highest). Cases for which data are unavailable are left blank.

Display (these options are located at the right side of the top button row):

Legend: This option provides the values represented by each level, known as the map legend, in a box at the lower right. Selecting this option a second time removes the legend.

Find: This option allows you to locate a particular case. When you select this option, a list of all cases will be shown. Click twice on the case you want to select so that an "x" appears to the left of the name. If the case you want to select is not shown in the window, scroll to it using the cursor keys or click the scroll bar at the right side of the window. Click [OK] to continue. The selected case is highlighted on the map and its name, value, and rank are shown at the bottom of the screen. To deselect this highlighted case, click the [Find] button again or click outside the border of the map.

Special Feature: Click a case. You may use the mouse to click a case. The selected case is shown in the highlight color and its name, value, and rank are shown at the bottom of the screen. To deselect this case, click outside the border of the map.

Spot: This view shows each case as a filled circle. The size of the spot, or circle, is relative to the value of the case—cases with higher values have larger spots. The color of the spot is the same as that used in the Map view. To return to the original map, click the [Spot] button again.

List [Rank]: This option allows you to rank the cases on the variable from high to low. The name of the variable, its rank, and its value are displayed. In addition, the map color for the case is shown to the left of the name. Since the initial screen shows only the highest cases, use the scroll bar at the right side of the window to see additional values.

List [Alpha]: This option works the same as [List: Rank], except that cases are shown in alphabetical order.

SCATTERPLOT

SELECTING VARIABLES

Select two variables according to the variable selection instructions provided in *Getting Started*, at the beginning of this book. The dependent variable will be represented by the *y*-axis on the graph and the independent variable will be represented by the *x*-axis.

If you want a subset of cases, see the instructions on selecting subsets at the beginning of this appendix. (If you need to erase all existing variable information for this task, click the [Clear All] option.)

Once your variables have been selected, click [OK] to obtain the scatterplot results.

VIEWS

The scatterplot task has only one view.

The scatterplot graph shows each case as a dot, with the *x*-axis representing the independent variable and the *y*-axis representing the dependent variable. The correlation coefficient (r) is shown at the lower left of the screen. One asterisk indicates a .05 level of statistical significance; two asterisks, a .01 level.

Display (these options are located in the Subview menu at the left of the screen):

Reg.Line: This option places the regression line on the scatterplot graph and gives the equation for the regression line below the graph. Selecting this option a second time removes the line.

Residuals: The residual for each case—a vertical line from the case to the regression line—is shown on the scatterplot graph. Selecting this option a second time removes the residual lines.

Find Case: This option allows you to identify—place a box around—the dot representing a particular case. When you select this option, a list of all cases will be shown. If the case you want to see is not immediately visible in the window, scroll to the appropriate case using the cursor keys or click the scroll bar at the right side of the window. To select a case, click it twice so that an "x" appears in the box to the left. Click [OK] to return to the scatterplot graph. Information on the selected case is shown in the window at the lower left—this window is described in the Special Features section, below.

Outlier: This option will identify—place a box around—the dot representing the outlier. In this application, the outlier is defined as the case that would make the greatest change in the correlation coefficient if it were removed. When you select this option, information on the outlier case is given in a window at the lower left—this window is described in Special Features, below.

Special Features

Click a dot: You may use the mouse to click a dot. A box is placed around this dot and information on the case is shown in the window at the lower left.

X button: If you click the X button at the bottom of the graph, the description of the independent variable will be shown below the graph. Click the "x" in the upper right corner of the description to close this window.

Y button: If you click the Y button at the left side of the graph, the description of the dependent variable will be shown below the graph. Click the "x" in the upper right corner of the description to close this window.

Window: When certain displays are selected from the scatterplot screen, a window appears that contains information on the case currently highlighted in the scatterplot. This window will appear when you use the [Outlier] option or the [Find case] option, or if you click a dot in the scatterplot. The name of the case and its value on the independent (or x) variable and on the dependent (or y) variable are shown. In addition, you are given the option of removing the case from the scatterplot. If you click the option [Remove Case from Graph], the case will be removed from the scatterplot and any statistics will be recalculated with that case removed. (The removal of this case is only temporary—the original data set is not modified.) The bottom line of the window tells you what the value and statistical significance of the correlation coefficient will be if the highlighted case is removed. Click the "x" in the upper right corner of this window to close it.

CORRELATION

SELECTING VARIABLES

Select two or more variables according to the variable selection instructions provided in *Getting Started*, at the beginning of this book. If you want a subset of cases, see instructions on selecting subsets at the beginning of this appendix. (If you need to erase all existing variable information for this task, click the [Clear All] option.) Once the variables have been selected, click [OK] to obtain the results of your analysis.

VIEWS

The CORRELATION task has only one view. If a correlation value (r) is statistically significant, it is followed by one asterisk (.05 level) or two asterisks (.01 level).

Note: The Windows version of Student ExplorIt allows you to toggle between pairwise and listwise deletion; you can also control whether a one-tailed or two-tailed test of significance is used.

REGRESSION

SELECTING VARIABLES

Select a dependent variable and one or more independent variables according to the variable selection instructions provided in *Getting Started*, at the beginning of this book. If you want a subset of cases, see instructions on selecting subsets at the beginning of this appendix. (If you need to erase all existing variable information for this task, click the [Clear All] option. To delete only a previously selected independent variable, click on the variable name and press the [Delete] or [Backspace] key on your keyboard.) Once the variables have been selected, click [OK] to obtain the results of your analysis.

VIEWS

Graph: The graph shows the effect of one or more independent variables on a ration or ordinal dependent variable. The individual correlations (r) between the independent variables and the dependent variable are shown, as are the beta values. If a beta value is statistically significant, it is followed by one asterisk (.05 level) or two asterisks (.01 level). Multiple R-squared is shown at the top right corner of the screen.

ANOVA: This option provides analysis of variance information including eta square, standardized and unstandardized betas, the sum of squares, degrees of freedom, mean square, F, the probability value, and more.

Correlation: This view provides a correlation matrix of all variables included in the analysis. If a correlation is statistically significant, it is followed by one asterisk (.05 level) or two asterisks (.01 level).

Means: This option provides the means and standard deviations for the variables included in the analysis.

HISTORICAL TRENDS

TRENDS

Select one or more "trends" using the same method used for selecting variables in other tasks. After you have selected at least one trend, click [OK] to continue.

VIEWS

Historical Trends has only one view.

A graph of the trends is shown. The range of years included in the graph are determined by the lowest and highest date for which data are available on one or more of the selected trends. A window at the bottom of the screen allows you to scroll major events that occurred in the twentieth century. The currently highlighted event is shown on the trend graph with a dotted, vertical line. See "Events" under special features below for additional information.

SPECIAL FEATURES

Description of trend: To see the description of a trend when the final trend graphic is showing on the screen, click on the small box located to the left of the trend name. The description of the trend will be shown below the graphic. Click on the "x" in the upper right of this description window to close the window.

Years: This option allows you to limit or expand the range of years covered in the graph. To change the range, select the [Years] option. You may then replace the current low year by typing another year in this box and pressing Enter or the Tab key. Then replace the high year in the same manner. Click on [OK] to see the new graph. (Data are available only for the twentieth century.)

Events: To scroll events, you may click the scroll bar at the right of the events window, or you may use the up and down cursor keys. To look at a specific year, approximate the location of the year on the graph and click that position on the ruler that appears just below the graph.

Search of events: If you wish to focus on a particular type of event, you may conduct a search of all events for a particular word or phrase. The resulting list of events will be limited to the subset of events that contains that word or phrase in its description. For example, you could search on the word *court* and you would get a list of events that have the word *court* in their descriptions. This new list replaces the full list. When you scroll or otherwise select events, only this sublist will now be used. To return to the full list of events, just click on [Full List].

Appendix C: Variable Names and Sources

Note for MicroCase Users: These data files may be used with MicroCase. If you are moving variables from these files into other MicroCase files, or vice versa, you may need to reorder the cases. Also note that files that have been modified in MicroCase will not function properly in Student ExplorIt.

◆ DATA FILE: COLLEGE ◆

1) TICKET
2) PICKED UP
3) SHOPLIFT
4) DRINK
5) FREQ MARIJ
6) EV MARIJ
7) FREQ COKE
8) THROW UP
9) CHEAT
10) OFT CHEAT
11) CHEAT WHEN
12) SMOKE
13) SUICIDE OK
14) EXECUTE
15) PC
16) STUDY TIME
17) HI STUDY
18) GRADES
19) HI GRADES
20) WHERE LIVE
21) SPORTS
22) EMPLOYED
23) MARITAL
24) FAMILY $
25) RACE
26) GENDER
27) RINGS
28) GO BALD
29) WEIGHT

◆ DATA FILE: GSS ◆

1) FEAR WALK
2) CAPPUN
3) COURTS
4) COURTS2
5) COP:CUSS
6) COP:KILL
7) COP:ESC
8) COP:ATT
9) CRIME$
10) DRUGS$
11) GRASS
12) GUNLAW
13) PORNLAW
14) IMMCRIM
15) POLVIEW
16) TRUST
17) PAID SEX
18) SEX PRTNRS
19) X MOVIE
20) ATT RELIG
21) PRAY
22) OWNGUN
23) HUNT
24) EAT OUT
25) HAPPY
26) CLASS
27) OCCUPATN
28) OCC PREST
29) HOME AT 16
30) MA WRKGRW
31) DAD OCC
32) SOUTH
33) PLACESIZE
34) SEX
35) RACE
36) POL PRTY
37) MARITAL
38) RELIGION
39) REGION
40) AGE
41) EDUCATION
42) INCOME

◆ DATA FILE: NCVS ◆

1) VICSEX
2) VICRACE
3) SETTING
4) HOWFAR
5) TIMEDAY
6) MULTOFF
7) STRANGER
8) OFFSEX
9) WEAPON
10) ATTACKED
11) PROTECT
12) HELPED
13) WORSE
14) REPORTED
15) COPS CAME
16) SPEED COPS
17) KNOWARR
18) AGEN.HELP

◆ DATA FILE: NYS ◆

1) SEX
2) ETHNIC
3) AGE
4) MARITAL
5) HITHEFT
6) HOTGOODS
7) HIDWEAP
8) ATTACK
9) MVTHEFT
10) BUYBOOZE
11) PUB DRUNK
12) DRUNK NUM
13) USED MARIJ
14) MARIJ NUM
15) DWI
16) ARRESTED
17) ARREST NUM
18) EVERMV
19) EVHITHFT
20) EVATTACK
21) EVBREAKN
22) EVSELL
23) SWORE PRT
24) THREAT PRT
25) THREW PRT
26) SHOVED PRT
27) SLAP PRT
28) HIT PRT
29) OBJCT PRT
30) BEAT PRT
31) GUN PRT
32) HIT PRT2
33) BLIKFRND
34) SHARFRND
35) LOYLFRND
36) ACTVPART
37) BLIKPART
38) SATFPART
39) WARMPART
40) LOYLPART
41) SUCCEED
42) GOODJOB
43) GRADCOLL
44) WRONGTAX
45) WRONGMJ
46) WRONG$5
47) WRONGHIT
48) WRONGSPD
49) FRNDTAX
50) FRNDMJ
51) FRND$5
52) FRND$50
53) FRNDSUGG

◆ DATA FILE: STATES ◆

1) STATE NAME
2) HOMICIDE
3) RAPE
4) ROBBERY
5) ASSAULT
6) BURGLARY
7) LARCENY
8) MV.THEFT
9) #LARCENIES
10) VIOCRIME
11) PROPCRIME
12) KID ABSE
13) COPS/10000
14) % PRISON
15) SOUTHNESS
16) WARM WINTR
17) ELEVATION
18) TORNADO RT
19) %FARMS
20) POPULATION
21) AVE. AGE
22) % OVER 64
23) %MALE
24) SEX RATIO
25) %BLACK
26) %ASIAN/PAC
27) %SPAN.SPK
28) %NON-ENG
29) IMMIGRANTS
30) %NO MOVE
31) %URBAN
32) %RURAL
33) POP GROWTH
34) HH CHANGE
35) BIRTHS
36) MOMS <20
37) VETERANS
38) MARRIAGES
39) DIVORCES
40) %SNG.MEN
41) COU.CHILD
42) FEM.HEAD
43) BOTH PARNT
44) %POOR
45) PER CAP$
46) MED.FAM$
47) % AFDC
48) UNEMPLMNT
49) %FEM.LABOR
50) % UNION
51) %ENTER.EST
52) NOT IN HS
53) COL.DEGREE
54) SAT VERBAL
55) MATH SAT
56) $ PUPILS
57) OWN HOME
58) TWO+/ROOM
59) PERSONS/HH
60) HOUS VALUE
61) HSE STARTS
62) MOB.HOMES
63) %HOMELESS
64) %NORELIG
65) CHURCH.MEM
66) COKEUSER
67) BEER
68) AIDS
69) HEART DEAD
70) ABORTIONS
71) SHRINKS
72) SUICIDES
73) CHILD MORT
74) SYPHILIS
75) HEALTH INS
76) PICKUPS
77) CARS/HOUSE
78) PUB.TRANS
79) MILES/CAP
80) CAR DEATHS
81) FATAL/DRV.
82) TV DISHES
83) HUNTING
84) F&STREAM
85) PLAYBOY
86) HOMICIDE18
87) GUN KILL18
88) ALC.DIE 18
89) POP GO1860
90) OLD WEST18
91) NEWNESS 18
92) CHURCHED18
93) S.RATIO 18
94) HERDS PC18
95) %BLACK1860
96) %LOCALS 20
97) BURGLARY23
98) LARCENY23
99) POP GO 20
100) BURGLARY40
101) LARCENY 40
102) POP GO 40
103) NOT MOVE40
104) BURGLARY60
105) LARCENY 60
106) NO MOVE 60
107) POP GO 60
108) POP GO 80
109) HOMICIDE82
110) ASSAULT 82
111) ROBBERY 82
112) BURGLARY82
113) LARCENY 82
114) MV.THEFT82

SOURCES

COLLEGE

The COLLEGE file is based on a survey of college freshmen administered in 1996. The college is located in the United States and is a fairly typical "state" college.

GSS

The GSS data file is based on selected variables from the National Opinion Research Center (University of Chicago) General Social Survey for 1996, distributed by The Roper Center and the Inter-university Consortium for Political and Social Research. The principal investigators are James A. Davis and Tom W. Smith.

HISTORY

The source of each variable is indicated in its long label in abbreviated form. A key to these abbreviations follows.

BJS: Bureau of Justice Statistics. 1994. *Criminal Victimization in the United States*, 1973–92. Washington, DC: U.S. Department of Justice.

GSS: These variables are taken from the National Opinion Research Center (University of Chicago), General Social Survey, distributed by The Roper Center and the Inter-university Consortium for Political and Social Research. The principal investigators are James A. Davis and Tom W. Smith.

NCHS: National Center for Health Statistics, Vital Statistics. U.S. Department of Health and Human Services.

UCR: Uniform Crime Reports, Federal Bureau of Investigation. U.S. Department of Justice.

NCVS

The NCVS file contains selected variables from the National Crime Victimization Survey. The file is based on robbery incidents for the years 1992–94. Some variables have been recoded, and question wording has been edited in places to enhance readability. These data were obtained from:

U.S. Department of Justice, Bureau of Justice Statistics. National Crime Victimization Survey, 1992–1994 [Computer file]. Conducted by the U.S. Department of Commerce, Bureau of the Census. 3rd. ICPSR ed. Ann Arbor, MI: Inter-university Consortium for Political and Social Research [producer and distributor], 1997.

NYS

The NYS file contains selected variables from the seventh wave of the National Youth Survey. The NYS is based on a national sample of American youth selected by area probability sampling. For this wave of the survey, young adults were interviewed in early 1987 about events and behavior occurring in calendar year 1986, when respondents were in their 20s. The principal investigator for the NYS was Delbert Elliott. Some variables have been recoded, and question wording has been edited in places to enhance readability. These data were obtained from:

Elliott, Delbert. National Youth Survey [United States]: Wave VII, 1987 [Computer file]. ICPSR version. Boulder, CO: Behavioral Research Institute [producer], 1995. Ann Arbor, MI: Inter-university Consortium for Political and Social Research [distributor], 1996.

STATES

The source of each variable is indicated in its long label. Often these are abbreviated. A complete key to these abbreviations follows.

ABC: Audit Bureau of Circulation's Blue Book for the indicated year.

CENSUS: The summary volumes of the U.S. Census for the indicated year.

CHURCH: *Churches and Church Membership in the United States*, published every 10 years by the Glenmary Research Center, Atlanta, for the year indicated.

DES: U.S. Dept. of Education, Digest of Education Statistics for the indicated year.

F & S: Roger Finke and Rodney Stark, *The Churching of America—1776–1990: Winners and Losers in Our Religious Economy* (Rutgers University Press, 1992).

HCSR: Health Care State Rankings (Morgan Quitno, Lawrence, KS) for the indicated year.

HIGHWAY: Federal Highway Administration, Highway Statistics for the indicated year.

KOSMIN: Barry A. Kosmin *Research Report: The National Survey of Religious Identification* (New York: CUNY Graduate Center, 1991).

MMWR: Morbidity and Mortality Weekly Report for the date indicated.

SA: Statistical Abstract of the United States for the indicated year.

UCR: Uniform Crime Reports for the indicated year.

Variables with no source shown are from U.S. Census publications.

LICENSE AGREEMENT

READ THIS LICENSE AGREEMENT CAREFULLY BEFORE OPENING THE SEALED SOFTWARE PACKAGE. BY OPENING THIS PACKAGE YOU ACCEPT THE TERMS OF THIS AGREEMENT.

MicroCase® Corporation, hereinafter called the Licensor, grants the purchaser of this software, hereinafter called the Licensee, the right to use and reproduce the following software: **Criminology: An Introduction Using ExplorIt, 4/e,** in accordance with the following terms and conditions.

Permitted Uses

- You may use this software only for educational purposes.
- You may use the software on any compatible computer, provided the software is used on only one computer and by one user at a time.
- You may make a backup copy of the diskette(s).

Prohibited Uses

- You may not use this software for any purposes other than educational purposes.
- You may not make copies of the documentation or program disk, except backup copies as described above.
- You may not distribute, rent, sub-license, or lease the software or documentation.
- You may not alter, modify, or adapt the software or documentation, including, but not limited to, translating, decompiling, disassembling, or creating derivative works.
- You may not use the software on a network, file server, or virtual disk.

THIS AGREEMENT IS EFFECTIVE UNTIL TERMINATED. IT WILL TERMINATE IF LICENSEE FAILS TO COMPLY WITH ANY TERM OR CONDITION OF THIS AGREEMENT. LICENSEE MAY TERMINATE IT AT ANY OTHER TIME BY DESTROYING THE SOFTWARE TOGETHER WITH ALL COPIES. IF THIS AGREEMENT IS TERMINATED BY LICENSOR, LICENSEE AGREES TO EITHER DESTROY OR RETURN THE ORIGINAL AND ALL EXISTING COPIES OF THE SOFTWARE TO THE LICENSOR WITHIN FIVE (5) DAYS AFTER RECEIVING NOTICE OF TERMINATION FROM THE LICENSOR.

MicroCase Corporation retains all rights not expressly granted in this License Agreement. Nothing in the License Agreement constitutes a waiver of MicroCase Corporation's rights under the U.S. copyright laws or any other federal or state law.

Should you have any questions concerning this Agreement, you may contact MicroCase Corporation by writing to MicroCase Corporation, 14110 N.E. 21st Street, Bellevue, WA 98007, Attn: College Publishing Division.